ANIMAL

CONSCIOUSNESS

Frontiers of Philosophy

Peter H. Hare, Series Editor

ADVISORY BOARD

ANIMAL
CONSCIOUSNESS

DAISIE AND MICHAEL RADNER

 **Prometheus Books**

59 John Glenn Drive
Amherst, New York 14228-2197

Published 1996 by Prometheus Books

00 99 98 97 96   5 4 3 2 1

Library of Congress Cataloging-in-Publication Data

Radner, Daisie.
    Animal consciousness / Daisie Radner and Michael Radner.
       p.   cm.
    Includes bibliographical references and index.
    ISBN 1–57392–114–9 (pbk.)
    1. Consciousness in animals. I. Radner, Michael. II. Title.
QL785.25.R34   1996
156′.3—dc20   96–29007
                                                    CIP

Contents

Introduction

In philosophy past and present, the prevailing attitude has been that any questions having to do with nonhuman animals are of decidedly secondary importance. Human nature poses one of the great problems of philosophy. By contrast, the problem of animal nature is a minor side issue, perhaps useful as an exercise in examining the limits of what it means to be human, but hardly worthy of extended treatment in its own right. Animals may be studied scientifically as part of the natural world, but their philosophical importance lies in what they lack. They are not just nonhuman, but less than human.

The time is long overdue for abandoning the anthropocentric approach to philosophy. Back in 1949 the *Journal of Philosophy* published an article entitled "The Messes Animals Make in Metaphysics." The author, B. A. G. Fuller, sketches some of the difficulties animals raise in various systems from the Stoics up to his own day. Animals have always threatened to make messes in philosophy. So long as animals are ignored, either as objects in the world or as perceivers, they will continue to make messes. As Fuller remarks at the end of his article, the animal issue illustrates "the treatment accorded by many a philosophy to inconvenient data, overlooked in the beginning, brazenly or with a blush, that turn up later to dispute and shock its pre-conceived notions. When the chickens come home to roost, it silently wrings their necks at the entrance to the coop, before they can get in and cackle" (Fuller 1949, 838).

Here we let the chickens cackle loud and clear. This book is about animals. We make no excuse that they are being studied in order to learn more about human nature. The zoocentric approach to philosophy is very fruitful. Certain issues in philosophy of science, philosophy of mind, even history of philosophy, take on new light when animals are given center stage.

The topic of animal consciousness cuts across disciplinary boundaries, from biology and ethology to psychology and on to philosophy. Science does not operate in a vacuum. In no area is this more true than in the study of animal mind and behavior. Scientists bring a lot of metaphysical and ideological baggage with them when they embark on this endeavor. The metaphysical baggage includes a theory of mind according to which consciousness is privately unassailable and publicly inaccessible, therefore scientifically useless. This concept of consciousness is usually traced back to Descartes, the father—and the anathema—of modern philosophy. The ideological baggage contains the time-honored precept of human uniqueness.

Only humans have or do x. The value of x has to be changed from time to time as more evidence comes in, but there must be an x because humans are unique. Only human beings conceptualize and perform abstractions. They alone make and use tools; have reason; have a sense of humor; practice deceit; count; communicate about things not in the here and now; are aware of their own existence; anticipate their own death; have a sense of beauty; have an ethical sense; have speech. Darwin (1874, 89) remarks that he once made a collection of such aphorisms and came up with over twenty, "but they are almost worthless, as their wide difference and number prove the difficulty, if not the impossibility, of the attempt." Nevertheless the attempt to build the insuperable barrier has continued (Thorpe 1974).

Obviously there are differences between humans and other species. *Every* species is different from every other species: this much is plain biology. The ideology lies not in the search for differences, but in the unwavering belief that humanity is defined by attributes that have absolutely no precedent in the rest of the biological world.

The metaphysical and ideological doctrines combine to generate a formidable challenge to the study of animal consciousness. How can we possibly know what animals are experiencing, when we have no direct access to their inner lives and the insuperable barrier between us and them undercuts any attempt at analogical reasoning from their behavior? One way to confront the challenge is to question the legitimacy of the doctrines on which it is based. That is what we propose to do.

Debates about animal consciousness fall into two periods: before and after Darwin. Cartesian metaphysics casts its shadow over both periods. The substance behind the shadow can be best understood by examining Descartes in his own time. The animal without consciousness—the beast-machine—was then preeminently a Cartesian creature. In Part One of the book we dissect this strange contrivance. We have two purposes for doing so. The first is negative: we take the machine apart so that it cannot be reassembled in working order. The Cartesian beast-machine breaks down under the weight of analysis within Descartes's own framework. The behavioral and theoretical case for it fails, and it fails for Cartesian reasons. Even the theological arguments for it are weak.

The second purpose is to gain a positive advantage for the study of animal consciousness. Part of the despair over making animal consciousness a subject of inquiry comes from a conviction that the only way to understand consciousness is along so-called Cartesian lines. We advocate a reexamination of what usually passes for the Cartesian concept of consciousness. We argue that there is in Descartes a distinction between two types of consciousness, reflective and nonreflective. This distinction averts certain notorious problems that critics and scholars have foisted on Descartes and on the notion of consciousness in general. Far from fostering the denial of consciousness to animals, the distinction makes it easier to talk about animals as having conscious experiences and easier to see how one can learn about them.

Part Two takes the debate on animal mind into the post-Darwinian era. The beast-machine did not curl up and die with the advent of Darwin. It assumed new guises, fueled by the continuing interest in human uniqueness and the continuing suspicion that consciousness does not fit into the natural world. Evolutionary biologists and psychologists of the nineteenth century were more than willing to attribute consciousness to animals. They needed animal mind in order to fit human mind into the evolutionary framework. Yet because they remained in the grip of Cartesian dualism, they ultimately failed to gain mind a rightful place in the causal network of biological processes. This opened the door to behaviorism. Cognitive psychology has rehabilitated mind but not consciousness.

Beast-machines come with two sets of options: with or without mental processes, and either metaphysical or methodological. The Cartesian choice was the metaphysical beast-machine without mental processes. Consciousness and thinking went hand in hand, and animals really had neither. Nowadays the prevailing view is that animals have mental processes, but these processes can be studied without bringing in the troublesome notion of consciousness (e.g., Terrace 1984). The favored model is the methodological beast-machine with mental components.

One would think that the doctrine of human uniqueness would have been finally laid to rest in the post-Darwinian era, but such is not the case. The lessons of Darwin have not been thoroughly absorbed even now. Humans still like to think of their species as above the biological turmoil. Those who try to combine evolution and humanism meet violent opposition from those who prefer their humanism untrammelled by biological facts. A properly Darwinian humanism does not seek to elevate humanity by denigrating animals.

In a Darwinian universe, the presence of human consciousness makes probable the presence of animal consciousness. A thoroughgoing evolutionary ethology should incorporate this aspect of animal life along with every other. To make room for consciousness in ethology, we must pass through dangerous territory. Potshots at the animals come from all sides—linguistics, artificial intelligence, behavioral ecology (a variant of sociobiology), and that branch of philosophy of mind that seeks to consign the whole notion of consciousness to the rubbish heap. Chapters 7, 8, and 9 are devoted to disarming these opponents.

In the final chapter we show how the study of animal consciousness can shed light on certain ethical questions concerning human intervention in nature.

Part One

The Breakdown of the Beast-Machine

Introduction

There is an old story about Thales' mule. The animal happened to stumble while fording a river. The sacks of salt it was carrying were soaked and the contents dissolved. Having noticed that its burden grew lighter in this instance, the mule, whenever it came to a stream, plunged in with its load. Thales outwitted the mule by having it loaded with sponges and wool. Thereafter it took great care to keep its cargo out of the water.

It is claimed that cattle in Susa, given the task of raising one hundred bucketfuls of water each day for the royal gardens, balked and would do no more once they reached their prescribed number.

The foxes of Thrace, refusing to cross a frozen river when they heard running water beneath the ice, were credited by the ancients with the following sorites: What makes noise is in motion; what is in motion is not frozen; what is not frozen is liquid; what is liquid gives way under weight; therefore what makes noise gives way under weight.

Elephants were considered to have religion, because they purify themselves in the sea and stand facing the rising sun with trunks lifted like hands in supplication.

In Aristotle's *History of Animals* (9.6.612a) it is written that wild goats of Crete, when wounded by arrows, go in search of dittany, which is supposed to have curative powers, and that the tortoise eats marjoram when it has partaken of a viper.

To illustrate the intelligence of small animals, Aristotle cites the nest-building of swallows. They mix mud and chaff together, and if they run short of mud, they douse themselves with water and roll in the dust (9.7.612b). He also reports that a mother nightingale has been observed to give singing lessons to her young (4.9.536b).

13

All this and more is related in Plutarch's *The Cleverness of Animals.*[1] The Greek author supplements his sources—Aristotle, Aelian, Pliny, and others—with observations of his own. Two of his anecdotes have to do with dogs. Once he saw a dog on a ship put pebbles into a half-empty jar until the oil in it rose high enough for the animal to reach it with his tongue (Plutarch 1957, 365–67). On another occasion he saw a play featuring a canine actor. The role called for the dog to feign death by poisoning. So realistic was the performance that the audience was amazed when, at the appropriate moment in the plot, the dog got up as though recovering from a deep sleep (1957, 405).

Such stories are repeated by Michel de Montaigne, the sixteenth-century French essayist and skeptic, in his "Apology for Raymond Sebond," one of his *Essays*, first published in 1580. Sebond was a fifteenth-century Spanish theologian who sought to establish the tenets of Christianity by reason. Montaigne "defends" him by undermining confidence that better arguments can be found. The point of the animal stories is to show that the separation of humanity from other creatures is just a vanity of the imagination. "There is more difference between a given man and a given man than between a given animal and a given man," declares the essayist (Montaigne 1957, 342).

Montaigne represents the sort of attitude toward animals that Descartes opposes. In one breath Montaigne advocates skepticism, while in another he trots out all the old legends of animal sagacity as though they were capable of providing evidence for something. He does not even rely on his own observations but contents himself with seeing the natural world through eyes long dead. Just as Descartes vindicates reason against skepticism, so too he defends the superiority of human nature against the unreasoned prejudices of common folk and ancient scholars. According to Descartes, both reason and experience support the conclusion that non-human animals are fundamentally different from human beings. The brutes are automata devoid of thought, understanding, or indeed awareness of any kind.

Descartes introduced his doctrine of animal automatism in the *Discourse on the Method* of 1637. His best-known and most widely read work, the *Meditations on First Philosophy,* contains no mention of the beast-machine. It does come up in the Objections and Replies published with the *Medita-*

---

1. Plutarch 1957, 389–91, 411, 377, 397, 407–9, 363, 401. The stories appear in Aelian's *On the Characteristics of Animals* (1958–59) as follows: Thales and the mule, 7.42; cattle of Susa, 7.1; foxes of Thrace, 7.24 (there is no mention of the sorites); elephant worship of the sun, 7.44; and of the moon, 4.10; tortoise and marjoram, 3.5.

tions in 1641, but only because some objectors, including the Port-Royal philosopher Antoine Arnauld and the atomist Pierre Gassendi, raised the issue.

Most of the standard books on Descartes follow the *Meditations* in their choice of topics and order of treatment. First comes Cartesian doubt, then knowledge of the self, then the argument for the existence of God and related issues, finally the material world and the relation between mind and body.[2] The problems that have received the major share of attention in the modern literature are those generated by the *Meditations*. As this work is primarily about skepticism and certainty, so the focus of modern scholarship has been on the epistemological and methodological aspects of Cartesian philosophy. A prime example is the Cartesian circle. Descartes uses the existence of a veracious God to guarantee the truth of clear and distinct ideas, but how can he prove that such a God exists without assuming that whatever is clearly and distinctly perceived is true? The charge of circularity was made by Arnauld in the Fourth Objections. Descartes believed he could get out of the circle. A number of scholars agree, though they disagree on exactly how it is done. A great deal of effort has been spent in the past few decades in extricating Descartes from the circle, because there are important methodological lessons to be learned in the exercise.

Philosophy does not live by methodology alone. Eventually one must get beyond the method to the content. In the case of Descartes's philosophy, there is a temptation to think that the method *is* the content. This is especially true when the content in question is his theory of mind. The "I" of the *Meditations,* the being in search of certain knowledge, is a thing that thinks, a thing that is united with the physical body known as "my" body. It is a soul or mind, which for Descartes is a substance, one of two kinds of created substance, the other being matter. In following the mind through its quest for certainty, one learns something of its nature and properties. In reconstructing the Cartesian theory of mind, however, one must be careful not to build into it the peculiar features of the I of the *Meditations.* That particular self is concerned about certainty, but the vast majority of selves are not. Moreover, the self of the *Meditations* reflects upon itself and its own thinking. We shall argue that this reflective thinking or self-consciousness is by no means essential to a Cartesian mind.

Descartes was right not to bring up the beast-machine in the *Meditations,* for this doctrine plays no role in the search for certainty. Yet the objectors

---

2. Books that follow this general format include Kenny 1968, Williams 1978, and M. D. Wilson 1978a.

were right to bring it up in their Objections, for it is relevant to the theory of mind implicit in the *Meditations*. We do not follow the order of the *Meditations* here because we want the beast-machine to be more than just a side issue. We approach Descartes's philosophy as readers who, having finished the *Meditations,* now seek to work out the implications of Cartesianism in one special area.

Our basic question is this. Once Descartes's theory of mind is properly reconstructed, is there any justification for denying a Cartesian mind to animals? The first chapter presents the Cartesian theory of mind with special emphasis on the relation between thought, which Descartes says is the essence of mind, and consciousness. The second chapter takes up Descartes's arguments in support of his claim that animals do not have minds. As we shall see, these arguments are specifically designed to show that animals lack one kind of thinking, namely, reason. In chapter 3 we consider what possible grounds Descartes could have for denying them sensations and feelings as well. Does sensation, construed as a mental faculty, depend upon reason as a necessary condition? That is, must a Cartesian mind have reason if it has sense perceptions? In this context we shall introduce another seventeenth-century French philosopher, Nicolas Malebranche, a priest of the Oratory. Working within the Cartesian metaphysical framework of substance and modification, mind and matter, Malebranche sought to correct what he saw as deficiencies in Descartes's system, to be clear and distinct where the master was not. One of the by-products of Malebranche's doctrine of ideas is a new tie between sensation and intellection. Is it strong enough to support the denial of sensation to animals? In chapter 4 we continue to follow Malebranche as he presents the theological arguments for the beast-machine. Descartes had merely hinted at them; it was left to Cartesians in the priesthood, such as Malebranche and Dilly, to develop them. In the end they fail to prove their point. Some seventeenth-century reactions to the beast-machine are considered in the fifth chapter.

All quotations from French and Latin sources are given in English translation. Where no published translation is available, we supply our own. For renderings of Descartes we rely chiefly on Cottingham, Stoothoff, and Murdoch (1984–85) and Kenny (1970). Our format for Descartes citations is as follows. First we give the reference to the French edition of Descartes's works edited by Adam and Tannery (1964–76). This is followed by references to the English translations. Since Haldane and Ross (1955) is still in wide use, we include it after Cottingham, Stoothoff, and Murdoch. On those few occasions where we think the Haldane and Ross rendering is better, we reverse the order. The following abbreviations are used: AT for Adam and Tannery

1964–76; CSM for Cottingham, Stoothoff, and Murdoch 1984–85; HR for Haldane and Ross 1955; K for Kenny 1970; and C for Cottingham 1976.

Malebranche references are to the standard French edition of *Oeuvres complètes* (1958–67), which is cited as OC. For Malebranche's *The Search after Truth* we use the Lennon and Olscamp translation (Malebranche 1980), cited as S.

1

Cartesian Consciousness

Descartes is notorious for his claim that the mind is a substance. Gilbert Ryle (1949) coined the phrase "the ghost in the machine" to describe Cartesian mental substance and its relation to the human body. The phrase conjures up an image from a horror story: something present in the body-machine, inhabiting it, making it do things it would not otherwise do. The image is apt so long as it is not pushed too far. Like a ghost in a Halloween story, the Cartesian mind is a thing or entity with properties of its own, capable of existing apart from the human body as a disembodied spirit, just as the body can exist without it as a corpse. Folklore is not clear on the question whether ghosts are completely nonmaterial or composed of some sort of ethereal matter (ectoplasm). Descartes, however, is quite emphatic on this score. Cartesian minds are immaterial entities. Since only material objects stand in spatial relations, minds cannot be spatially related to other things. Ghosts in haunted houses are frequently given spatial positions— in the kitchen behind the chair, for example. Cartesian minds are not like that. Although Descartes speaks of the soul as being "in" the body and as having its "seat" in the pineal gland, he insists that such terms are not to be taken in their usual spatial sense. The mind's "presence" in the body it inhabits is not local but causal presence: it acts upon the body and the body acts upon it.

Descartes defines "substance" in Part One of the *Principles of Philosophy*: "By substance, we can understand nothing else than a thing which so exists that it needs no other thing in order to exist" (AT 8A:24; HR 1:239; CSM

1:210). Substances are contrasted with modes, which do need another thing in order to exist. Physical objects, or rather the physical world as a whole, and minds are substances; so is God. Matter and minds are finite substances, God is infinite. Examples of modes are motion, shape, and magnitude of bodies; feeling, understanding, imagination, and volition in minds.

What does it mean to say that one thing does or does not *need* another in order to exist? In Cartesian philosophy "x needs y" has two meanings. The first is that x is causally dependent on y. Strictly speaking, God is the only being that needs nothing else in this sense, for he is the only one that depends upon nothing else as cause. Nevertheless, one can still distinguish finite substances from modes in terms of this sense of "need" by adding the stipulation that y refers to created things only. Finite substances are causally dependent on no other creature. Extended matter and individual minds are produced directly by God. Modes are causally dependent on things in the created realm. To answer the question "Why does this substance have this particular mode?" one must look at the situation in which the substance acquires the mode. The mind's feeling of pain, for instance, is acquired when the body to which it is united is disturbed.

The second meaning of "x needs y" is more general than the first. It is that x cannot exist without y. If y does not exist or ceases to exist, then x does not exist or ceases to exist. In the letter to Hyperaspistes (August 1641) Descartes writes that a created substance "is a thing of a kind to exist without any other creature; and this is something that cannot be said about the modes of things, like shape and number" (AT 3:429; K 116). Modes need substances in the sense that no particular mode can exist without that particular substance whose mode it is. According to Descartes, my pain cannot exist without my mind. I may imagine a unicorn exactly as you do, but my act of imagining is numerically distinct from yours. If I cease to exist then so does my imagining. The same holds for the modes of bodies: two balls can have identical motions but not literally the same mode.[1] Created substances need no other thing in the sense that there is no particular thing, whether created substance or mode, such that if the thing ceased to exist, the original substance would thereby cease to exist. A Cartesian mind can exist without the particular body to which it is joined. It can also exist without the particular thoughts it is now having.

It cannot, however, exist without any thought at all (AT 5:150; C 8). Thought is the nature or essence of mind as extension is the essence of

---

1. Descartes's nominalism lies behind his assertion to Henry More (August 1649) that there is no "transmigration" of motion or rest from one body to another (AT 5:405; K 258).

matter. Descartes defines "nature and essence" in the *Principles* as that "principal property" of substance "to which all its other properties are referred" (AT 8A:25; CSM 1:210; HR 1:240). No substance can exist without its essence. Lest we conclude that substances are not really substances after all since they need their essences in order to exist, Descartes goes on to explain that the difference between a substance and its essence is only a distinction of reason. When we consider thought and extension as constituting the natures of mental and corporeal substance, respectively, "they must then be considered as nothing else but thinking substance itself and extended substance itself—that is, as mind and body" (AT 8A:30–31; CSM 1:215; HR 1:245–46).

What exactly does Descartes mean by "thought," and in what sense do all the other properties of the mind depend upon it? Although the question arises in the context of a substance ontology, it can be answered without making any reference to the notion of substance at all. In this respect it is different from the notorious problem of Cartesian mind-body interaction.

The latter problem is, for Descartes, one of the intelligibility of a certain relation between two substances. How can mental and material substances act upon one another, especially since Descartes's own general theory of causation seems to require communication from one substance to another, and thus some sort of likeness between the two substances (Radner 1971, 1985)? If minds were not substances in the first place, the problem would not arise, at least not in this form; for then there would be no communication from one substance to another and hence no conflict with the causal theory.

By contrast, even if there is no mental substance, even if the mind is nothing apart from the body, so long as there is thinking going on, it still makes sense to ask "What is thinking?" Descartes's answer to this question can still be assessed on its own merits. So for the time being, let us set aside the troublesome notion of substance and treat Descartes's theory of mind as though it were neutral on the question of whether the mind is a substance. We do not mean to suggest that Descartes himself was ever neutral on it. Obviously he was not. All we are saying is that it is possible to analyze Cartesian thought and the so-called modes of thought without bringing in the view that the thinker is an immaterial substance or "ghost in a machine."

THOUGHT

Descartes defines "thought" in the *Principles* and in the Second Replies to the *Meditations*. In both places the definition is followed by a list of the sorts of operations that count as thinking. Here is the passage from the first part of the *Principles:* "By the term *thought* I understand all those things which, we being conscious, occur in us, insofar as the consciousness of them is in us. So not only understanding, willing and imagining, but also sensing, are the same here as thinking" (AT 8A:7; HR 1:222; CSM 1:195).[2] He puts it thus in the Second Replies: "*Thought* is a word that covers everything that exists in us in such a way that we are immediately conscious of it. Thus all the operations of will, intellect, imagination, and of the senses are thoughts" (AT 7:160; HR 2:52; CSM 2:113).

The inclusion of sensation in the list needs some explanation. The word "sensation" is ambiguous for Descartes. On the one hand, it can refer to the corporeal process of transmission of impulses by the nerves to the brain. In the case of the external senses, the impulses usually arise from the action of external objects upon the sense organs. When I see light, for example, an image is produced by an external source on my retina and is in turn conveyed to the brain; or at least the brain is affected as if the image had come from an outside source. In the case of internal sensations—this includes natural appetites such as hunger, as well as passions such as fear and joy—the nerve impulses come from internal organs. On the other hand, the word "sensation" can also refer to the awareness that is associated with the corporeal process. This is the meaning Descartes has in mind when he says that sensing is thinking.

Immediately after listing the modes of thought in the *Principles,* Descartes distinguishes physical seeing from the consciousness of seeing. The latter, he says, can function as the "I think" in "I think, therefore I am," whereas the corporeal process cannot. This echoes the Second Meditation. Even if I am only dreaming that I see light, hear noise, and feel heat, still "I certainly *seem* to see, to hear, and to be warmed." Its seeming to me that I see light is the same as my being conscious of seeing light. "What is called 'having a sensory perception' is strictly just this, and in this restricted sense of the term it is simply thinking" (AT 7:29; CSM 2:19; HR 1:153).

---

2. Here we give the translation in Curley 1978, 179, which is more accurate than either Cottingham, Stoothoff, and Murdoch, or Haldane and Ross. The Latin term *conscientia,* given by Curley as "consciousness," is rendered likewise by Haldane and Ross as well as by Miller and Miller (1983); Cottingham, Stoothoff, and Murdoch favor "awareness." For the most part we shall use "consciousness."

In the phrase "conscious of seeing," the object of consciousness is a process going on in the body: we are conscious of corporeal seeing. Descartes underscores this point by treating consciousness of seeing on a par with consciousness of walking. Thus in the *Principles* he rejects "I see, or I walk, therefore I am" when seeing and walking refer to bodily activities. "But if I take 'seeing' or 'walking' to apply to the actual sense or awareness of seeing or walking, then the conclusion is quite certain, since it relates to the mind, which alone has the sensation or thought that it is seeing or walking" (AT 8A:7–8; CSM 1:195; HR 1:222).

Now according to the definition of "thought" given above, anything in us of which we are conscious is a thought. Although Descartes admits that we are conscious of corporeal seeing, he does not mean to include it among the modes of thinking. On the contrary, he insists that it is our *consciousness* of the bodily process which is a form of thinking. Had he simply defined thinking as being conscious, there would be no problem here; for then the corporeal process would be both that which I think of and that of which I am conscious. Descartes complicates matters by defining thought as that in us of which we are conscious. If my consciousness of seeing is a thought, and thought is that of which I am conscious, then it seems that I must be conscious of my consciousness of seeing.

The term "consciousness" or "awareness" (Latin *conscientia,* French *conscience*) seems to be playing two different roles in Descartes's theory of mind. In one role it is roughly synonymous with "thought" (Latin *cogitatio,* French *pensée*). A passage in the Third Replies explicitly equates them: "There are other acts which we call 'acts of thought,' such as understanding, willing, imagining, having sensory perceptions, and so on: these all fall under the common concept of thought or perception or consciousness" (AT 7:176; CSM 2:124; HR 2:64). In the other role consciousness is used to define thought without being synonymous with it. The definition in the *Principles* and the Second Replies reads not that thought *is* consciousness but that thought is that *of which* we are conscious. Thought "exists in such a way that we are immediately conscious of it," that is, we are conscious of *the thought.*[3]

One might be tempted to account for the distinction implicit in the definition by saying that "consciousness" refers to the act of being conscious,

---

3. Some commentators think that the definition makes "thought" and "consciousness" synonymous. See, for example, Laporte 1950, 78. Robert McRae (1972, 55 n. 2) questions this interpretation. We maintain that it is clearly wrong. The definition does not say that in having a thought of *x,* I am conscious of *x;* rather, it says that in having a thought of *x,* I am conscious of the thought.

whereas "thought" refers to the object of the act. Thus when I think of a thing, my thought is the object I am thinking of and my consciousness is the act of thinking of it. Descartes rules out this interpretation, however, by the sentences that come immediately after the definition. "And so not only understanding, willing, and imagining, but also sensing, are here the same as thinking," he writes in the *Principles,* and it is clear that he is referring to acts of thinking. This is also clear in the Second Replies: "Thus all the operations of will, intellect, imagination, and of the senses are thoughts." Operations of the mind are acts of the mind, not objects. From the definition of thought it follows that for any thought, if I have it, I must be conscious of it. Thus Descartes declares in the Fourth Replies that "we cannot have any thought of which we are not aware at the very moment when it is in us" (AT 7:246; CSM 1:171; HR 2:115). What this means is not that we are aware of all the things we think of, but that we are aware of all our acts of thinking. This is evident from his subsequent statement that "although *we are always actually aware of the acts or operations of our minds,* we are not always aware of the mind's faculties or powers, except potentially" (AT 7:246; CSM 2:172; HR 2:115, emphasis added).

Is it possible to draw a viable distinction between the consciousness that *is* thinking (as in the phrase "consciousness of walking") and consciousness *of* thinking? If not, then Descartes's theory of mind leads to an infinite regress. Given his definition of thought, it follows that for any act of thinking, if I have it, I must be conscious of it. When we are conscious of walking at the time of walking, our act of consciousness is clearly different from the object of consciousness, namely, walking. If we are conscious of thinking in the same way that we are of walking, then we will be conscious of thinking by a separate mental act. Whenever we think of anything, there would have to be two acts in us: the act of thinking and that of being conscious of thinking. But since this latter act is itself a mode of thinking, we must also be conscious of it, conscious of our consciousness of it, and so on.

The English philosopher Thomas Hobbes raised the problem of infinite regress in connection with the cogito: "Moreover, I do not infer that I am thinking by means of another thought. For although someone may think that he *was* thinking (for his thought is simply an act of remembering), it is quite impossible for him to think that he *is* thinking, or to know that he is knowing. For then an infinite chain of questions would arise: 'How do you know that you know that you know . . . ?' " (AT 7:173; CSM 2:122–23; HR 2:62). The problem goes far beyond the cogito. According to Descartes's definition of thought, in order to think at all, one must be conscious of thinking. But if being conscious is thinking, then does not every thought require another thought?

This question was put to Descartes by Frans Burman, a young man who visited the philosopher in 1648 and recorded the conversation. It is interesting to compare Descartes's answer to Burman with that to Hobbes. In reply to Hobbes, Descartes seems bent on denying that one thought can be of another: "It is irrelevant for the philosopher to say that one thought cannot be the subject of another thought. For who, besides himself, ever supposed this?" (AT 7:175; CSM 2:124; HR 2:64).[4] As E. M. Curley (1978) notes, the latter sentence is ambiguous. It can mean either that no one but Hobbes ever supposed that one thought *could* be the subject of another, or that no one but he ever supposed that it *could not* be. The reply to Burman suggests that one thought can indeed be of another thought: "It is correct that to be aware is both to think and to reflect on one's thought. But it is false that this reflection cannot occur while the previous thought is still there. This is because . . . the soul is capable of thinking of more than one thing at the same time, and of continuing with a particular thought which it has. It has the power to reflect on its thoughts as often as it likes, and to be aware of its thought in this way" (AT 5:149; C 7). One must be careful not to put too much weight on a work not from Descartes's own hand. Still, it is safe to use this passage as evidence that for Descartes, we are conscious of at least some of our thoughts by reflective acts of thinking.

In order for the infinite regress to arise, however, it is not enough that we are conscious of some of our thoughts in this way. It is necessary that we should be conscious of all our thoughts by separate acts of thinking. Does Descartes's definition of thought commit him to this stronger claim? Not if the appropriate distinction can be drawn between consciousness of thinking and consciousness that consists in thinking. We intend to show that it can be drawn. We do not claim that Descartes ever explicitly acknowledged such a distinction, but only that it is implicit in his writings and that certain problems can be averted by bringing it out into the open. The two notions of consciousness coexist in his theory of mind, and he does not confuse them. It is always possible to determine which one is being referred to in a given passage.

---

4. The last sentence is the translation of Curley (1978, 182). Cottingham, Stoothoff, and Murdoch obscure the ambiguity that is present in the original by rendering it thus: "For who, apart from him, ever supposed that it could be?" Haldane and Ross's rendering is no better: "Who, except my antagonist himself, ever imagined that it could?"

TWO TYPES OF CONSCIOUSNESS

We shall begin with the consciousness that is thinking: the sort referred to in the phrase "consciousness of seeing or of walking." As we have already noted, the object of consciousness here is a bodily activity. This sort of consciousness is a mode of thinking, and it is equivalent to its seeming to me that a certain corporeal process is going on. Now it can seem to me that I am walking when in fact I am not, for example, in a dream. Moreover, I can actually be walking even though it does not seem to me that I am, as occurs in sleepwalking unaccompanied by a dream of walking. The same holds for consciousness as Descartes uses the term in this context. I can be conscious of walking without walking, and I can walk without being conscious of it.

In ordinary language "I am aware of walking" does not have quite the same meaning as "it seems to me that I am walking." Expressions of the form "I am aware of x" or "I am conscious of x" are normally used in contexts in which x actually exists or occurs. So, often, are their denials. Thus one might say, for example, "I picked up the knife without being conscious of doing so." The form "it seems to me that x" is usually reserved for contexts where the speaker would hesitate to assert that x is really happening, as in "It seems to me that I am flying, but it must be an effect of the monkshood root I ate a little while ago." Descartes is not interested in adapting his terminology to reflect such nuances of ordinary language. He is concerned only with the logical connection between the mental act and its object, and this connection is contingent in both cases. The act of being conscious of x, or of its seeming to me that x, can occur without the object x existing, and conversely, the object can exist without the act.

Let us call this sort of consciousness C1. My consciousness is of the C1 variety if and only if the following two relations hold between it and its object x:

(i) It is possible that I am conscious of x and x does not exist.
(ii) It is possible that x exists and I am not conscious of x.

This may appear to be a circular definition but in fact it is not. The aim is not to define consciousness but to distinguish between two types of it in order to resolve a problem of textual intepretation. The situation is in one respect similar to that of defining an obtuse triangle as a triangle having an angle greater than a right angle. Although the word "triangle" appears in both the term to be defined and the phrase defining it, the definition is not circular since it is meant to distinguish a certain kind of triangle from others such as right and equilateral triangles. There is, however, an important dissimilarity. One can go on to define the word "triangle." Descartes offers a definition of thought but never one of consciousness. For him the term "consciousness" functions as a primitive. It can be defined, if at all, only ostensively.

The existence of an act of C1 is neither a necessary nor a sufficient condition for the existence of its object. In a full-blown doctrine of representative realism, such as Malebranche holds and Berkeley criticizes, physical objects are perceived by the mediation of ideas. We are directly aware of the ideas, only indirectly aware of the objects they represent. Material objects need not exist in order to be perceived, and they need not be perceived in order to exist (Radner 1977, 1978). Thus for a representative realist, our consciousness of the material world is of type C1. It is open to question whether Descartes was himself committed to the representative realist thesis that ideas are entities perceived instead of bodies (Costa 1983). It is not necessary, however, for him to subscribe to this thesis in order to hold that our consciousness of material things is of the C1 variety. One can grant that it is possible to perceive what is not really there, and yet deny that one's awareness of the thing is by means of some mental object perceived instead of it. Antoine Arnauld, arguing against Malebranche, granted the first and denied the second, and believed that he was being true to Descartes's teaching (Arnauld 1775–83, 38:220–21).

Suppose that I am conscious of something in such a way that the negations of the C1 relations hold. Let us call this sort of consciousness C2. My consciousness is of the C2 variety if and only if the following conditions hold:

(iii) Necessarily, if I am conscious of x, then x exists.
(iv) Necessarily, if x exists, then I am conscious of x.

The existence of an act of C2 is both necessary and sufficient for the existence of its object. C2 has condition (iii) in common with the immediate perceptions of representative realism. No one is more emphatic than Malebranche about this feature of immediate perception. He contrasts immediate and mediate perception as follows in Book Four of *The Search after Truth*:

> To see nothing is not to see; to think of nothing is not to think. . . . Now it follows from this that nothingness is not perceptible, and that everything we see clearly, directly, immediately, necessarily exists. I say what we immediately see, attest to, or conceive; for to speak strictly, the objects we immediately see are very different from those we see externally, or rather from those we

think we see or look at; for . . . we can see, or rather believe we see, external objects that are not there, notwithstanding the fact that nothingness is not perceptible. But there is a contradiction in saying that we can immediately see what does not exist, for this is to say that at the same time we see and do not see. (OC 2:99; S 320)

Some representative realists would also affirm condition (iv) of immediate perceptions; for the objects of immediate perception are ideas, whose existence, as Berkeley notes, consists in being perceived. If they are my ideas then they must be perceived by me. For Malebranche, however, the ideas I perceive are not mine but God's, and they are in God whether or not I am perceiving them (Radner 1978).

Is Descartes committed to representative realism, with ideas intermediate between the mind and the world, in holding that we have consciousness C2? Not if the x referred to in the conditions is something other than an idea in the representative realist sense. For Descartes it is indeed something else.

When Descartes defines thought in terms of consciousness and says that we are conscious of all our acts of thinking, he cannot be referring to C1 but must instead be referring to C2. Since thought is all that exists in us in such a way that we are conscious of it, there can be no thought in me of which I am not conscious. If I am thinking, I must be conscious of thinking. This is condition (iv). Furthermore, since acts of thinking are entities that occur in us "insofar as the consciousness of them is in us," it cannot be the case that I am conscious of such an act but it does not exist in me. If I am conscious of thinking, I must be thinking. This is condition (iii). Notice that the x here stands for an act or operation of thinking, not for the object of such an act as it does for the representative realist.

Acts of thinking, acts of which we have C2, fall into two major classes: perceptions and volitions. Included in the first class are sense perceptions, imaginations, feelings, and emotions. These mental processes have corresponding physiological states. Also included are conceptions or acts of "pure intellect." These are "pure" in that they have no neurological counterparts. When the mind conceives of a triangle by contemplating the definition of it, as opposed to imagining it by representing to itself three lines enclosing a definite space, nothing special goes on in the brain: no corporeal image is formed in it and no traces are left in it.[5] The second class pertains to the faculty of will. It includes desires and aversions as well as operations of judging: affirming, denying, and doubting (AT 8A:17; CSM 1:204; HR 1:232).

Among our acts of thinking are perceptions of what goes on in our own body and in the world around us. Such perceptions are acts of C1. They are neither necessary nor sufficient for the existence of the corporeal things or processes that are their objects. These acts of C1 are in turn things of which we are conscious (C2). Our being conscious (C2) of them is both necessary and sufficient for their existence.

Acts of C1 are modes of thought, whereas acts of C2 are not themselves modes of thought but ingredients of such modes. My perception or awareness (C1) of a rabbit sitting in the grass is an act of thinking. My awareness (C2) of perceiving a rabbit is not a mental act separate from that of perceiving. Whenever I think of any object *x*, I am, according to Descartes, conscious (C2) of thinking of *x;* but there are not two acts, one having *x* as its object, the other with my act of thinking as its object. There is only one act, the act of thinking of *x*, which has *x* as its primary object and itself as secondary object. Object *x* is primary, in the sense that it is, properly speaking, what I am thinking about or what my thought is directed toward. The act reveals itself along with this object as a kind of by-product, albeit an essential one.

When our act of C1 has as its object a mental rather than a physical process, it is an act of reflective thinking, or thinking of thinking, and gives us knowledge of what goes on in our mind.

If we were conscious of all our acts of thinking by separate acts, then the charge of infinite regress would be justified. Suppose that whenever I am conscious of a mental act, there is another mental act, namely, that of being conscious of the first act. This second act will also be a mode of thought and hence something of which I am conscious, since according to Descartes we are conscious of all our thoughts. But my consciousness of the second act requires yet another act, of which I am also conscious, and so on. The way out of the regress is to deny the premise upon which it is based: that consciousness of every act of thinking consists in a separate

---

5. Sixth Meditation, AT 7:72–73; CSM 2:50–51; HR 1:185–86; Fifth Replies, AT 7:358; CSM 2:248; HR 2:212. For Descartes, then, mental processes are not only different from physical processes; some of them have no physical counterparts. In this respect Descartes's dualism is more radical than "Cartesian dualism" as that term is ordinarily understood. See M. D. Wilson 1978b.

mental act. The distinction between C1 and C2 makes it possible to reconcile Descartes's reply to Hobbes with his suggestion elsewhere that one thought can indeed be the object of another. The key statement in the reply to Hobbes is that it is "irrelevant . . . to say that one thought cannot be the subject of another thought." It is *irrelevant* to say this, because the consciousness that accompanies all thought is C2, a kind that does not require any act of thinking over and above the original act. Hobbes's error is to suppose that it would have to be C1, in which the object, in this case a thought, is something distinct from the awareness of it.

In order to counter the charge of infinite regress, it is not necessary to deny that one thought is ever the object of another thought. There are occasions on which we think about or reflect upon our thoughts, and in these cases one act of thinking does have another as its object. For instance, when I remember what it was like to see a rabbit on the grass, as opposed to remembering the rabbit, my act of remembering has as its object my prior act of perceiving. Similarly, when I reflect upon what I am doing when I conceive a triangle, the object of my thought is the act of conceiving. We do not think about every act of thinking, either while it is happening or afterwards. When we see things around us, we usually do not think "I'm seeing this." When we do have such thoughts it is in some special context. For example, what I see may be so bizarre that I have to wonder whether I am really seeing it or only imagining it. Or I may reflect upon my mental states as an exercise in Cartesian philosophy, to try to learn something about the nature of the mind.

Every thought is an object of C2, but not every thought is an object of another thought. Thus, even in those cases in which we do think about our thinking, when one act becomes the object of another, an infinite regress does not arise, since the act of thinking of thinking does not itself have to be the object of a further act. As a mode of thought, it must be an object of C2, but the act of which it is the object of C2 is none other than itself.

The claim is sometimes made, by philosophers and nonphilosophers alike, that all consciousness is self-consciousness. Applied to Descartes's theory, this claim is false for C1 and misleading in regard to C2. Acts of C1 can have—indeed most of them do have—objects other than the self and its own thoughts. Relatively little of one's mental activity consists of reflecting upon one's own thoughts or upon the fact that it is oneself who is having them. As for C2, it is true that everything of which I am conscious is a thought of mine. But in being conscious (C2) of my thinking, I may not realize that these thoughts are mine or that it is I myself who am thinking. This sort of self-knowledge comes only with reflective thinking. One can easily imagine a being who never happens upon this particular thought, either through lack of intellectual development or for want of application.

INCORRIGIBILITY AND EVIDENCE

It is commonly held that the Cartesian theory of mind involves two problematic theses.[6] The first is that one cannot be mistaken about one's own mental states. If I believe that I am in a certain state, then I am in that state. For instance, if I believe that I am in pain, then I really am in pain; nothing a doctor might say about my physical or psychological condition can prove me wrong. This is known as the incorrigibility thesis. The second thesis is that every mental state is evident to the one who has it. If I am in a certain state, then I know that I am in that state. If I am in pain, I know I am; I cannot have a painful feeling without knowing it. This is the evidence thesis. An important consequence of our analysis of Cartesian consciousness is that Descartes is committed to neither of these theses.

Let us start with the incorrigibility thesis: if I believe I am in a certain state, then I am in that state. Twentieth-century philosophers tend to favor a dispositional analysis of belief, according to which a statement such as "She believes that men are all alike" means that if in appropriate circumstances she is asked whether men are all alike, she answers yes. Descartes, however, treats belief as a mental act. To believe a proposition is to accept or assent to it. Belief is by no means equivalent to C2. When a person believes that a certain mode of thought exists, two acts of thinking are distinguishable: the act of belief and the mental act that is believed to exist. The former act is neither necessary nor sufficient for the existence of the latter.

To illustrate, suppose you think of God as a gaseous vertebrate. You may believe that you are thereby conceiving of God, but you are really only imagining him. You are conscious (C2) of your act of imagining, but you believe that it is an act of conceiving. Thus you have an act of imagining but do not believe that you have one, and you do not have

---

6. The following hold this view in one form or another: Kenny 1968, 72–73; Ryle 1949, 13–14, 154–60; Williams 1978, 49–50, 80–84; M. D. Wilson 1978a, 151. For criticism of Wilson's version of the evidence thesis, see Radner 1988.

an act of conceiving though you believe you do. Descartes is perfectly willing to acknowledge that such things happen. In his July 1641 letter to Mersenne he remarks that a certain correspondent "is not a man to think he cannot conceive a thing when he cannot imagine it, as if this was the only way we have of thinking and conceiving" (AT 3:393; K 105). Presumably there are people who do make this sort of mistake, and such people are also likely to have false beliefs about their own acts of thinking.

Suppose we try to save the incorrigibility thesis by adding a qualification. If I believe I am in state x and I understand what it means to be in state x, then I am in state x. Provided that I know what the word "conceive" means, surely I cannot be mistaken in believing that I am conceiving. In ordinary cases of identification, it is quite possible for one to identify a thing incorrectly even though one knows perfectly well what the term means. I know that a chiliagon is a thousand-sided figure, yet I may apply the term to a nine-hundred-ninety-eight-sided figure, having miscounted the sides. Can this sort of thing happen with one's own mental states? There is every reason to think that it can.

The best candidates for this sort of misidentification are cases in which it takes a lot of reflection to determine whether the term applies. Take the passion of repentance. Descartes defines it in *The Passions of the Soul* as "a kind of sadness, which results from our believing that we have done some evil deed" (AT 11:472; CSM 1:396; HR 1:417). A little study will make this definition clear. Once it is well understood, there is still the problem of determining whether it accurately describes what one is now feeling. One may not be in a condition to do this. As Descartes notes in the *Passions*, "experience shows that those who are the most strongly agitated by their passions are not those who know them best" (AT 11:349; CSM 1:339; HR 1:344). I may believe that I feel repentance whereas what I really feel is remorse, defined by Descartes as "a kind of sadness which results from our doubting that something we are doing, or have done, is good" (AT 11:464; CSM 1:392; HR 1:412).

Suppose we reformulate the incorrigibility thesis so that it makes no reference to the specific type of mental state. Let it simply read: If I believe I am in a mental state, then I am in a mental state. On this formulation I can mistakenly believe that I am in state x rather than y, where x and y stand for subclasses of mental states such as conceiving and imagining. But I cannot err in my belief that it is a mental state. Does Descartes subscribe to this amended version of the incorrigibility thesis? Yes he does, but only as an instance of the form "if I . . . , then I am in a mental state." Fill in the blank with any act of which you have C2 and you get a true statement. Any of the following will do for a starter: "doubt that I am in a mental state"; "believe that you are in a mental state"; "believe that the Easter bunny exists"; "imagine a golden mountain"; "feel remorse." The statement "if I believe I am in a mental state, then I am in a mental state" is on exactly the same footing as any other true substitution instance. Its truth depends on belief's being a mode of thought, not on any special status for a certain class of beliefs. As an incorrigibility thesis it is vacuous.

We turn now to the evidence thesis: if I am in a certain state, then I know that I am in that state. According to Anthony Kenny (1968, 49) this thesis follows from Descartes's definition of thought, for "according to Descartes's definition, if we wish to find whether a given verb φ, which is applied to human beings, signifies a kind of thought or not, we must ask 'is it true that when I φ I know that I φ?' Descartes therefore makes it true by definition that if I think, I know that I think." On our interpretation it is true by definition that if I think, I am conscious (C2) of thinking. C2 does not consist in knowledge, nor is it a sufficient condition for knowledge. This is certainly true if knowledge means actual cognizance, for then knowing that one thinks would require a separate mental act. Descartes makes it quite plain that we do not know all our modes of thought in this sense. In the third part of the *Discourse on the Method* he acknowledges that people are often ignorant of their beliefs. He goes on to explain that "believing something and knowing that one believes it are different acts of thinking, and the one often occurs without the other" (AT 6:23; CSM 1:122; HR 1:95).

What if knowledge is given a dispositional meaning? In that case I could still be said to know I am in a certain state even though I am not actually taking cognizance of the fact that I am in it. There need not be an *act* of knowing in me; it is enough that I am able to respond appropriately if questioned.

We ordinarily attribute knowledge to a person only if that person can recall the information over some time interval. A student who allegedly knows the Pythagorean theorem ought to be able to answer questions about it on the upcoming examination. One can, of course, know something and subsequently forget it. Suppose, then, we refine the evidence thesis along the following lines: If I am in a certain state, and I am asked about it within a reasonable time interval, I will be able to answer that I am or was in that state. What time interval is reasonable? Twenty years is obviously too long. What about twenty minutes—or twenty seconds? In the letter for Arnauld dated 29 July 1648, Descartes asserts that mental states are sometimes forgotten immediately after they occur: "Being conscious of our thoughts at the time when we are thinking them is not the same as remembering them afterwards. Thus, we do not have any thoughts in sleep without being conscious of them at the moment they occur; though commonly we forget them immediately" (AT 5:221; K 235). If by "reasonable time interval" we mean any interval, no matter how short, after the mental event has occurred, then Descartes does not subscribe to this version of the evidence thesis. According to him, a person can be in a mental state at one moment, be asked about it immediately afterwards, and not be able to say what state it was.

Suppose we further amend the evidence thesis so that it only applies while the mental episode is actually occurring. If I am in a certain state, and I am asked about it while I am in it, I will be able to answer that I am in that state. If I am asked about it at a later time, I may or may not be able to anwswer. This version is no more acceptable than the previous one. We have already noted Descartes's statement in the *Passions* that those who are most agitated by their passions are not those who know them best. When one is agitated, one's perceptions of one's mental states are apt to be obscure and confused, rendering correct identification difficult if not impossible. An astute and sympathetic questioner can be of aid in the introspective process. After calming down the agitated person, the questioner can draw attention to the identifying features of the relevant mental states—by asking, for example, "Do you believe that what you did was evil, or do you merely doubt whether it was good?" In the course of answering, the person may come to realize that he is feeling regret rather than repentance. This seems to suggest yet another version of the evidence thesis: If I am in a certain state, then I can learn that I am in that state. There is, however, nothing special about such "knowledge" of one's own mental states, for one has exactly the same sort of "knowledge" of the truths of mathematics and indeed of anything knowable. As an evidence thesis it is worthless.

INFANT THOUGHT

If all thinking involved reflection on one's own mental states, then any being that failed to think about its own thinking would fail to think at all; in other words, it would be mindless. In such a case it would be fairly easy to argue that animals do not think. One would simply have to point out that they lack the wherewithal to engage in introspection. Having no concepts of pain, anger, and so on, they cannot be said to identify their own feelings and passions. Thus they cannot form the belief that they are in this state rather than that. Moreover, having no concept of self, they cannot be said to know that they have mental states at all.

This easy argument against animal thinking is not open to Descartes. Cartesian thought is by definition that of which the thinker has C2, and C2 is different from reflective thinking. From the statement that all minds are conscious (C2) of their thoughts, it by no means follows that all minds have introspective awareness of their own states. Descartes admits that there are individuals who think without reflecting upon their thoughts. They are human infants, among whom he includes babes in the womb. "I do not doubt," he writes in the Fourth Replies, "that the mind begins to think as soon as it is implanted in the body of an infant, and that it is immediately aware of its thoughts, even though it does not remember this afterwards because the impressions of these thoughts do not remain in the memory" (AT 7:246; CSM 2:171–72; HR 2:115). Thus the thoughts of infants are like the unremembered dreams of adults. "I had reason to assent," he writes to Hyperaspistes (August 1641), "that the human soul, wherever it be, even in the mother's womb, is always thinking. . . . This does not mean that I believe that the mind of an infant meditates on metaphysics in its mother's womb; not at all. . . . it seems most reasonable to think that a mind newly united to an infant's body is wholly occupied in perceiving or feeling the ideas of pain, pleasure, heat, cold and other similar ideas which arise from its union and intermingling with the body" (AT 3:423–24; K 111). He goes on to propose that the fetal mind has implicit knowledge of God, itself, and self-evident truths "in the same way as adult humans have when they are not attending to them. . . . I have no doubt that if it were taken out of the prison of the body it would find them within itself" (AT 3:424; K 111).

Malebranche develops the Cartesian position on fetal thought in the second book of *The Search after Truth*. He explains that although the soul of the fetus is separate from the mother's soul, its body is attached to hers, and because of this attachment the fetus is subject to the same sensations and passions that arise in the mother's mind due to its union with the body. "Thus, children see what their mothers see, hear the same cries, receive the same impressions from objects, and are aroused by the same passions" (OC 1:234; S 113). The delicate body of the fetus is vulnerable to disorder as a result of the mother's traumatic experiences. Malebranche cites the instance of a mother who witnessed the execution of a criminal. The disturbance to her brain was magnified in her unborn child and affected its physical and mental development. The child came into the world insane and with his body broken in the same way as the criminal's (OC 1:239;

S 115). Even when no physical deformity results, there is enough influence on the tiny brain to produce thoughts in the fetal mind like those of the mother: "If the mother imagines and strongly desires to eat pears, for example, the unborn . . . imagines them and desires them just as ardently" (OC 1:242; S 117). Since "there are few women without some weakness, or who have not been disturbed by some passion during pregnancy, there must be very few children whose minds are not distorted in some way, and who are not dominated by some passion" (OC 1:246; S 119). The corruption of the mother's nature is passed on to the child, directing its thoughts and inclinations away from God and toward material things.

Why attribute thoughts to fetuses and yet deny them to animals? Granted, animals do not think of God and eternal truths and have no potential to think of these things. But why insist that they lack thought and consciousness altogether? If the disposition of the lamb to flee the wolf can be communicated to it in its mother's womb, as Malebranche suggests (OC 1:242; S 117), why cannot the lamb acquire the passion of fear to go along with the disposition?

In his letter to Henry More of 15 April 1649, Descartes makes an interesting case for positing a metaphysical difference between animals and human infants: "I should not judge that infants had minds unless I saw that they were of the same nature as adults; but animals never grow up enough for any certain sign of thought to be detected in them" (AT 5: 345; K 251). What are these signs of thought that no animal ever "grows up enough" to exhibit? We explore Descartes's answer in the next chapter.

2

Descartes's Two Tests

Early in the seventeenth century, visitors to the royal gardens of Saint-Germain-en-Laye watched life-sized statues behave in surprisingly lifelike ways. In one grotto Orpheus made lovely music on his lyre while birds sang and animals danced around him. In another a girl in contemporary dress played the organ. In the grotto of Perseus and Andromeda, Perseus struck the head of the dragon, forcing it to sink into the water. Constructed by the Italian engineer Thomas Francini for Henry IV of Navarre, the machines worked by hydraulic action. When visitors stepped on a concealed panel, a valve opened and water rushed through a network of pipes in the statue, causing it to move (Gruyer 1922; Hautecoeur 1959; Prasteau 1968).

In the *Treatise on Man* Descartes draws an analogy between the human body and the automata in the royal gardens. He compares the nerves and animal spirits with pipes and water, the heart with the source of water, the cavities of the brain with storage tanks, the muscles and tendons with the devices and springs that move the parts of the statue.[1] The stimulation of the sense organs by external objects, he says, is like the triggering of automata movement by visitors inadvertently stepping on the hidden tiles. He gives the example of a bathing Diana who flees into the reeds; if the visitor tries to follow her, a Neptune comes forth and brandishes his trident (AT 11:131; CSM 1:100-101).

---

1. "The parts of the blood which penetrate as far as the brain serve . . . to produce in it a certain very fine wind, or rather a very lively and pure flame, which is called the *animal spirits*" (AT 11:129; CSM 1:100).

The *Treatise on Man* was published posthumously in 1664. It was originally intended to be part of a larger work along with *The World*. Descartes abandoned this project when Galileo was condemned by the Church in 1633. Like *The World*, the *Treatise on Man* is presented as a fable. Descartes says that he is going to describe "men who resemble us," people "composed, as we are, of a soul and a body." It is to these surrogates that he refers when he states: "I suppose the body to be nothing but a statue or machine made of earth, which God forms with the explicit intention of making it as much as possible like us" (AT 11:120; CSM 1:99). As in *The World*, the fable is a subterfuge. Descartes is talking about real human bodies.

Obviously not every aspect of human anatomy has a counterpart in the moving statues in the royal gardens. Human physiology is not simply a branch of hydraulic engineering. Nevertheless, the human body, being part of the extended world, is composed entirely of extended parts, and these parts move according to the same laws of motion as the rest of the material world. In this sense the human body may be considered a "machine made of earth."

Remarkable as she was, it is highly unlikely that the Diana in the royal grotto would have been mistaken for a real person—at least not for long. It would be unnecessary to open her up and observe the plumbing to be convinced of her mechanical nature. Simply observe her in action. Enter the grotto a dozen times; she is always equally "surprised" and "hides" in exactly the same way. Without denigrating the genius of her creator, it is possible to imagine an even more intricate mechanism enabling the automaton to respond differently under different conditions. One can, for instance, imagine a Diana who sometimes flees, sometimes gets dressed, and sometimes just stands and waves. No matter how complex a mechanism we imagine, insists Descartes, it will invariably lack something that real humans possess. A human body is a "machine made of earth," but a *human being* is "composed of a soul and a body." To have soul or mind is to think. Human beings think, whereas mere machines do not.

Surely the mechanical animals at Saint-Germain-en-Laye were just as inflexible in their actions as the mechanical people. It would take a more intricate design to achieve a more lifelike effect. To this extent the human and animal cases are similar, but here the comparison ends. According to Descartes, there is nothing in real animals that cannot, at least in principle, be duplicated in their mechanical counterparts. The added element in human nature—soul or mind—is missing in animals.

"It seems incredible," remarks Arnauld in the Fourth Objections, "that it can come about, without the assistance of any soul, that the light reflected from the body of a wolf onto the eyes of a sheep should move the minute fibers of the optic nerves, and that on reaching the brain this motion should spread the animal spirits throughout the nerves in the manner necessary to precipitate the sheep's flight" (AT 7:205; CSM 2:144; HR 2:85-86). In reply, Descartes points out that the physiology of motion is purely mechanical in humans as well as in animals. Not even those movements we call voluntary are brought about by direct action of the mind upon the limbs. The mind merely alters the course of the animal spirits as they flow past its "principal seat," the pineal gland, and the spirits go into the muscles, causing them to distend and contract (cf. AT 11:354-55; CSM 1:341; HR 1:347). "Now a very large number of the motions occurring inside us do not depend in any way on the mind. These include heartbeat, digestion, nutrition, respiration when we are asleep, and also such waking actions as walking, singing and the like, when these occur without the mind attending to them" (AT 7:229-30; CSM 2:161; HR 2:103-4). He compares the sheep's flight at the sight of a wolf to a man's act of thrusting out his hand to protect his head at the sight of an impending fall. Such a motion is produced "without any mental volition, just as it would be produced in a machine" (AT 7:230; CSM 2:161; HR 2:104). What Descartes means is that the man does not act deliberately; the movement is not initiated by a desire to put the hand in this position. Likewise there is no sheep correlate of "Feets, do your stuff" when the eyes take in the wolf image.

Descartes may have satisfied Arnauld's objection about the necessity of conscious intervention for the movement of the limbs, but he has not established that either the man or the sheep lacks awareness of the situation and desires pertaining to it. If in falling the thought flashes through your mind, "Oh no, here I go," could not the sheep also be experiencing something like apprehension or fear as it runs away?

The more general issue of animal awareness is raised by unnamed theologians and philosophers in the Sixth Objections. In the course of defending the doctrine that the soul is corporeal, they declare that dogs "know that they are running" when awake, "just as in their dreams they know that they are barking." The opposite view has no proof. "If you say that a dog does not know that it is running or thinking, then this is an assertion that cannot be proved; the dog might well make a similar judgement about us, and suppose that when we are running or thinking, we do not know that we are running or thinking" (AT 7:414; CSM 2:279; HR 2:235). The phrase "know that it is running or thinking" unnecessarily confuses the issue in two ways. First, the question is whether animals think at all, not whether they know that they are thinking. Second, the dog does not have to know that it is running, insofar as knowledge involves a judgment based on reasons. It only has to be aware of running.

Descartes answers that the advocates of animal thinking are the ones who have no proof of their assertion. They say to him, "You do not see the dog's internal mode of operation any more than he sees yours" (AT 7:414; CSM 2:279; HR 2:235). Yet they do not hesitate to attribute all manner of inner states to dogs "as if they were present in the animals' hearts" (AT 7:426; CSM 2:288; HR 2:244). In order to prove that animals possess thought, it is not enough to notice that they behave in ways that in us are accompanied by thought. That is, the following argument from analogy will not do: Animals engage in behavior x; humans engage in behavior x; behavior x is accompanied by thought in humans; therefore behavior x is accompanied by thought in animals. Let behavior x be sneezing. When we sneeze we are usually aware of it, but our sneezes do not depend on our awareness of them. They can be explained solely in terms of the laws of physiology, which are at bottom mechanical laws. We can speculate that dogs and cats are similarly aware of their sneezes, but this is only speculation, or as Descartes puts it, "saying something without proving it" (AT 7:426; CSM 2:288; HR 2:244). Unlike our own case, where we can reflect on our inner experience, all we have to go on is their behavior, and there is nothing about this particular case that requires us to posit awareness.

As for myself, says Descartes, I did not merely assert that brutes possess no thought, but I "proved it by very strong arguments which no one has refuted up till now" (AT 7:426; CSM 2:287-88; HR 2:244). He is referring to Part Five of the *Discourse on the Method*. In reconstructing his argument we shall not limit ourselves to this work but shall call upon other sources as well, especially the letters to Reneri for Pollot (April 1638), the Marquess of Newcastle (23 November 1646), and Henry More (5 February 1649).

In the *Discourse* Descartes offers "two very certain means" of recognizing that machines imitating humans are not real people. "The first is that they could never use words, or put together other signs, as we do in order to declare our thoughts to others." What is important, he explains, is not merely the ability to utter different phrases in response to different stimuli, but the ability to "produce different arrangements of words so as to give an appropriately meaningful answer to whatever is said in its presence." The second way is that "even though such machines might do some things as well as we do them, or perhaps even better, they would inevitably fail in others, which would reveal that they were acting not through understanding but only from the disposition of their organs" (AT 6:56-57; CSM 1:139-40; HR 1:116).

He goes on to argue that animals differ from people in precisely the same two ways. No animal is capable of "arranging various words together and forming an utterance from them" as even the dullest people can do to express their thoughts. "This shows not merely that the beasts have less reason than men, but that they have no reason at all." Furthermore, "although many animals show more skill than we do in some of their actions, yet the same animals show none at all in many others; so what they do better does not prove that they have any intelligence. . . . It proves rather that they have no intelligence at all, and that it is nature which acts in them according to the disposition of their organs" (AT 6:57-59; CSM 1:140-41; HR 1:116-17).

There is little doubt that for Descartes the "two very certain means" function as tests that real people pass and machines fail.[2] But if these are tests then two questions naturally arise. First, tests of what? And second, what counts as passing them? Descartes is not entirely clear about either answer. As for the first question, it is not clear whether they are supposed to be behavioral tests for the presence of thought in general, of reason in particular, or, as Chomsky (1966, 78) suggests, tests "by which we can determine whether a device is really human." As for the second, it is not clear what a machine would have to do to use language as we do, nor what degree of skill it must display in what kinds of actions. The role of the tests in the beast-machine argument hinges on the answers to these questions. Following Gunderson (1964), we shall call the two tests the *language test* and the *action test*, respectively.

THE LANGUAGE TEST

The language test involves the ability to put words together in different ways that are appropriate to a wide variety of situations. Noam Chomsky in his *Cartesian Linguistics* (1966, 4-5) credits Descartes with having recognized "the 'creative aspect' of ordinary language use—its property being both unbounded in scope and stimulus-free." By "stimulus-free" he means "free from control by identifiable external stimuli or internal physiological states" (11). It is true that, for Descartes, a necessary condition for passing the language test is that at least some of one's utterances must be stimulus-free. A machine so constructed that "if you touch it in one spot it asks

---

2. Haldane and Ross's rendering of "deux moyens trés certains" as "two very certain tests," though not literally correct, nevertheless agrees with the spirit of Descartes's teaching.

what you want of it, if you touch it in another it cries out that you are hurting it, and so on" would fail the language test since there are many occasions on which such automatic utterances are not "appropriately meaningful" (AT 6:56-57; CSM 1:140; HR 1:116). It is questionable, however, whether Descartes would agree that an unbounded scope of responses is necessary. What is important for him is that the responses should be able to suit an unlimited range of *occasions*. A limited (albeit large) linguistic repertoire may suffice for this purpose. A single utterance such as "I don't understand" may serve as an "appropriately meaningful answer" in an endless variety of situations.

Manifestation of what Chomsky calls the "creative aspect" of language use is clearly not sufficient for passing Descartes's language test. Noting that "the properties of being unbounded and being stimulus-free are independent," Chomsky gives an example of a machine whose responses are stimulus-free but not unbounded: "An automaton may have only two responses that are produced randomly" (1966, 77). Consider a more complicated machine: one that, having been fed a large vocabulary and programmed to follow the basic rules of English grammar, randomly generates sentences such as "In the wet green grass was the large fat frog" and "This is the dog that chased the cow that chased the horse that ate the mouse." The utterances of such a machine would be both stimulus-free and unbounded. They would not, however, be "appropriately meaningful." Thus the machine would fail the language test.

Occasionally the output of a computer is mistaken for that of a real human being. The programs capable of such deception are, of course, far more sophisticated than the mechanical designs envisaged by Descartes. Yet we fall prey to the deception and are able to unmask it precisely as Descartes said. What fools us is the uncanny appropriateness of the replies. When they become grossly out of place, we are fooled no longer. Our test of the humanlikeness of computer-generated conversation is how well it accords with our intuitions about what is and is not appropriate in a given linguistic situation.

ELIZA is the name of a family of language analysis programs developed in the mid-1960s by Joseph Weizenbaum of MIT. ELIZA consists of devices for locating key words, reassembling fragments into sentences, and so on. When given a script that parodies the interview techniques of Rogerian nondirective psychotherapy, ELIZA elicits information about the human participant's state of mind. For instance, to the statement "Perhaps I could learn to get along with my mother" comes the response "Tell me more about your family." When no key terms (e.g., "mother," "depressed") are forthcoming, ELIZA falls back on formulas such as "What makes you think that . . ." and "Does that have anything to do with . . . ," referring to earlier statements (Weizenbaum 1966, 1976).

In 1968 a vice-president of a high-tech firm typed a message into a teletype, believing that it would be received by a programmer in his company. Unbeknown to him, the computer was running a version of ELIZA. Here is the dialogue that ensued:

V.P.: Do you think that I can use the computer this morning?

ELIZA: Why do you ask?

V.P.: I might be able to make some additional telcomp sales.

ELIZA: Why aren't you sure?

V.P.: My prospective customers have never seen a demonstration of the system.

ELIZA: Does this mean very much to you?

V.P.: Of course it does.

ELIZA: You seem very positive about that.

V.P.: This is ridiculous.

ELIZA: What do you mean this is ridiculous?

V.P.:Is there any reason why I can't use the computer now?

ELIZA: Tell me more about your prospective customers.

(Heppenheimer 1985, 66)

The sort of reply that seems eminently suitable and enlightening in the therapeutic setting appears perverse in the context of business. Yet the remarks were not so completely out of place as to raise the vice-president's suspicions. After all, people do sometimes respond in an obtuse or teasing manner. Indeed, when the vice-president, having had enough, finally telephoned the programmer, the latter, whether deliberately or not, gave a reply that could easily have come from ELIZA:

V.P.: Why are you being so snotty to me?

PROGRAMMER: What do you mean, why am I being so snotty to you?

ELIZA's mechanical nature is fully revealed when it engages in that brand of off-the-wall conversation that so typifies the computer. Here is an excerpt from a dialogue reported by Colby, Watt, and Gilbert:

> PROGRAM: We want to focus on your relationships with people who bother you most.
>
> PERSON: That is easy. At the moment it is a surfeit of children in too small a space.
>
> PROGRAM: Is it.
>
> PERSON: Yes.
>
> PROGRAM: Can you describe an example.
>
> PERSON: Of what.
>
> PROGRAM: I see.
>
> PERSON: No you do not.
>
> PROGRAM: Can you elaborate.
>
> PERSON: What on.
>
> PROGRAM: Let's explore further your feelings about it.
>
> (1966, 151-52)

To be sure, one can conjure up imaginary situations in which a human being might make the same degenerate conversational moves that the program makes here. The person may, for example, be trying to imitate a computer, in which case the responses are perfectly appropriate. In the dialogue above, the program is supposed to behave like a nondirective psychotherapist interviewing a patient. The output is inappropriate in this context. The moral of this tale is that in order to determine whether utterances are appropriate to the situation, one must first determine what the situation is. This lesson becomes important when we apply the language test to animals.

According to Descartes, the same two tests that distinguish machines from people also serve to distinguish animals from people. Of the language test, he writes in the *Discourse*: "For it is quite remarkable that there are no men so dull-witted or stupid—and this includes even madmen—that they are incapable of arranging various words together and forming an utterance from them in order to make their thoughts understood; whereas there is no other animal, however perfect and well-endowed it may be, that can do the like" (AT 6:57; CSM 1:140; HR 1:116-17). This difference between man and beast cannot be explained by the presence or absence of speech organs. Some animals, namely, parrots and magpies, have the ability to utter words; and some people, namely, deaf-mutes, lack this ability yet "invent their own signs to make themselves understood by those who, being regularly in their company, have the time to learn their language" (AT 6:58; CSM 1:140; HR 1:117).

Following conventional wisdom, Descartes focuses on the words of avian mimics as the most ostensively languagelike of animal vocalizations. The utterances of parrots do not function like human speech. In his letter of 23 November 1646 to the Marquess of Newcastle, Descartes explains that parrots' words do not count as speech because they are not "relevant." By contrast, even the ravings of madmen are "relevant to particular topics" though they do not "follow reason" (AT 4:574; K 206).

"Nor should we think," continues the *Discourse*, "like some of the ancients, that the beasts speak, although we do not understand their language. For if that were true, then since they have many organs that correspond to ours, they could make themselves understood by us as well as by their fellows" (AT 6:58; CSM 1:141; HR 1:117). From the reference to similar organs and the phrase "make themselves understood," it is evident that Descartes is here contrasting animals to human deaf-mutes who, despite their failure to master conventional speech, nevertheless "invent their own signs to make themselves understood." In other words, if the animals cannot master our language, then let them invent one that we can understand.

The onus on the animals is greater than on deaf-mutes, for the latter have as their audience "those who, being regularly in their company, have the time to learn their language." If we expect animals to make themselves understood by us, the least we can do is to make the effort to be regularly in their company. We should take the time to learn their natural communication systems instead of expecting them to learn our signs or to invent new ones for our benefit. Perhaps Gassendi had something like this in mind when he objected that Descartes was being unfair to the animals: "You may say that even a delirious man can still string words together to express his meaning, which even the wisest of the brutes cannot do. But surely you are not being fair if you expect the brutes to employ human language and are not prepared to consider their own kind of language" (AT 7:271; CSM 2:189; HR 2:146).

What happens when the natural communication systems of animals are subjected to the language test? In answering the question, we must keep in mind that for Descartes the important thing about language as the expression of thought is the meaningful appropriateness of the utterances, rather than their formulation by grammatical rules.

Machines fail the language test because there are many situations in which their responses are inappropriate.[3] Talking birds fail because their speech is not relevant. What about the natural cries and gestures of animals? No matter what situation an animal is in, does it not behave in a way that is somehow appropriate to the situation? To be sure, its responses are sometimes the wrong ones to make; for example, it may give an alarm call when there really is no danger. But do not humans make the same sorts of errors? Appropriate responses are not necessarily correct responses.

Suppose a man walks up to a bird and says, "Little bird, what is the meaning of life?" "Dee dee dee," says the bird. From the man's point of view this is neither a wrong answer nor a cryptic one; it is not an answer at all. From the bird's perspective, however, the call fits the circumstances: it is exactly the right thing to say. Unlike the ELIZA case, this is no conversational breakdown. On the contrary, it is an accidental juxtaposition of utterances from two different communication systems, each with its own criteria of relevance.[4] In order to determine whether an animal's cries and gestures are appropriate, one must evaluate them in terms of the animal's world, not ours.

Descartes counters this line of argument by introducing a modification in the language test. He cautions in the *Discourse* against confusing speech with "the natural movements which express passions and which can be imitated by machines as well as by animals" (AT 6: 58; CSM 1: 140-41; HR 1: 117). Remember the imaginary machine that, when touched in a certain spot, cries out that you are hurting it. When he reiterates the language test in the letter to Newcastle, Descartes states that the external actions that show the presence of thought are "words, or other signs that are relevant to particular topics without expressing any passion. . . . I add also that these words or signs must not express any passion, to rule out not only cries of joy or sadness and the like, but also whatever can be taught by training to animals" (AT 4: 574; K 206-7).

---

3. Whether or not a computer has yet passed Descartes's language test, or ever will, is not at issue here. Descartes introduced the test as a way of distinguishing machines from people. If a computer ever does pass, then Descartes's argument must be posthumously modified in one of two ways: either machines can think or else the language test is not a test of the presence of thought.

4. The "chick-a-dee" call system of the black-capped chickadee has recently been shown to have a computable syntax. It is an open system in that the number of possible call-types that compute as grammatical is limitless. The semantics of the system has yet to be determined. See Hailman and Ficken 1986.

The magpie's "hello" is ruled out because it is just an expression of the bird's hope of receiving a tidbit. According to Descartes, all animal responses fall into the class of expressions of passion and for this reason cannot provide behavioral evidence of thought.

At first it seemed as though a creature passes the language test if and only if, for an endless variety of situations, the creature forms utterances appropriate to the situations. Now it appears that a creature passes the test if and only if, in a variety of situations, it forms utterances that are appropriate but do not express any passion.

One must be careful in the phrasing, lest more is demanded of animals than is forthcoming in human beings. Human assertions that are about things other than the speaker's internal state may be passionately expressed. For example, a child may shout, "The square of the hypotenuse is equal to the sum of the squares of the other two sides!" giving vent to his anger at another's obstinate denial of this obvious truth. One would be disinclined indeed to say that the child's behavior in this instance gives no indication of the presence of thought. Nor would one be any more inclined to say such a thing if the child *always* spoke with passion. To allow for this consideration, let us try the following reformulation of the language test: A creature passes the language test if and only if, in a variety of situations, the creature forms utterances that are appropriate and not solely expressions of passion.

The reformulation cannot stop here. It must rule out utterances that convey factual information about the world; otherwise many animals would pass the test. It would be anachronistic to fault Descartes for not taking into account the dance language of honeybees or the different alarm calls that some species have for different classes of predators. Nevertheless, twentieth-century ethological field research has yielded data of a kind that is well within the range of seventeenth-century experience.

A Thomson's gazelle, seeing a predator lurking in the distance, assumes an alert posture and gives a soft snort. The other gazelles near enough to hear it immediately stop grazing and took in the same direction (Walther 1969). The alarm signal serves not only to communicate the signaler's fear but also to convey information about the location of the fear-producing stimulus. The message is not simply "I'm scared," but more like "There's something scary over there in that direction."[5] Descartes cannot object that the animal's intent is only to express fear and that the factual information is just a by-product of its expression. As far as Descartes is concerned,

---

5. The example and the analysis are borrowed from Griffin 1984, 80.

intent does not enter into the picture at all. For him there can be no distinction between what an animal expresses and what its confederates pick up from its behavior. In this instance they pick up information about the world, not just about the snorter's inner physiological state.

In order to keep animals from passing the language test, Descartes must find some feature that is lacking in animal cries and gestures no matter how varied they are, how appropriate to the animal's situation, and how much information they convey. According to Descartes, what is missing is that animals never communicate anything pertaining to pure thought. Thus he writes to Henry More (5 February 1649):

> Yet, although all animals easily communicate to us, by voice or bodily movement, their natural impulses of anger, fear, hunger and so on, it has never yet been observed that any brute animal reached the stage of using real speech, that is to say, of indicating by word or sign something pertaining to pure thought and not to natural impulse. Such speech is the only certain sign of thought hidden in a body. All men use it, however stupid and insane they may be, and though they may lack tongue and organs of voice; but no animals do. Consequently it can be taken as a real specific difference between men and dumb animals. (AT 5:278; K 244-45)

By *pure thought* he means thought unaccompanied by any corporeal process. The apprehension of a predator in a certain direction has a strong sensible component and hence does not qualify as pure thought. The apprehension of mathematical and metaphysical truths is pure thought so long as the imagination is not involved. The reason Descartes singles out the expression of pure thought is that it is the only sort of linguistic behavior that cannot in his view be fully explained mechanistically. The reformulation then must read as follows: A creature passes the language test if and only if, in a variety of situations, the creature forms appropriate utterances that are not solely expressions of passion and that pertain to pure thought.

The language test started out as a way of distinguishing between human beings and machines resembling them. That is to say, it was a test of genuine humanness. When applied to animals, its role is not simply to establish that they are not human; everyone already knows they aren't. Descartes uses the language test to draw a further conclusion about animals. The conclusion is variously stated. In the *Discourse* it is that animals "have no reason"; in the letter to Newcastle, "that they have no thoughts." In the letter to Reneri for Pollot, which we have yet to discuss, he goes further and suggests that animals lack "any real feeling or emotion" (AT 2:41; K 54), a puzzling statement in light of his insistence elsewhere that they express only their passions. The language test in its final formulation concerns only one class of mental acts, namely, acts of pure understanding. Strictly speaking, failure to pass it is evidence for the absence of pure thought only. Yet in drawing his conclusion about animals, Descartes slips into the wider meaning of "thought" as all that of which the subject is conscious. A similar slippage occurs with the action test.

THE ACTION TEST

The second way in which machines differ from humans is that although machines do some things as well or better than we do, they invariably fail at others. This shows that they act "not through understanding but only from the disposition of their organs" (AT 6:57; CSM 1:140; HR 1:116). If you want to determine whether a creature acts through reason, you observe whether there are any areas in which it falls short of human performance. If there are, then the creature acts not through reason but only from the disposition of its organs, that is to say, mechanically.

To fall short of human performance obviously does not mean to do something worse than an individual person. Otherwise all of us would fail the test, since everyone is excelled by someone at something. Most of us are worse than Bobby Fischer at chess, and Bobby Fischer is worse than Itzhak Perlman at playing the violin. Nor does it mean doing something worse than any known human being. A chess-playing pig would be remarkable even if it played worse than any human player. As with the language test, where the telling case is conversational breakdown, so with the action test the issue is whether a certain type of action can be performed at all.

It is essential to the formulation that the creature under test be compared with human beings. To see why this is so, consider what happens when we try to formulate the test in more general terms as follows: In order to determine whether a creature of type A is acting through reason, you observe whether there are any areas in which it falls short of the performance of creatures of another type B. If there are, then it does not act through reason but only from the disposition of its organs. Let A stand for monarch butterflies and B for humans. Butterflies cannot calculate square roots or dance the samba, therefore they do not act through reason. So far so good. But notice what happens when A stands for humans and B for monarch butterflies. Monarchs can spin cocoons, and they can find their way to the mountains of Michoacán near Mexico City from thousands of miles away without a map. Humans fall woefully short of butterfly performance in these areas. Therefore they do not act through reason but only from the disposition of their organs.

The seventeenth-century French poet Cyrano de Bergerac makes fun of the Cartesian argument by turning it upside down in a similar way. In *The States and Empires of the Sun* the birds argue that man cannot possibly be endowed with reason:—"man, whose mind is so perceptive, but who cannot tell sugar from arsenic, and will swallow hemlock, which his fine judgment tells him is parsley." That was how the wisest among them argued. As for the rest, they murmured: "It has neither beak, nor feathers, nor claws—and yet its soul is supposed to be spiritual! O gods! What impertinence!" (Cyrano de Bergerac 1965, 171).

Comparison of A's actions with B's cannot provide evidence for or against reason in A unless it is already established that B acts through reason. The action test can be stated thus: In order to determine whether a creature of type A is acting through reason, you compare its performance with that of creatures that do act through reason. If A's performance falls short of B's, where B is a creature that acts through reason, then A does not act through reason but only from the disposition of its organs. The B always stands for human beings because they are the only beings known for sure to have reason. Only in the human case do we have direct access to the reasoning process.

Linguistic performance is a kind of action. Any creature that falls short of human linguistic performance does some things worse than people. It would seem, then, that if a creature fails the language test, it ipso facto fails the action test. It is possible, however, for a creature to fail the action test without failing the language test; it may equal human linguistic performance yet fall short in some nonlinguistic area. Gunderson (1964, 199) endorses this view of the relation between the two tests. In our view, failing the language test is a sufficient condition for failing the action test, only because the latter rests on too narrow a conception of acting through reason.

Descartes distinguishes acting through reason from acting through the disposition of the organs in terms of reason's universal applicability. "For whereas reason is a universal instrument which can be used in all kinds of situations, these organs need some particular disposition for each particular action" (AT 6:57; CSM 1:140; HR 1:116). This is not to say that an individual possessing reason will actually apply it in every situation. If having reason meant always acting through reason, then none of us could be said to have reason, for we often act mechanically. In one of Descartes's favorite examples of human mechanical action, the disposition of the organs conflicts with what reason prescribes, and the organs win out over reason. He writes in *The Passions of the Soul:* "If someone suddenly thrusts his hand in front of our eyes as if to strike us, then even if we know that he is our friend, that he is doing this only in fun, and that he will take care not to harm us, we still find it difficult to prevent ourselves from closing our eyes" (AT 11:338-39; CSM 1:333; HR 1:338).

It is necessary to distinguish between acting through reason and acting in accordance with reason. The former requires that the agent possess the faculty of reason but the latter does not. Actions *in accordance with* reason are actions that are justifiable in terms of some set of principles. It is possible for a rational observer to demonstrate that the act is optimal in regard to a given end. The agent, however, has no awareness of the principles and does not reason from them. To act *through* reason is to base one's action on the principles. One must be able to apprehend the principles, determine what follows from them, and use this information to decide on a course of action.

It is hard to tell whether a single act is being performed through reason or merely in accordance with reason. Taken case by case, there is no difference on the level of behavior. An observer can figure out that the action is optimal under the circumstances, but it remains an open question whether the agent did it because it was optimal. In order to determine whether the agent acted through reason or merely in accordance with it, one must observe how the agent behaves in other related contexts. If the agent acted on the basis of principles in the original case, it may be expected to use them in other cases where they are applicable and to determine its action accordingly.

Descartes claims that "although many animals show more skill than we do in some of their actions," this "does not prove that they have any intelligence, for if it did then they would have more intelligence than any of us and would excel us in everything" (AT 6:58-59; CSM 1:141; HR 1:117). M. D. Wilson (1978, 184) treats this passage as hyperbole: "His point, surely, is only that if animals used something like human reason to accomplish their various remarkable feats, then they should show qualities of adaptability, and learning abilities, far beyond any they actually exhibit." In other words, what he means is not that animals would be smarter than people, but only that they would be smarter than they are now.

Gunderson (1964) suggests that Descartes's main point remains intact when "everything" is replaced by "many other things" or "a wide range of things" (208). Gunderson's assessment of the passage, thus interpreted, is that the reasoning is "fundamentally sound and important" (206). One of Gunderson's examples is bird migration. We cannot assume that swallows are "good at maps, terrain, landmarks, or anything else in general. . . . The case of the swallows is not like the case of the fellow who is good at maps, but would be like the case of a fellow who was only able to get from Princeton to Capistrano to Princeton to..........etc." (209).

Descartes brings up swallows in the letter to Newcastle: "I know that animals do many things better than we do, but this does not surprise me. It can even be used to prove they act naturally and mechanically, like a clock which tells the time better than our judgment does. Doubtless when the swallows come in spring, they operate like clocks. The actions of honeybees are of the same nature, and the discipline of cranes in flight, and of apes in fighting, if it is true that they keep discipline" (AT 4:575; K 207). Having cited these instances of perfectly executed behavior, he switches to imperfectly executed behavior, namely, the instinct "of dogs and cats who scratch the earth for the purpose of burying their excrement; they hardly ever actually bury it, which shows that they act only by instinct and without thinking" (AT 4:576; K 207).

Animals, it seems, are damned if they do and damned if they don't. If cats and dogs thoroughly covered their droppings virtually every time, Descartes would cry mechanism just the same. The reason is that neither success nor failure is correlated with success or failure in other more or less closely related tasks. Dogs fail to bury their excrement yet they are perfectly capable of burying and digging up bones.

There are cases in which people act pretty much like Descartes's dogs and cats. Take young children brushing their teeth. The object of the exercise is to clean the teeth, yet few of them do a thorough job of it. They go through the motions without concern for completing the task, like the dogs and cats with their scratchings. Should we conclude that the children act mechanically and "without thinking"? Obviously they are not thinking in terms of the principles of oral hygiene. But there is another principle that is relevant here, namely, that one is supposed to brush one's teeth, and it is this principle which guides their action. Since they are acting through understanding—albeit to a very limited extent—they can be expected to show a similar understanding in other contexts, where there is something else that one is supposed to do.

If two agents A and B both do *x* through reason, then both must be applying some set of principles—but not necessarily the same set. How much competence they display in other areas will depend on which principles they use. Consider a child who learns to get from home to school, home to the corner store, and so on, by memorizing directions based on landmarks. She knows enough about navigation to adjust the directions to the situation.

For example, she knows how to proceed from a point halfway to school without having to begin at home. When a small detour is needed or a shortcut presents itself, she can work it into her routine without requiring a new set of directions. Her navigational principles will not take her very far in a strange neighborhood; she could never match the performance of someone proficient at maps and compass. Yet it would be a mistake to conclude that she uses no principles at all and does not act by reason.

The action test is set up on the assumption that the possession of reason is an all-or-nothing affair. At the beginning of the *Discourse* Descartes ventures the opinion that reason "exists whole and complete in each of us." He is speaking here of the faculty of reason, which he defines as "the power of judging well and of distinguishing the true from the false" (AT 6:2; CSM 1:111-12; HR 1:81-82). Although this faculty exists in all of us, we do not exercise it equally well. Indeed the aim of the *Discourse* is to show us how to conduct our reason better. The action test assumes more than just full possession of the *faculty* of reason, however. It also assumes that there is only one way to exercise the faculty in a given context—only one set of principles, skills, and techniques that can achieve a certain kind of result. If a creature does not use this set in this situation, it does not use reason at all. Without this assumption, A's failure to match B's performance, where B acts through reason, would not show that A fails to act through reason. The most that one could conclude is this: Either A does not act through reason, or A is using a different set of principles and techniques with a narrower range of application.

Given the assumption that there is only one way to exercise reason in a given context, it follows that if A does something better than B and does it through reason, then A is exercising reason better than B in this instance. Since A has proved itself a better reasoner in this case, one expects A to excel in other cases as well. This line of argument, we believe, lies behind Descartes's assertion about animals excelling us at everything. Animals do some things far better than any of us. If they did them by reason, Descartes is saying, then they have a method of conducting their reason that is far superior to any that humanity has so far devised. The birds flit among the branches, deftly avoiding obstacles with split-second maneuvers. To do this by instantaneously calculating velocities and trajectories would take superhuman mental agility and discipline.[6] If birds have reason, then they

---

6. The same holds for human feats of dexterity such as juggling. The Cartesian view is that such feats are accomplished not through reason but through acquired dispositions of the organs. In *The Search after Truth* 6.2.3 (OC 2:315; S 449-50) and the *Méditations chrétiennes*

direct it so well that their demonstrations approach intuitive knowledge in speed and accuracy. Think of what a rational being could accomplish with such a method at its disposal.

Descartes tells the Marquess of Newcastle that animals "only imitate or surpass us in those of our actions which are not guided by our thoughts" (AT 4:573; K 206). This is not strictly true. Descartes supplies examples of human mechanical actions: "It often happens that we walk or eat without thinking at all about what we are doing; and similarly, without using our reason, we reject things which are harmful for us, and parry the blows aimed at us" (AT 4:573; K 206). These examples fail to show that animals duplicate *only* our mechanical actions. One must look instead at human actions that are guided by thought and see whether animals ever imitate or surpass any of them. Dogs track by scent, which counts as a mechanical process. People's senses are not so keen, so they must resort to reason in tracking their quarry. In some kinds of situations dogs track better than men. So animals do sometimes surpass us in those of our actions that are guided by our thoughts.

There is an obvious contrast between acts we perform mechanically, such as fending off blows, and acts we perform through pure thought, such as solving mathematical equations. Descartes makes much of this contrast. There is, however, an extensive middle ground between these two extremes, an area which seems to get lost in the Cartesian shuffle. It comprises acts performed through reasoning from very limited and possibly faulty principles.

Once we allow that reason can manifest itself in limited ways, we must admit the possibility that a creature might act through reason in one area yet fall short of human performance in many other areas. Instead of comparing the creature's actions to what humans would do in similar circumstances, we should tailor the test to the species. Descartes's action test would be fairer to the brutes if it read like this: In order to determine whether a creature is acting through reason, find out whether it is using a set of principles. Consider all likely sets of principles on which the action could be based. Determine what would follow from them in other related contexts. See whether the creature acts accordingly in those contexts, assuming of course that it is physically capable of performing the acts. If the creature does not act in accordance with any of the alternative sets of principles in their relevant contexts, then this is prima facie evidence that it is not acting through reason.

---

et métaphysiques 6.11 (OC 10:62), Malebranche remarks that a juggler who knows nothing of anatomy can move his arms more skillfully than the most learned anatomist.

THE MAN WHO NEVER SAW ANIMALS

About a year after the publication of the *Discourse,* Pollot wrote a letter
to Reneri for Descartes (February 1638). In it he notes animal behaviors
that seem to belie the beast-machine doctrine. Animals make known their
affections and passions by signs, including "their regret at having done wrong."
He cites the story in Aristotle's *History of Animals* 9.47 about the horse
that hurled himself down a precipice when he discovered that he had mated
with his mother. Animals act "by a principle more excellent than by the
necessity arising from the disposition of their organs, namely by an instinct,
which is never found in a machine or in a clock, which have neither passion
nor affection, as animals do" (AT 1:514).

In reply (April 1638) Descartes presents a fable. Consider, he says, a
man raised in a place where he never saw animals other than humans. The
man helped to construct automata, some in human form, others shaped like
horses, dogs, birds, and so on. The mechanical animals were made to imitate
their living counterparts as far as possible, although the builders had no
firsthand knowledge of real animals and perhaps did not even know that
there were any such creatures actually in existence. Sometimes the man
encountered creatures in human form and wondered whether they were real
people. Experience taught him that there were two ways to tell machines
from real people: "first, that these automata never answered in word or sign,
except by chance, to questions put to them; and secondly, that though their
movements were often more regular and certain than those of the wisest
men, yet in many things which they would have to do to imitate us, they
failed more disastrously than the greatest fools" (AT 2:40; K 53–54). Having
noticed the intricate composition of plants, the man realized that the works
of God were far superior to the products of human industry. He surmised
that if God or nature made automata to imitate human actions, they would
be more skillfully constructed than his own artifacts. "Now suppose," ventures
Descartes, "that this man were to see the animals we have, and noticed in
their actions the same two things which make them differ from us, and which
he had already been accustomed to notice in his automata. There is no doubt
that he would not come to the conclusion that there was any real feeling
or emotion in them, but would think they were automata, which, being made
by nature, were incomparably more accomplished than any of those he had
previously made himself" (AT 2:41; K 54).

This story is remarkable in three respects. First, the question of how
to tell the difference between real and mechanical animals never comes up.
The man is accustomed to raise the question about people-shaped creatures.

Yet when he learns that his clockwork animals have natural archetypes just as clockwork people do, it somehow never occurs to him to ask whether the real animals exhibit any types of behaviors that are not duplicated in the machines. Had he asked, the answer would obviously have been yes. No seventeenth-century machine was capable of learning. Even if we suppose the technology of the mythical kingdom to be two hundred years advanced beyond Descartes's time, their machines would still have lacked this capacity. In the letter to Newcastle, Descartes cavalierly dismisses the tricks taught to animals as "only expressions of their fear, their hope, or their joy" and consequently capable of being "performed without any thought" (AT 4:574–75; K 207). Since for Descartes whatever occurs without thought occurs mechanically, the implication is that it is possible to construct a machine that duplicates animal tricks. It is not enough, however, to build a machine to *do* them; the machine must be able to *learn* to do them. As for the man in the fable, experience would soon teach him that there was at least one way to distinguish real horses and dogs from their clockwork counterparts: the real animals can learn.

To illustrate the inherent superiority of natural machines over artificial ones, the fable introduces the notion of automata made by God to imitate human actions. Divinely made mechanical people are conceptually intermediate between real people and man-made mechanical people. They are not to be confused with the imaginary people of the *Treatise on Man,* who are composed of soul and body just as we are. The point is not that people imitate people better than automata imitate people. It is rather that automata made by nature would imitate people better than man-made automata do.

This brings us to the second remarkable thing about the fable. The question of how to tell one of these hypothetical God-made person-machines from a real person never comes up. The man has observed that his clockwork people differ in two ways from real people, but when he raises the possibility of natural human automata, it never occurs to him to wonder whether they would pass the tests that his own machines fail. Would their superior imitation of our actions extend to all areas, including language use? Experience has nothing to say on the matter, for such machines have never been observed. The answer must rest on conceptual grounds.

Consider first the affirmative answer: a naturally constructed human automaton, though soulless and hence lacking understanding, could nevertheless perfectly imitate all human behavior, including linguistic behavior. On this alternative, failing the two tests still shows an absence of reason, but passing them does not show its presence. There can be behavioral evidence that machines do *not* think, but no amount of successful behavior would constitute evidence that they *do* think. To this extent the Cartesian doctrine becomes unfalsifiable.

Suppose our Cartesian gentleman goes for the opposite answer, that the natural automata would fail to imitate us in those of our actions by which we display our reason. It is difficult to see what the justification is for putting this limitation on the mechanical model.[7] Such a conclusion cannot be based upon considerations of human anatomy alone, for an automaton in human form need not be an exact replica of a human body. The aim is to imitate our actions, not our organs. Is human language so complex that no mechanism, not even one more intricate than our own brain, could not generate it in a meaningfully appropriate manner?

The most remarkable thing of all about the fable is the inference drawn from the observation of animal behavior. Instead of comparing real animals with mechanical animals, the man compares them with people and notices that they differ from them in the same two ways that automata in human form do. Animals, too, never answer in word or sign, except by chance, to questions put to them; and although their movements are often more regular and certain than ours, yet in many things they would have to do to imitate us, they fail disastrously. As we have seen, failing the first test indicates a lack of pure thought only, and failing the second, that the actions are not performed through reason in the Cartesian sense. Yet the man does not simply conclude that animals are devoid of pure thought or reason. He undoubtedly notices that animals express feelings and emotions in ways that seem appropriate to the circumstances and, being a good Cartesian, he knows that feelings are modes of thought. He refuses to conclude "that there was any real feeling or emotion in them" since the behavioral effects could in principle, he supposes, be duplicated by machines, even if his own creations fall short. Instead of remaining agnostic on the issue of animal feeling, however, he concludes that animals are true automata, that is to say, bodies without Cartesian thought.

As the argument stands in the fable, the conclusion is not warranted. From the fact that animals differ from people in the aforementioned ways, all that follows is that animals are not people, as machines in human form

---

7. Philosophers in the Cartesian tradition had differing opinions about what could and could not be accomplished by mechanical means. Malebranche for one rejected the whole idea of living organisms having been constructed by natural means alone, on the ground that organized bodies cannot be produced solely by the laws of the communication of motion. God must have created the first plants and animals by particular volitions and put in them the seeds of all future generations. See *Méditations chrétiennes et métaphysiques* 7.7 (OC 10:71) and *Entretiens sur la métaphysique et sur la religion* 10.3 (OC 12:229).

are not people. It does not follow that animals are totally lacking in consciousness. In order to arrive at this conclusion, another premise is needed, namely, that having pure thought or reason is somehow a necessary condition for having thought at all. Whether or not this premise is justifiable on Cartesian grounds remains to be seen.

3

Senseless Brutes

Nicolas Malebranche was born in 1638, one year after Descartes published his *Discourse on the Method.* At the age of twenty-two Malebranche entered the congregation of the Oratory. In 1664, walking one day along the quai des Augustins (Some say it was the rue Saint-Jacques), he asked a bookseller if there were any new books. He was handed Descartes's posthumous *Treatise on Man.* He immediately began to read it and, as he later told his friends, the excitement of learning so many new discoveries caused him such violent palpitations of the heart that he was periodically obliged to set the book aside in order to catch his breath (André 1970, 11–12).

In *The Search after Truth,* first published in 1674–75, Malebranche credits Descartes with having discovered more truths in thirty years than all previous philosophers (OC 1:64; S 15). Descartes provided the right method for the conduct of reason. Moreover, he laid the proper foundation for metaphysics with his ontology of substance and modification and his mind-body dualism. True, Descartes made a few mistakes; among them were his beliefs that the nature of mind is better known than that of matter (OC 3:163–71; S 633–38) and that a body at rest has a force to resist motion (OC 2:444; S 524). Malebranche sought to improve upon the Cartesian philosophy by applying the method more strictly than its founder had done.

Malebranche wholeheartedly embraced the doctrine of animal automatism. He was quite emphatic in denying all modes of thought to animals— not just pure intellections, but sensations, feelings, and volitions as well. "The Cartesians," among whom he includes himself, "do not think that animals feel pain or pleasure, or that they hate or love anything, because they do not admit anything but the material in animals, and they do not believe that either sensations or passions are properties of matter in whatever form" (OC 2:391; S 493). Animals "eat without pleasure, cry without pain, grow without knowing it; they desire nothing, fear nothing, know nothing" (OC 2:394; S 494–95). In the *Entretiens sur la mort* (Dialogues on Death) the character Theodore says that to suppose that a dog knows and loves its master and that it is capable of pleasure and pain "is to humanize it. It is to make your dog a little man with big ears and four paws, which differs from us only by the external shape and conformation of its limbs" (OC 13:373).

History tells us that Descartes had a dog named Monsieur Grat whom he treated with great kindness. The Malebranche lore contains no such frivolities. The Oratorian apparently was as relentless toward animals as he was toward philosophy. According to Trublet (1761, 115), Bernard le Bovier de Fontenelle once visited the Oratory on the rue Saint-Honoré and saw Malebranche kick a pregnant dog rolling at his feet. The dog let out a cry of pain and Fontenelle a cry of compassion, whereupon Malebranche said: "Well! Don't you know that it does not feel?"

Malebranche obviously thought that in denying animals any conscious experience, he was merely following the teaching of Descartes. There is some question, however, whether Descartes actually held so radical a doctrine and, if so, whether he had any justification for holding it. Cottingham (1978) maintains that Descartes never went so far as to deny all feelings and passions to animals. We shall first consider whether Cottingham succeeds in making his case. Then we shall take up the issue of whether a lack of pure thought entails a lack of sensation in Descartes's theory of mind. Finally, we return to Malebranche and show why he has more reason than Descartes to support a full-fledged beast-machine doctrine.

NO REAL FEELING?

Cottingham grants that animals are machines for Descartes but denies that this rules out the presence of sensations or feelings. "In fact it is important to notice that the *human* body is, for Descartes, a machine in exactly the same sense as the animal body" (1978, 552). Cottingham further grants that Cartesian animals are automata but denies that this implies the absence of feeling. An automaton is simply a self-moving machine, a thing that operates on its own without the intervention of an external cause. Nothing in the definition implies that the thing is insensible. The point of calling animals "natural automata" is that "the mere complexity of their movements is no more a bar to explanation in terms of inner mechanical structure than is the case with the responses of the trident-brandishing 'Neptune' " (554).

Cottingham overlooks an important dissimilarity between human and animal machines. Descartes characterizes the human *body* as a machine, but he never refers to human *beings* as either machines or automata. Human beings are composed of body and soul. It is by virtue of this soul-body union that they have sensations and passions. Descartes states in the *Principles* that appetites, emotions, and sensations "must not be referred either to the mind alone or to the body alone. These arise . . . from the close and intimate union of our mind with the body" (AT 8A:23; CSM 1:209; HR 1:238). The human body is a machine, to be sure, but the body is not what has the feelings. The person—the being composed of soul and body—has them. The question whether animals have feelings cannot be settled by pointing out that animal *bodies* are machines. To this extent Cottingham is right. Yet it is a fundamental principle of Cartesian philosophy that matter cannot have modes of thought; and machines, including self-moving machines, are material things. Consequently, if not just animal bodies but the animals themselves are machines, then they cannot have sensations and passions of the sort referred to in the *Principles*. The inference from "X is just a machine and nothing more" to "X is incapable of feeling" is warranted on Cartesian grounds.

Cottingham suggests that for Descartes the term "automaton" meant not necessarily a self-moving *machine,* but any object that operates on its own. If this is so, then a mind-body complex is an automaton, and such a complex can of course have feelings. The fact that Descartes never refers to the human mind-body complex as an automaton is evidence that he did not use the term in this way. Even if the term "carried no more than its strict Greek meaning of 'self-moving thing,' " as Cottingham proposes (553), motion is a property that pertains to matter alone. Thus a self-moving thing is a body that moves itself without the intervention of any external cause, including soul. An automaton is a machine in spite of itself.

Cottingham grants that Descartes held that animals do not think but questions the move from this thesis to the "monstrous thesis" that animals do not feel. Does not Cartesian thinking include feeling? Descartes tells Mersenne (May 1637) that "willing, understanding, imagining, sensing and so on are just different ways of thinking, and all belong to the soul" (AT 1:366; K 32). In the letter to Reneri for Pollot (April 1638) he asserts that "not only meditations and acts of the will, but the activities of seeing and hearing and deciding on one movement rather than another, so far as depends on the soul, are all thoughts" (AT 2:36; K 51). Nevertheless, insists Cottingham, "It is misleading to say, *tout court,* that *cogitatio* 'includes' sensations and feelings" (555). He cites *Principles* I, 9, where Descartes says of "I am seeing, or I am walking, therefore I exist" that the conclusion is not certain unless the terms "seeing" and "walking" are taken "to apply to the actual sense or awareness of seeing or walking" (AT 8A:7–8; CSM 1:195; HR 1:222). Cottingham comments: "The only sense in which a sensation like seeing is a true *cogitatio* is the sense in which it may involve the reflective mental awareness which Descartes calls *conscientia*—the self-conscious apprehension of the mind that it is aware of seeing" (555). He concludes that Descartes's assertion that animals do not think "need not commit him to denying any feeling or sensation to animals—for example a level of feeling or sensation that falls short of reflective mental awareness" (556).

It is revealing that Cottingham omits the part about walking when he discusses the passage in *Principles* I, 9. The mind is aware of walking in the same way that it is aware of seeing, but "walking" is never listed among the things that pertain to thought. Since "seeing" is coupled here with "walking," it must refer to the physical process of seeing. As we noted in chapter 1, consciousness of corporeal seeing is an act of C1. It is not a case of reflective awareness, since the object of C1 is not itself a mental act. Like many other commentators, Cottingham fails to distinguish between reflective awareness and the awareness that is present in every act of thinking. One is always conscious (C2) of one's consciousness (C1) of seeing, but one need not self-consciously apprehend that one is aware of seeing. Seeing as "a true *cogitatio*," i.e., mental seeing, requires only C2, not "reflective mental awareness."

Does Descartes's assertion that animals do not think commit him to the "monstrous thesis" that they are totally without feeling? Cottingham thinks not. Cartesian animals can, he suggests, have feeling and sensation on a level that "falls short of reflective mental awareness." What level might this be?

In the Sixth Replies Descartes distinguishes three grades of sensory response. The first is the mechanical process by which external objects affect the sense organs and the resulting motions are transmitted to the brain. The second "comprises all the immediate effects produced in the mind as a result of its being united with a bodily organ which is affected in this way. Such effects include the perceptions of pain, pleasure, thirst, hunger, colors, sound, taste, smell, heat, cold and the like, which arise from the union and as it were the intermingling of mind and body" (AT 7:437; CSM

2:294; HR 2:251). The third grade involves judgments concerning the existence and properties of external objects. This grade, strictly speaking, pertains to the intellect rather than to sensation since it involves reasoning. Now the first grade is not at issue in the "monstrous thesis," for Descartes freely acknowledges that it "is common to us and the brutes" (AT 7:437; CSM 2:295; HR 2:252). Moreover, the thesis that animals do not think implies that they lack the third grade. Descartes is quite emphatic that the brutes do not have reason. This leaves the second grade.

Descartes seems to attribute this grade of sensation to animals in his letter to Henry More of 5 February 1649. He writes: "Please note that I am speaking of thought, and not of life or sensation. I do not deny life to animals, since I regard it as consisting simply in the heat of the heart; and I do not deny sensation, in so far as it depends on a bodily organ" (AT 5:278; K 245). Cottingham takes this passage as evidence that Descartes separates sensation, considered as a form of awareness, from thought and denies only thought to animals (557). The phrase "in so far as it depends on a bodily organ" is reminiscent of the description of the second grade as being "produced in the mind as a result of its being united with a bodily organ." Notice, however, the crucial phrase "in the mind." When sensation is considered as a form of awareness, as it is in the second grade, it is distinguished not from thought, of which it is a mode, but from *pure* thought or intellect.

Like all thoughts, sensations and feelings belong to the mind, even though they arise from the mind's union with the body. Thus Descartes informs Regius (January 1642) that "sensations such as pain are not pure thoughts of a mind distinct from a body, but confused perceptions of a mind really united to one" (AT 3:493; K 127–28). Similarly, to Gibieuf (19 January 1642) he writes: "I do not see any difficulty in allowing on the one hand that the faculties of imagination and sensation belong to the soul, because they are species of thoughts, and on the other hand that they belong to the soul only as joined to the body, because they are kinds of thoughts without which one can conceive the soul entirely pure" (AT 3:479; K 125–26).

The second grade of sensation cannot occur without the presence of a mind or soul, since the sensations are produced in the mind, albeit only as a result of its union with the body. Descartes declares in the Fifth Replies that animals have no incorporeal soul (AT 7:355; CSM 2:246; HR 2:210). He tells a correspondent that he prefers "to say with the Bible (Deuteronomy 12, 23) that blood is their soul" since the rarefied parts of the blood move the body (AT 4:65; K 146; cf. AT 1:414; K 36). The blood is not "soul" in the literal Cartesian sense, for it is corporeal and does not think. Only "soul" in the literal sense, that is to say, incorporeal and thinking soul, has sensations and feelings as a result of its union with the body. Descartes's assertion that animals do not think therefore commits him to the thesis that animals are devoid of feelings and sensations except for the first grade, which is purely mechanical. The second grade, sensation as a form of awareness, is closed to them. Cottingham has failed to extricate Descartes from the "monstrous thesis."

THE METAPHOR OF INATTENTION

Writing to Plempius for Fromondus (3 October 1637), Descartes criticizes the latter for supposing "that I think that animals see just as we do, i.e. feeling or thinking that they see." It should be evident from the *Discourse* "that my view is that animals do not see as we do when we are aware that we see, but only as we do when our mind is elsewhere. In such a case the images of external objects are depicted on our retinas, and perhaps the impressions they leave in the optic nerves cause our limbs to make various movements, although we are quite unaware of them. In such a case we too move just like automata . . ." (AT 1:413–14; K 36). The passage is similar to that in the Fourth Replies where he compares the sheep's flight from the wolf to the human act of thrusting out one's hand in a fall (AT 7:230; CSM 2:161; HR 2:104). The emphasis is different, however. His aim in the Fourth Replies is to show that even in human beings many motions do not depend on the will, so he focuses on the movement of the limbs in response to the sensation. In the letter to Plempius, on the contrary, the issue is the nature of animal sensation.

At first glance the passage seems to provide a way out of the "monstrous thesis," for it indicates that mechanical action does not necessarily preclude consciousness. After all, one must have a mind in order for it to be elsewhere. Descartes, however, does not say that when animals see, their minds are elsewhere. Rather, he says that animals see as we do when our minds are elsewhere. What exactly does this mean?

Consider the following case of human seeing. A man is driving home from work, his mind still on the day's events at the office. He sees the road and the traffic and responds to what he sees—for example, he changes lanes to pass slower vehicles—but he is not thinking about what he sees. Suddenly he sees a flashing light up ahead and comes out of his reverie. Is it an accident? the police? Oh, it is just a tow truck pulling a car. His mind goes back to office politics.

Is this how animals see? Of course, since they lack thought, according to Descartes, they cannot ever "come out of their reveries" but must remain in a continual state of absentmindedness. Unlike the proverbial absentminded professor, they are not preoccupied with other more lofty matters. Their absentmindedness consists not in the mind's being elsewhere but in its being nowhere.

In the human case there is more than a subjective difference between seeing when the mind is elsewhere and seeing when the mind is on what one sees. A person whose mind is elsewhere acts differently. Certain things that ought to elicit a reaction fail to do so or elicit the wrong reaction. Mommy tells Daddy that Johnny broke a lamp today and Daddy, whose hearing is excellent, mumbles from behind his newspaper, "That's nice." The preoccupied driver, normally solicitous of his car's suspension, runs smack into a vast pothole and expresses surprise. "The mind is elsewhere" means that the person is not paying attention, and one can determine whether or not another person is paying attention by examining that individual's behavior.

If Descartes means that animals never pay attention to what they see and hear, then his claim is clearly false. Animals exhibit selective attentiveness, just as humans do, and an astute observer of animal behavior can determine exactly what features of their sensory environment draw their attention.

Descartes is obviously not thinking of the behavioral difference between attending and not attending to what one sees. He is only interested in the phenomenological difference. Attention functions as a metaphor for awareness. A person who is not paying attention will be unaware of many things although the person sees them in the physiological sense and may even react to them. The driver, for instance, was not aware of the pothole until he hit it even though its image struck his retina and was transmitted to his brain. Animal seeing is like human seeing without attention in that the corporeal process occurs without a corresponding state of consciousness. Just as we are not aware of what we see when our minds are elsewhere, so animals are never aware of the objects whose images strike their retinas. Behavior that shows selective attention on their part can be explained purely mechanically; there is no need to posit consciousness.

SENSATION AND INTELLECTION

Descartes tells Plempius that his position on animal seeing is explained "quite explicitly" in the fifth part of the *Discourse*. As we have already noted, neither the language test nor the action test directly establishes the absence of sense perception in animals. At best they show that animals lack pure thought or reason. In order to arrive at the conclusion that animals have no sensory awareness, a further premise is needed, one that links sensation to pure thought. There is, of course, a necessary connection between having sensations, construed as modes of thought, and having Cartesian thought in the general sense. A being that lacks Cartesian thought must also lack every mode of thought, including sensation. The question, however, is whether the absence of a certain kind of Cartesian thought, namely, pure thought or intellection, entails the absence of another kind, namely, sensory awareness. If so, then it is at least implicit in the *Discourse* that animals see without awareness. If not, then there is no justification for Descartes's claim to have established anything about animal sensation in the *Discourse*.

The Sixth Meditation contains an interesting statement about the relation between sensation and intellection. There, having established the real distinction between mind and body, Descartes goes on to consider the faculties of imagination and sensory perception. He notes that the mind can be conceived without these faculties, but that they cannot be conceived "without me, that is, without an intellectual substance to inhere in. This is because there is an intellectual act included in their essential definition" (AT 7:78; CSM 2:54; HR1:190).

How is intellection included in the definition of sensation and imagination? One possible answer is that given by M. D. Wilson (1978, 201). When Descartes states that his essence is thought, by "thought" he means "*intellectus purus*, pure understanding," that is to say, thought carried on independently of all bodily processes. If Wilson is right, it would follow that no creature can have sensation and imagination as modes of thinking without having pure intellect as the principal property to which they are referred.

Wilson cites a passage from the Sixth Meditation (AT 7:73) as textual support for her interpretation. Her translation is: "I consider that this power of imagining which is in me, is different from the power of understanding, in that it is not requisite to the essence of myself, that is of my mind" (200–201). On this rendering, Descartes seems to be saying that the power of understanding *is* requisite to the essence of the mind. Compare the more accurate translation of Cottingham, Stoothoff, and Murdoch: "I consider that this power of imagining which is in me, differing as it does from the power of understanding, is not a necessary constituent of my own essence, that is, of the essence of my mind" (CSM 2:51). And this from Haldane and Ross: "I remark besides that this power of imagination which is in one, inasmuch as it differs from the power of understanding, is in no wise a necessary element in my nature, or in . . . the essence of my mind" (HR 1:186). The latter two renderings are open to the following interpretation: The power of imagining is different from the power of (pure) understanding, and it is not necessary to my nature. This is not to say that pure understanding *is* a necessary constituent of my nature.

A sentence from the Second Meditation seems to lend better support to Wilson's equation of Cartesian thought with pure intellect: "I am, then, in the strict sense only a thing that thinks; that is, I am a mind, or intelligence, or intellect, or reason—words whose meaning I have been ignorant of until now" (AT 7:27; CSM 2:18; HR 1:152). Here Descartes treats mind and intellect as though they were synonymous. Yet barely two paragraphs later, he includes intellect or understanding among the modes of thinking: "But what then am I? A thing that thinks. What is that? A thing that doubts, understands, affirms, denies, is willing, is unwilling, and also imagines and has sensory perceptions" (AT 7:28; CSM 2:19; HR 1:153). If intellection is just another mode of thinking, why was it singled out for special consideration above?

Pure intellect is emphasized in the *Meditations* because that is how the mind knows itself, God, and matter best. By means of this faculty the mind recognizes itself to be a substance really distinct from the body and capable of existing apart from it. Pure cognitions, unlike acts of sensation and imagination, have no corresponding physiological processes in the body to which the mind is united. The mind could therefore, in principle, continue to think in this way when separated from the body. This much is true for Descartes. None of it implies that the essence of mind is pure intellect. A substance cannot exist without its essence; no mind can exist without thinking. Consequently, if the essence of the mind is to think in such a way that its thoughts have no physical counterparts, then all minds would have to think this way and always think thus, even when they are not engaged in reflective thinking. The aforesaid passages provide no evidence that Descartes believed this to be the case.

Norman Malcolm (1973) offers a different answer to the question of how sensation and imagination include intellection in their definition. As Malcolm interprets Descartes, every thought must have a propositional content. "Indeed, I suggest that for Descartes the distinction between the 'mental' and the 'physical' is *defined* by the presence or absence of propositional content" (11). Descartes uses the term "idea" to refer to this content. Malcolm gives an example: "The idea of God . . . might be expressed by the sentence, 'There is a Supremely Perfect Being,' or by the nominalized phrase, 'the existence of a Supremely Perfect Being.' In either case, what was expressed could be affirmed or denied" (7). Every mental episode—every feeling, sensation, desire, and so on—has a propositional content. In order to have any mental episodes at all, one must be able to " 'apprehend,' 'entertain,' 'contemplate,' or, in plain language, think of, *propositions*" (13). In order to do this one must have language. Cartesian animals are automata for want of ability to handle propositions. They do not see light because they cannot entertain the propositional content expressed by the sentence "It seems to me that I see light." They do not feel pain because they cannot think "I feel pain" (10).

The problem with Malcolm's account is that there is no textual basis for it; indeed there is textual evidence against it. Malcolm's suggestion that the idea of God is expressed by the sentence "A supremely perfect being exists" is explicitly rejected by Descartes in his letter to Mersenne of July 1641. "It is true that the simple consideration of such a Being leads us so easily to the knowledge of His existence that it is almost the same thing to conceive God and to conceive that He exists; but nonetheless the idea we have of God as a supremely perfect Being is quite different from the proposition 'God exists,' so that the one can serve as a means or premise to prove the other" (AT 3:396; K 107).

Descartes's position on fetal thought belies Malcolm's claim that Cartesian thought necessarily involves the entertaining of propositions. In the Fourth Replies Descartes maintains that infants in the womb think and are conscious of their thoughts although they do not remember them afterwards (AT 7:246; CSM 2:171–72; HR 2:115). If Cartesian thought consisted in thinking of propositions, as Malcolm insists, then human fetuses would be no more capable of mental episodes than animals are, for they lack language just as animals do. True, they have the potential to acquire language, whereas animals do not. But an appeal to potentiality will not suffice here, since on Malcolm's view actual thinking requires the actual possession of language. Nor does it help to bring up Descartes's remark in the 15 April 1649 letter to Henry More: "I should not judge that infants had minds unless I saw that they were of the same nature as adults" (AT 5:345; K 251). There the issue is whether or not they show any behavioral evidence or, in Descartes's words, "any certain sign of thought." Here, on the contrary, the issue is whether or not the ascription of mental episodes to them is consistent with Descartes's theory of mind. Malcolm's interpretation of Cartesian thought puts human fetuses and animals on the same footing.

A third attempt to explain how sensation and imagination include intellection is that by Robert McRae (1972). This answer draws upon a passage from the Fifth Replies, where Descartes refuses to concede that the ideas of geometrical figures enter the mind through the senses. In order to recognize a triangle from a group of lines on paper, argues Descartes, we must already possess the idea of it from another source. It is like recognizing a drawing as being of a man's face, which could not happen unless we already knew the human face by other means (AT 7:381–82; CSM 2: 262; HR 2:227–28). According to McRae, this shows that for Descartes all sense perception presupposes intellection. Even in the case of feelings such as joy and anger, pain and warmth, we always relate the feeling to something, whether it be our own body, an external body, or the soul. "This necessary relating of feelings in one of three ways,—to my own body, to an external body, or to the soul—is, according to Descartes, a judgment; and it would appear then that there is no such thing in experience as a pure sense datum or feeling datum in isolation from a judgment. All judging involves conception—in the cases under consideration, conceptions of our bodies, of external bodies, or of our soul" (65). Therefore all sensation and feeling involves conception.

Descartes's statements about fetal thought raise problems once again. Does not Descartes tell Arnauld (4 June 1648) that he is "convinced that in the mind of an infant there have never been any pure acts of understanding, but only confused sensations" (AT 5:192; K 231)? Either infants sense without recognizing the object sensed, or they recognize it in a way that does not involve intellection. Descartes speculates in the letter to Hyperaspistes (August 1641) that babes in the womb feel pain, pleasure, heat, and cold (AT 3:424; K 111). If they relate these feelings to their own bodies, then their judgment is based upon a confused sensation rather than a conception of their bodies. If they merely feel and do not relate the feeling to anything, then their feeling exists in isolation from a judgment. In either case conception is not involved. McRae's account may hold for adult human beings, but it does not work for Cartesian infants in the womb. So there is no reason to insist on it for animals—no reason to deny them sensation and feeling just because they fail to exhibit the powers of recognition and judgment of a human adult.

The comparison in the Fifth Replies between perceiving a face and a triangle raises an important issue concerning the relation between sensation and pure understanding. When we see three not-quite-straight lines on paper, we recognize them to represent a mathematically perfect figure, something we have never seen. This could not happen, says Descartes, unless "the idea of the true triangle was already in us." It is, he says, "just the same as" when we look at some lines drawn in ink on paper and apprehend a man's face. This too could not happen "unless the human face were already known to us from some other source." Yet when we compare the two cases, it becomes evident that they are not the same on Descartes's terms. The object represented by the three lines, "the true triangle," is apprehended by an act of pure intellection in which corporeal images play no role. As Descartes explains in the Sixth Meditation, in pure understanding one contemplates the definition of the geometrical figure without imagining it; I do not "see the three lines with my mind's eye as if they were present before me" (AT 7:72; CSM 2:50; HR 1:185). There is no precise definition of a human face as there is of a triangle. Looking at the drawing, we recognize a face because we have prior knowledge of the human face, but this knowledge does not consist in intellectual apprehension of what it means for something to be a face. Pure understanding is needed to recognize a mathematical figure from a depiction because it is the faculty by which we know the original. Since faces are not apprehended in this way, there is prima facie no reason why an individual must be endowed with pure intellect to recognize one.

The recognition of an object from lines drawn on paper is not without parallel in the animal kingdom. Animals often react to schemata as they do to the object represented. For instance, ducks respond to decoys as though they were real ducks sitting on the water below them. Of course, the duck does not realize that the decoy is not a true duck but only a representation, whereas a person viewing a drawing is well aware that it is not a real man. But this step is by no means essential for the process of recognition. All that is necessary is that the representation produce in the individual an idea of the thing represented. Recognition takes place by matching the present sensation with an idea already in the mind. So long as the idea brought to mind is not one of pure intellect, there is no need to posit intellection as an ingredient in the mental process of recognition.

ANIMALS AND THE VISION IN GOD
(OR WHY MALEBRANCHE KICKED THE DOG)

Despite his esteem for Descartes, Malebranche was dissatisfied with Descartes's theory of ideas: "I claim that this great Philosopher has not thoroughly examined in what the nature of ideas consists" (OC 6:214). Malebranche devotes considerable attention to this topic in his own writings. His contribution, the doctrine of seeing all things in God, has been vilified in the philosophical literature, along with his equally infamous doctrine of occasionalism, according to which God is the true cause of all that happens in the world (Radner 1978). Cartesian philosophers such as Antoine Arnauld and Pierre-Sylvain Régis bitterly opposed Malebranche's alleged refinement of the Cartesian theory of ideas. In the heat of the controversy no one, least of all Malebranche, worried about the beast-machine. More important issues were at stake. Yet when Malebranche's epistemology is examined in light of its implications for animals, it turns out that the "monstrous thesis" has even greater significance for Malebranche than it had for Descartes. Seeing and feeling take on a whole new dimension in Malebranche's system.

What, exactly, is the vision in God and why would anyone hold such a strange view?

Malebranche starts with the common notion that every act of perception has an object, or that to perceive is to perceive something. As he puts it, "nothingness is not perceptible" (OC 2:99; S 320; OC 4:72; 9:953); "to see nothing is not to see" (OC 2:99; 6:202; 9:1009); "to think of nothing is not to think" (OC 9:910); "to perceive nothing and not to perceive are the same thing" (OC 15:5). He takes this common notion to imply that whenever the mind perceives, there is some actually existing object that it perceives directly. Now one can perceive bodies that do not exist. This often happens, he says, during sleep and high fever. When I see a body that is not really there, something must exist as the object of my perception. Otherwise I would see nothing, which is to say, I would not see. There must, then, be something else that I perceive immediately and directly when I say I perceive the body (OC 2:99; S 320; OC 4:72–73; 9:1065–67; 15:5).

We do not simply fail to have direct perceptions of nonexistent bodies; we have no direct perceptions of bodies at all, not even when the bodies exist. Malebranche's argument for this position may be summarized as follows. The mind can directly perceive an object external to it only if that object is present to or united with the mind. Bodies are not present to the mind in the requisite manner. Therefore they cannot be directly perceived by the mind. At one point in *The Search after Truth* Malebranche gives the impression that the kind of presence required for direct perception is local presence: "We see the sun, the stars, and an infinity of objects external to us; and it is not likely that the soul should leave the body to stroll about in the heavens, as it were, in order to behold all these objects. Thus, it does not see them by themselves . . ." (OC 1:413; S 217). Elsewhere he in effect acknowledges that even if the soul were to sally forth into the heavens, it would not help. After all, the mind is "in" the brain, yet it does not perceive the composition of the brain (OC 2:100; S 320; OC 4:30).

In some passages he indicates that bodies cannot be present to the mind because there is no "relation" between mind and matter (OC 1:417; S 219; OC 4:28). What is crucial is not the lack of similarity or resemblance between the mental and the physical, but the absence of a necessary connection between the existence of anything mental and the existence of anything physical. The fact that we sometimes see bodies that do not exist demonstrates that there can be an act of perceiving a body without the body's existing. There cannot, however, be an act of *directly* perceiving an object unless the object actually exists. Thus bodies are not objects directly perceived. Whenever we perceive a body, we are always directly acquainted with some object other than the body. Thus the above-quoted passage from the *Search* continues: ". . . and our mind's immediate object when it sees the sun, for example, is not the sun, but something that is intimately joined to our soul, and this is what I call an *idea*" (OC 1:413–14; S 217).

As Malebranche analyzes the perceiving situation, there are three entities: the act of perceiving, the idea, and the object represented by the idea. When I see the sun, there is in me a certain act of perceiving. This act, usually referred to by Malebranche as the "perception," is a mode or modification of my mind. The existence of the idea is a necessary condition for the existence of the act of perceiving it. One cannot perceive a nonexistent idea. The idea represents or makes known the sun. The sort of relation between the idea and the sun is different from that between the act of perceiving and the idea. The existence of the sun is not a necessary condition for the existence of the idea of the sun. An idea can represent a nonexistent object.

Acts of perceiving are definitely in the mind since they are modes of it. The material objects represented by the ideas are definitely not in the mind. What about the ideas? Malebranche has several reasons, some theological, for maintaining that ideas are not in our minds but in God's. The principal argument has to do with the generality of ideas.

Every creature, says Malebranche, is a particular being. Created things can have many different properties, but insofar as they have some, they are thereby precluded from having others. A body that is round cannot at the same time be square. A circular object with a diameter of five meters cannot also have a diameter of some other magnitude. Ideas, the objects of our immediate perceptions, are not subject to this sort of limitation. The idea of a circle in general represents all possible circles at once. "For to think of a circle in general is to perceive infinite circles as a single circle" (OC 12:53).

General ideas are not formed by abstraction from an assemblage of particular ideas, as many philosophers believe. On the contrary, asserts Malebranche, particular ideas are formed by taking something away from general ideas. The idea of a circle of a particular diameter is included, along with an infinite number of other ideas of particular circles, in the general idea of a circle. The latter idea is in turn included in the more general idea of figure. All ideas are included in the idea of being in general; they are, in Malebranche's words, "participations in the general idea of the infinite" (OC 1:441; S 232). Since all created things are particular and the idea of the infinite is general, this idea is not created. And since all ideas are included in it, none of them is created either. Anything in a human mind would have to be, like it, created and particular. Hence, ideas are not in human minds.

What is not in the mind can be perceived by the mind only if it is present to it. Earlier we said that local presence is not the sort that is required. What then? Presence to the mind consists in a capacity for self-revelation. An object is present to the mind if and only if it is capable of producing a perception of itself in the mind. According to Malebranche, only God can produce perceptions, for by the principles of occasionalism God alone is capable of producing a mode in a substance. "All our ideas, therefore, must be located in the efficacious substance of the Divinity, which alone is intelligible or capable of enlightening us, because it alone can affect intelligences" (OC 1:442; S 232).

The vision in God is by no means confined to the conception of mathematical entities and general features of extension. It also includes sense perceptions of particular material things. When we look out over a meadow, the ontology of the situation is as follows. Out there are the actual trees, flowers, and grass that God has created. We do not perceive any of these things directly. Neither does God for that matter: "God derives His light only from Himself; He sees the material world only in the inteligible world He contains and in the knowledge He has of His volitions, which actually give existence and motion to all things (OC 3:61; S 573; cf. OC 6:62, 118; 9:959; 10:97). On the occasion of our standing before the meadow with eyes open, God creates in us sensible perceptions of the ideas of the things out there. The perceptions are modifications of our minds. The ideas are in God (OC 1:445; S 234).

The extension we see, the so-called visual field, is the same idea of extension or intelligible extension that is the object of study in geometry. Extension conceived and extension sensed are one and the same. Whether it is conceived or sensed depends upon what kinds of perceptions it produces in the mind. Malebranche explains in the *Conversations chrétiennes:*

> When the idea of extension affects or modifies the mind with a pure perception, then the mind simply conceives this extension. But when the idea of extension

> touches the mind more sharply, and affects it with a sensible perception, then the mind sees or feels the extension. The mind sees it when this perception is a sentiment of color; and it feels it or perceives it even more vividly when the perception with which intelligible extension modifies it is a pain. For color, pain and all other sentiments are only sensible perceptions, produced in intelligences by intelligible ideas. (OC 4:75–76)

Sensible perceptions serve to differentiate portions of intelligible extension, whereas pure perceptions do not. When I conceive a circle, I consider a portion of intelligible extension all the extremities of which are equidistant from a point that is the center. The question of which portion it is does not enter in. When I see a circular object, my perception of it singles out a portion of intelligible extension and "renders it particular" in such a way that it becomes meaningful to ask where it is with respect to surrounding objects (OC 6:61). Returning to the *Conversations chrétiennes:*

> It is color alone which makes objects visible: it is solely by the variety of colors that we see and distinguish the diversity of objects. Now when we see bodies, the idea of extension modifies us with diverse sentiments of color, and we agree that this idea is found only in God. . . . It is therefore necessary to say that in the instant that we open our eyes in the middle of a field, God . . . by the idea of extension contained in him, touches our mind with this variety of colors by which we judge of the actual existence and diversity of objects; of their grandeur, their position, their distance, their movement and rest. (OC 4:76)

The expression "sentiments of color" is misleading insofar as it suggests that colors are included among the ideas or objects of the mind's acts of perceiving. This is not the case. Sensible qualities such as color and pain are not objects of sensible perception, but sensible perceptions of an object. Malebranche makes this clear in the letter to Arnauld of 19 March 1699: "For, in short, the soul's perception in one who sees or feels an arm is only the perception, which is called either color or pain, of the extension which composes the arm; I mean the immediate and direct perception of the ideal extension of the arm, without which one can neither see nor feel it, as experience teaches us" (OC 9:961–62). Similarly he writes to Dortous de Mairan (12 June 1714): "For it is certain that sensible perceptions are only modifications of the soul different from the idea or the object immediately perceived. Thus if I look at my hand, I will have the perception of it, color; if I regard it in water, I will have the perception of it, coldness; and if I have gout at the same time I regard it in water, I will have the modification or perception of it, pain" (OC 19:884). The Cartesian thesis that sensible qualities are only in the mind has twofold significance in Malebranche's system. It means that there is nothing like sensible qualities in the physical realm: bodies are not colored; pain is not in the hand. It also means that sensible qualities are species of mental acts.

According to Descartes, the objects of conception are different from those of sensation. Geometrical figures are conceived but not sensed. For Malebranche, on the contrary, the objects of pure and sensible perceptions are the same. Geometrical figures can be sensed, albeit not as figures in general. Descartes held that we come by our idea of a geometrical triangle in a different way from how we come by our idea of a depicted triangle. In Malebranche's system all ideas are in God and all perceptions of them come from him. Prima facie, there is no reason why God could not give a creature sensible perceptions without ever giving it pure perceptions. Such a creature would not recognize the figures it sees as conforming or failing to conform to certain geometrical definitions, but it would see the figures all the same and could discriminate among them.

A boy stands in the middle of a field with his dog at his side. The boy sees a variety of objects by virtue of the fact that different portions of intelligible extension are "rendered particular" by different colors. The boy is too young to have studied geometry. He has never conceived the idea of extension; that is to say, God has never given him pure perceptions of it. The boy can see and discriminate objects nonetheless. What is wrong with maintaining the same about the dog? Cannot the process of seeing all things in God be extended to animals as well as people? In principle, yes, provided that animals have minds. This makes it all the more impera- tive for Malebranche to defend animal automatism against the sympathizers of kicked dogs. Malebranche needs the beast-machine in order to rescue the doctrine of the vision in God from theologically paradoxical consequences.

Malebranche sets great store upon the theological advantages of his system. The vision in God "places created minds in a position of complete dependence on God—the most complete there can be. For on this view, not only could we see nothing but what He wills that we see, but we could see nothing but what He makes us see" (OC 1:439; S 231). It agrees with Scripture: "Not that we are sufficient of ourselves to think any thing as of ourselves; but our sufficiency is of God" (2 Cor. 3:5); "For in him we live, and move, and have our being" (Acts 17:28). It explains how God is "the Father of lights" (James 1:17), "he that teacheth man knowledge" (Ps. 94:10), "the true Light, which lighteth every man that cometh into the world" (John 1:9).

What happens if animals are allowed sentiments of color, pain, and so on? Such mental acts must have objects, for to see nothing is not to see and to feel nothing is not to feel. The objects cannot be material, otherwise animals would have immediate and direct knowledge of bodies—a feat which not even God himself can accomplish. The objects of animal perceptions must be either in the animals' minds or else outside them but capable of acting upon them. If animals directly perceive ideas in their own minds, then all ideas are not included in the general idea of the infinite, all ideas are not uncreated, and Malebranche's reason for keeping particular ideas out of human minds is seriously undermined. If the analysis of generality is not to be undermined, animals must be granted access to the ideas in the efficacious substance of the Divinity. Animals, too, would sense nothing but what God makes them sense. In him they too would live and move and have their being. He would be the true light that enlightens every animal.

Even worse, it could be argued that God sometimes shows preferential treatment in giving them access to his ideas. Granted, only people receive pure perceptions, so only they can know the general properties of intelligible extension. Nevertheless, when it comes to detecting particular features of material and sensible things, animals often outshine us.

According to Malebranche, although we see all things by God's ideas, and God created the world according to his ideas, we do not necessarily see material objects as they really are. The sun, for instance, appears larger near the horizon than when it is far away from it, yet the sun itself does not change size (OC 3:151; S 626). When we look out over a meadow, our sentiments of color do not single out the full variety of objects there. A hawk's visual acuity is much greater than ours. Now suppose that the hawk has mental episodes and that its seeing consists in God's giving it sensible perceptions of his ideas. Then when the hawk surveys the meadow, God shows it more of what he has created than he reveals to us in similar circumstances. A dog's olfactory ability far exceeds ours. If an act of perceiving occurs when molecules enter its nose, and some general idea in God's mind is "rendered particular" thereby, then the dog has direct access to a small feature of God's plan—a feature that humans can only detect indirectly, for example, by chemical analysis.

In the letter to Plempius for Fromondus (3 October 1637), Descartes voiced the concern that once animals are allowed sense-cognition, which is supposedly "a matter of simple apprehension and therefore cannot be false," it seems that "the senses of animals are closer to the knowledge of God and the angels than human reasoning is" (AT 1:415; K 37). What humans must go through long and tortuous steps to discover is granted to animals in a single intuitive act. The issue becomes all the more pressing in Malebranche's system, where sense perception gives access to the very ideas according to which the world was created. For in seeing, the animal learns something of what God has made and, in a small and limited way, something of God himself. Malebranche has to deny sensation and feeling to animals, lest they, too, "see through a glass, darkly" even if never "face to face" (1 Cor. 13:12).

4

God and the Beast-Machine

The more we examine the theory of animal automatism the flimsier it seems, even within the context of Cartesianism. Descartes claims in the Sixth Replies to have "proved it by very strong arguments" (AT 7:426; CSM 2:287; HR 2:244). He is referring to the argument based on the two tests of thought. In order to keep animals from passing the tests, he has to interpret "thought" in the narrow sense of pure thought or reason. To conclude that animals lack thought in the wider sense, he needs the additional premise that all modes of thinking, including sensations and feelings, presuppose pure thought as a necessary condition. This premise we found to be unwarranted by Cartesian principles.

Descartes seems to adopt a more cautious position on animals in his correspondence with Henry More. He writes in the letter of 5 February 1649: "But though I regard it as established that we cannot prove there is any thought in animals, I do not think it is thereby proved that there is not, since the human mind does not reach into their hearts" (AT 5:276–77; K 244). This is not so much a change of view as a shift in the meaning of "proof." Because we do not "reach into their hearts" and have direct apprehension of their subjective experiences, if any, we cannot settle the question whether or not they think with the same assurance as in our own case. We cannot "prove" they lack thought in the sense in which things are proved in the *Meditations*—that is, proved beyond the shadow of a metaphysical doubt. We can, however, "prove" it in the sense in which things are proved in natural philosophy: we can set up a hypothesis, derive consequences from it, and put them to the test. Descartes acknowledges the inductive nature of the case when he states in the Fifth Replies that the question of animal thinking must be settled "by an *a posteriori* investigation of their behavior" (AT 7:358; CSM 2:248; HR 2:211). In the letter to More he compares the inductive arguments for and against animal thinking and proclaims the latter stronger. "But when I investigate what is most probable in this matter, I see no argument for animals having thoughts except the fact that since they have eyes, ears, tongues, and other sense-organs like ours, it seems likely that they have sensation like us; and since thought is included in our mode of sensation, similar thought seems to be attributable to them. . . . But there are other arguments, stronger and more numerous, but not so obvious to everyone, which strongly urge the opposite" (AT 5:277; K244).

The list of arguments in the letter to More includes two that we have already considered: one from the sufficiency of physiology to explain animal behavior, the other from animals' lack of speech. Descartes also adduces a third reason: "that it is more probable that worms and flies and caterpillars move mechanically than that they all have immortal souls" (AT 5:277; K 244).

The reference to immortal souls betrays a theological concern. This concern is not prominent in Descartes's writings on animals, but it is certainly there waiting to be developed. Descartes's followers took the hint and came up with a set of theological arguments to support the doctrine of animal automatism. These arguments acquire greater importance once it is recognized how weak Descartes's own nontheological arguments really are.

Among the Cartesians who presented theological support for the beast-machine were Nicolas Malebranche and Antoine Dilly.[1] Malebranche we have already introduced. About all that is known of Dilly is that he was a priest of Ambrun, that his book *De l'ame des bêtes* (On the Soul of Beasts) was published at Lyons in 1676, and that he died shortly thereafter (Rosenfield 1968, 269). *De l'ame des bêtes* is primarily directed against the *Discours de la connoissance des bestes* (Discourse on the Knowledge of Beasts), written four years earlier by the Jesuit priest Ignace Gaston Pardies. Dilly's book was quite popular at the time and went through several editions.

Of Cartesians who considered the beast-machine from a theological perspective, not all followed Dilly and Malebranche in their reliance upon reason to settle the issue. Pierre-Sylvain Régis, a scientist and teacher of Cartesianism, believed that ultimately one must have recourse to faith to uphold the doctrine of animal automatism.

---

1. For a complete list see Rosenfield 1968, 45–50, 265–99.

We shall consider three theological arguments for the beast-machine. The first argument originates in Descartes's letter to the Marquess of Newcastle (23 November 1646). Addressing the possibility that animals with organs like ours might have thoughts like ours, "but of a very much less perfect kind," Descartes writes: "To which I have nothing to reply except that if they thought as we do, they would have an immortal soul like us. This is unlikely, because there is no reason to believe it of some animals without believing it of all, and many of them such as oysters and sponges are too imperfect for this to be credible" (AT 4: 576; K 208). We call this the oyster argument. For the other two arguments we have more prosaic names: the argument from divine recompense and the argument from human dominion.

THE OYSTER ARGUMENT

The oyster argument has the form of a reductio ad absurdum. It proceeds as follows: Suppose that (1) animals with organs similar to ours have subjective experiences like we do. For example, animals with eyes have visual experiences, those with ears have auditory experiences, and so on. The more their sense organs are like ours, the more similar their sensations are to ours. Having brains less complex than ours, they do not reach our level of thinking, but they are capable of "less perfect" thoughts. Since (2) whatever thinks has an immortal soul, it follows that (3) such animals have immortal souls. But this leads to the consequence that (4) oysters and sponges have immortal souls, which is ridiculous. Therefore (5) no animals have subjective experiences.

This argument is clearly fallacious. The move from (3) to (4) is utterly unwarranted. The animals referred to in (3) are animals with organs like ours; oysters and sponges have no such organs. Furthermore, the absurdity of (4) fails to provide any support for (5). The most that can be concluded is that oysters and sponges do not have conscious experiences. Since the original premise only concerned animals with organs similar to ours, the reductio must establish that *those* animals do not have thoughts. To argue that they do not because oysters do not is a non sequitur.

Descartes's excuse for picking on oysters, that there is no reason to believe some animals have immortal souls without believing they all do, is extremely lame in the circumstances. The reason given for the belief that some animals have souls has to do with similarities to human physiology and behavior. Where the similarities are lacking, so is the support for the belief in soul.

The oyster argument stands in need of major reconstruction. First and foremost, one must get rid of the oysters. Perhaps because he was trying for maximum impact, Descartes singled out organisms that even the most ardent animal lover would be loath to welcome into heaven. This psychological persuasiveness is gained at the expense of logic. It may not be quite so incredible that dogs and monkeys have immortal souls, but in order to get to the desired conclusion (5), one must argue from the absurdity of attributing such souls to the higher animals.

Another problem with the oyster argument is that premise (2) is questionable. Even if we grant that whatever thinks or has conscious experiences has a soul, and that soul is something distinct from the body, why must we add the adjective "immortal"? The opposing view is prima facie a viable alternative. Indeed it had influential advocates during the seventeenth century. The Aristotelian or Peripatetic philosophers ascribed soul and sensory awareness to animals but insisted that this soul was material and died with the animal's body. According to them, animal souls differed from human minds or spirits not merely in degree but in kind; only the latter survived the death of the body. Since the oyster argument hinges on the absurdity not merely of animal souls but of immortal animal souls, premise (2) must be defended against the Peripatetic alternative.

By combining the contributions of Dilly and Régis, it is possible to construct a cleaned-up version of the oyster argument. Whether this new version is free of fallacy remains to be seen.

The first step is to counter the Peripatetic doctrine of the materiality of animal soul. Both Dilly and Régis do this, but since Régis does it better, we shall use him.

In Book Seven of the *Cours entier de philosophie* Régis declares that it is unreasonable to attribute to brutes a soul that is both really distinct from the body and incapable of existing apart from it. Such a soul, he reasons, would be both a substance and a mode: a substance insofar as it is really distinct from the body, and a mode because it needs the body in order to exist. Moreover, it is inconceivable that animal soul is of a different nature from human soul, for we can conceive of nothing that is not body or spirit or a mode of one of these two substances (Régis 1970, 2:631).

What about the view that animal soul is an immaterial thinking substance, distinct from the body and capable of existing apart from it—in other words, that animal soul is of the same nature as human soul though less perfect in its thoughts? According to Régis this opinion, which he calls Pythagorean, is by no means inconceivable. There is no evidence to support it, since all animal behavior can be explained mechanically; but there is no "certain proof" against it either. Reason can show that the Peripatetic alternative is absurd but not that the Pythagorean view is. If we prefer the Cartesian view to the Pythagorean, explains Régis, it is only because we do not wish to assume responsibility for the undesirable consequences of the latter, such as "that the soul of beasts is immortal, that it thinks, wills, loves and so on. . . . That is why, whatever inclination we may have to give beasts a soul distinct from the body, we prefer to suspend our judgment in this regard" (Régis 1970, 2:632).

Jean du Hamel objected that it was unreasonable for Régis to advocate suspension of judgment on animal soul after having dismissed it as untenable. Régis replies that suspension of judgment is appropriate with regard to immaterial animal soul, whereas the judgment of untenability refers to animal soul as material. "The reason is that on the one hand I am not convinced that the brutes have a soul like that which the Pythagoreans give them; faith itself assures me that they do not. On the other hand, reason clearly shows me that the soul which the Peripatetics give to beasts is a pure chimera" (Régis 1692, 223).

Unlike Régis, Dilly is not content to leave the last word to faith. For reasons similar to Régis's, he rejects the Peripatetic view as incoherent. He goes on to reactivate the oyster argument, replacing "immortal" in premise (2) with "immaterial." From the revised version of (2) he derives (2a) that whatever thinks has an indivisible soul. For Descartes's oysters and sponges he substitutes the worm that so puzzled Saint Augustine in chapter 30 of *The Greatness of the Soul*.

When the worm is cut in half each piece moves of its own accord. There are in effect two worms. Now suppose, reasons Dilly, that the worm has an immaterial soul and that at the time of bisection it has some sentiment or imagines something. Either the soul is divided along with the body or else it is indivisible. The first alternative is incomprehensible. How can sensations and imaginations be divided? The second alternative is equally inadmissible. If the worm's soul remains one and the same before and after the division, then it exists in a manner even more noble and incomprehensible than the human soul, which is, as Descartes says, "coextensive with the body—the whole mind in the whole body and the whole mind in any one of its parts" (AT 7:442; CSM 2:298; HR 2:255). The soul of the worm would be coextensive with both pieces after the division—a mode of existence suitable only for the sacramental body of Jesus Christ in the Eucharist (Dilly 1676, 67-68). Moreover, the worm would feel the division "and each half has to say afterwards, 'I who am only half of what I was a moment earlier, I who am part here and part there, in short, I who am separated from myself' " (69).

This little scenario of worm cogitation is a bit off the mark. The one who is saying these things to itself is not the bisected worm but its alleged soul. The soul is not "half of what it was" since it has not been divided. Nor is it "part here and part there" but whole in each part. Nor is it literally "separated from itself" insofar as this implies spatial location. It is, however, "separated from itself" in the metaphorical sense that it now has two distinct sets of experiences. For Dilly's purposes this is incomprehensible enough.[2]

The oyster argument has been transformed into the worm argument. The latter may be summarized thus. Suppose (1) animals that move and have at least rudimentary sense organs also have conscious experiences, in short, they think. Since (2) whatever thinks has an immaterial soul—the Peripatetic alternative being inconceivable—and thus (2a) whatever thinks has an indivisible soul, it follows that (3) such animals have indivisible souls. But this leads to the absurd consequence that (4) worms have indivisible souls. Therefore (5) no animals think.

Because worms are included among the animals referred to in premise (1), the argument is not a blatant non sequitur like the original oyster argument. Nevertheless, it commits the fallacy of hasty generalization since the worm is an atypical case. The heroes of the traditional tales of animal sagacity were mostly mammals, birds, fish, reptiles, and insects. In these classes a division of the body has one of three results: the animal dies, or it goes on living without the missing segment, or it regenerates a new segment. In each case there is only one living body.[3] Given that these animals do not share the worm's remarkable ability to lead two separate lives, there is no prima facie absurdity in attributing indivisible souls to them.

Perhaps the oyster argument has been changed too much. Why not stick with immortality and simply change "oysters and sponges" to, say, "fish and fowl" or "cats and rats"?

The problem with this tactic is that immortality does not logically follow from immateriality. True, one of the main concerns behind the Cartesian dualism was to provide a foundation for the religious doctrine of immortality of the soul. Yet inasmuch as Cartesian souls are substances created by God, and creation is a continuous process, God can annihilate souls at any time, individually or collectively, just as he can put an end to the material world.

---

2. For a fanciful description of a person in a similar situation see "Where Am I?" in Dennett 1978, 310–23; reprinted in Hofstadter and Dennett 1981, 217–29.

3. Cloning as a means of reproduction creates no special quandary here. From the point of view of dualist metaphysics, it is no more problematic than ordinary sexual reproduction, in which the Cartesian God endows the newly formed body with a soul of its own.

From the thesis that souls are thinking, unextended substances, the most that follows is that they cannot be destroyed by natural processes as organized bodies can. Malebranche is quite explicit on this score. The character Theodore explains in the *Entretiens sur la mort*: "I grant you that God can annihilate our souls at death, but their immortality is sufficiently demonstrated once it has been proved that they are substances distinct from the body. For the destruction of substances is naturally impossible. . . . No doubt God can, if he so wills, annihilate our souls when they leave the body; but I am quite certain that he will never will this" (OC 13:369). Should God, however, choose to annihilate the souls of brutes upon the death of their bodies, there is no philosophical or theological reason to prevent it.

Or is there? This brings us to the second argument.

THE ARGUMENT FROM DIVINE RECOMPENSE

In the fourth book of *The Search after Truth* Malebranche offers a "demonstration which proves that animals are insensible, to wit, being innocent, as everyone agrees and I assume, if they were capable of feeling, this would mean that under an infinitely just and omnipotent God, an innocent creature would suffer pain, which is a penalty and a punishment for some sin" (OC 2:104; S 323). He is rather pessimistic about the psychological persuasiveness of this argument, since it is based on abstract principles which are usually "taken for illusions and chimeras" (OC 2:104; S 323). Because animals cry out when they are struck, we are inclined to believe they suffer pain. Most people would rather go with this inclination than listen to the voice of reason. "For all the most certain and most evident arguments of the pure understanding will never persuade them against the obscure proofs they have through their senses. Indeed, one risks exposing oneself to the laughter of superficial and inattentive minds if one pretends to prove to them, by moderately abstract arguments, that animals do not sense" (OC 2:106; S 324).

The abstract principle on which the aforesaid argument is based is that "under a just God one cannot be miserable without having merited it." Augustine used this principle against Julian to demonstrate original sin (OC 2:104; S 323). The saint failed to realize that it also had implications for animals. Malebranche clarifies his position with respect to Augustine in the Fifteenth Elucidation:

> It is certain . . . that Saint Augustine always spoke of animals as if they had souls—I do not say a corporeal soul, for this holy doctor knew too well to

distinguish the soul from the body to think that there could be corporeal souls. I say a spiritual soul, for matter is incapable of sensation. Nonetheless, I believe that it is more reasonable to use the authority of Saint Augustine to prove that animals have no soul than to prove that they do; for from the principles he carefully examined and securely established, it manifestly follows that they do not, as Ambrosius Victor shows in his sixth volume of the *Philosophia Christiana*. (OC 3:236–37; S 676)

The most complete statement of the argument from divine recompense is found in a 1682 piece by Malebranche entitled *Défense de l'autheur de la Recherche de la vérité contre l'accusation de Monsr. de la Ville* (OC 17-1:509-31). Dilly, too, gives the argument (1676, 96–99), but as usual he displays less philosophical acumen than his more illustrious contemporary. In both Malebranche's *Défense* and Dilly's book, it is apparent that the argument relies on more than Augustine's principle about the relation between misery and divine justice.

The following is our reconstruction of the argument from divine recompense. The argument has six premises:

(1) If God is just, then no creature is miserable without deserving it.

(2) No sinless creature deserves misery.

(3) Suffering without recompense is misery.

(4) Animals are not granted recompense for suffering.

(5) Animals are sinless.

(6) God is just.

Premise (1) is Augustine's principle. Premise (2) is also Augustinian, at least on Malebranche's reading, for in order to demonstrate original sin it must be assumed that being a sinner is a necessary condition for meriting misery, or that only sinners deserve to be miserable.

Premise (3) is needed to establish a relation between ordinary suffering and the more global state referred to by Augustine. Otherwise it could be argued that animal suffering does not constitute the sort of misery that is prohibited to undeserving creatures. On premise (3) suffering becomes misery when it must be endured without compensation. For many animals, there is obviously no compensation for suffering in this life, so their reward would have to come after death. But they have no animal heaven to look forward to: in other words, premise (4). Malebranche writes in the *Défense:*

"Moreover, there is this difference between men and beasts, that men after their death can receive a happiness which pays them for the sufferings they have endured in life. But the beasts lose everything at death: they have been unhappy and innocent, and there is no recompense awaiting them" (OC 17-1:514).

As for premise (5), we already noted Malebranche's remark in the *Search* that the innocence of the beasts is something he assumes and everyone agrees on. Sin, by his definition, consists in making bad use of one's freedom by confining one's love to particular goods, rather than following the impression God gives toward the good in general, that is, toward himself (OC 2: 314–15; 3:19; S 449, 548). Animals cannot make bad use of their freedom since they have none in the first place. Hence they cannot sin.

Of the final premise, (6) that God is just, suffice it to say that it is a basic tenet of religion.

The rest of the argument is fairly straightforward. Given that (2) no sinless creatures deserve misery and (5) all animals are sinless, it follows that

(7) no animals deserve misery.

Moreover, since (3) suffering without recompense is misery and (4) animals receive no recompense, it follows that

(8) if animals suffer, then they are miserable although they do not deserve to be so.

Contraposition of premise (1) yields:

(9) if any creature is miserable without deserving it, then God is not just.

From (8) and (9) it follows that

(10) if animals suffer, then God is not just.

But God is just, by premise (6). Therefore

(11) animals do not suffer.

Given Malebranche's interpretation of the Augustinian principles, the following statements cannot all be true: "animals are sinless"; "animals are not granted recompense for their suffering"; "God is just"; and "animals suffer." Any one of these statements can be demonstrated to be false using the other three as premises.

To illustrate, let us replace premise (6) in the original argument with the premise that animals suffer.[4] This yields the following argument:

(1) If God is just, then no creature is miserable without deserving it.

(2) No sinless creature deserves misery.

(3) Suffering without recompense is misery.

(4) Animals are not granted recompense for suffering.

(5) Animals are sinless.

(6) Animals suffer.

(7) Animals do not deserve misery (from 2, 5).

(8) If animals suffer, then they are miserable without deserving it (from 3, 4, 7).

(9) If animals are miserable without deserving it, then God is not just (from 1).

(10) If animals suffer, then God is not just (from 8, 9).

(11) God is not just (from 6, 10).

Alternatively, let us keep the original premise (6) and put the premise about animal suffering in place of (5). Now the argument proceeds thus:

(1) If God is just, then no creature is miserable without deserving it.

(2) No sinless creature deserves misery.

---

4. In this and the subsequent two arguments, the new premise can be glossed as either "all animals suffer" or "some animals suffer." The conclusion of the present argument remains the same on either reading. On the alternative "some animals suffer," the conclusion of the next argument becomes "some animals are not sinless"—bad enough for Malebranche's purposes. The conclusion of the third argument is "those animals that suffer are given recompense for it."

(3) Suffering without recompense is misery.

(4) Animals are not granted recompense for suffering.

(5) Animals suffer.

(6) God is just.

(7) No creature is miserable without deserving it (from 1, 6).

(8) Animals are miserable (from 3, 4, 5).

(9) Animals deserve their misery (from 7, 8).

(10) Animals are not sinless (from 2,9).

Finally, by substituting the premise about animal suffering for the original premise (4), we get this argument:

(1) If God is just, then no creature is miserable without deserving it.

(2) No sinless creature deserves misery.

(3) Suffering without recompense is misery.

(4) Animals suffer.

(5) Animals are sinless.

(6) God is just.

(7) No creature is miserable without deserving it (from 1, 6).

(8) Animals do not deserve misery (from 2, 5).

(9) Animals are not miserable (from 7, 8).

(10) If animals suffer, they are given recompense for it (from 3, 9).

(11) Animals are given recompense for their suffering (from 4, 10).

Malebranche claims that if we accept the common opinion on animal suffering, then Augustinian principles force us to conclude that God is not just, a consequence opposed to faith (OC 17–1:514). Malebranche goes a little too fast. What follows from the common opinion is that God is not just, or animals are guilty of sin, or animals are granted recompense for their suffering. Admittedly, the first alternative is theologically disastrous, but what about the other two? Everyone agrees that animals are without sin. Or almost everyone, for a person named Rabin was said to have held that all animals ate of the forbidden fruit except the phoenix (Rosenfield 1968, 293). There are two main theological objections to animal sin. First, it requires that animals have free will, for by Malebranche's definition of sin, one must have freedom in order to sin. This undermines human uniqueness. Second, animal sin creates a need for animal redemption. Would God provide for our salvation and not for theirs? Did Christ die for kangaroo and caribou as well as for mankind? Must we send missionaries to the lions and, like Saint Francis, preach to the fish?

The third alternative, recompense for animal suffering, cannot be dismissed so easily as the other two, for the theological ramifications, though unsettling, are far from disastrous. None of the essential tenets of Christianity is contradicted by it. The uniqueness of humanity in creation remains intact. Only humans are free and they alone are in need of salvation. Moreover, the traditional attributes of God are unchallenged. The divine justice and goodness are preserved. To be sure, it does not say anywhere in the Bible that animals receive compensation for their suffering. There is no reason why Scripture should provide an answer one way or the other on this matter, since nothing hinges on it as far as human salvation is concerned. It is strictly between God and the brutes.

The notion that God should take on some sort of obligation with respect to animals is not without precedent in Scripture. After the Flood, God establishes a covenant not only with Noah and his descendents, but also "with every living creature that is with you, of the fowl, of the cattle, and of every beast of the earth with you; from all that go out of the ark, to every beast of the earth" (Gen. 9:10). Every time the covenant is mentioned, animals are specifically included: "This is the token of the covenant which I make between me and you and every living creature that is with you" (Gen. 9:12); "And I will remember my covenant, which is between me and you and every living creature of all flesh" (Gen. 9:15); "the everlasting covenant between God and every living creature of all flesh that is upon the earth" (Gen. 9:16); "the covenant, which I have established between me and all flesh that is upon the earth" (Gen. 9:17). It is revealing that when Malebranche discusses the covenant of the rainbow in connection with natural laws, he refers to it simply as God's covenant with man (OC 10:80). Most clergy do the same. If their justification is that only the human part is relevant to human concerns, their point is well taken. By the same token, however, it must be admitted that there is no reason why we would have to be informed of any additional covenant God might have made exclusively with his brute creation.

One might be tempted to take a cue from Descartes and bring up oysters in protest. Where do you draw the line? Do oysters and sponges stand in need of compensation? Are worms miserable? Of course, if it were up to us to decide which animals suffer and which do not, we would undoubtedly make mistakes. But under the present scenario it is not up to us. Our justice is not at stake, God's is. Surely an omniscient being can handle the task of determining what sensations and feelings each organism is capable of and, accordingly, which creatures qualify for compensation.

The persuasive force of the argument from divine recompense depends on the acceptability of its premises. Its major rival is the argument for recompense of animals. The two arguments differ in that the denial of a premise of one is the conclusion of the other. Which of the two arguments has more force? It depends on which is more plausible as a premise: that animals are not given recompense or that animals suffer. Malebranche provides no defense of his premise (4) but relies instead on our disinclination to grant the brutes a place in heaven. Descartes, too, appealed to this same reluctance in the original oyster argument. The choice then is between two prejudices, one against animals in heaven, the other about animal suffering. In order for Malebranche's argument to win out over the rival argument, it must be shown either that reason opposes the extension of recompense to animals, or else that reason opposes the belief in animal suffering. Malebranche fails to do the former. As for the latter, it will not do for him to offer his own argument from divine recompense in support of it, since acceptance of that argument already assumes an answer to the question of which premise is more plausible. Malebranche needs some independent grounds for rejecting the crucial premise of the rival argument. The argument from divine recompense cannot uphold the beast-machine on its own.

THE ARGUMENT FROM HUMAN DOMINION

Dilly writes in chapter 11 of *De l'ame des bêtes:*

> Finally, what right do the like of us men have over the beasts, to ill-treat them and to have their life and their death at our sovereign command as we do? Is it not a very great cruelty to torment them without reason and quite often to deprive them of the innocent pleasures which they are capable of enjoying? One can reply that man is the King of the animals, that he can make use of them as he sees fit, and that God has given him this right. It is true that innocent man would be their legitimate sovereign, but we are their tyrants, and our loss of innocence deprives us of the rightful authority that we had

over all sensible creatures. Thus I do not see reasons which can justify our conduct with regard to the beasts, and from whatever side I consider the matter, whether from God's or from ours, I find everywhere again reasons to strengthen me in my thought and to persuade me that the beasts have no soul. (1676, 100–101)

It is interesting to compare this passage with Descartes's statement to Henry More: "Thus my opinion is not so much cruel to animals as indulgent to men—at least to those who are not given to the superstitions of Pythagoras—since it absolves them from the suspicion of crime when they eat or kill animals" (AT 5:278–79; K 245). Descartes is not giving an argument for the beast-machine but merely noting an advantage of his view. If there is an argument at all here, it is a moral one: the doctrine of animal automatism serves as a premise to support the conclusion that the killing and eating of animals is morally permissible. Dilly's argument works the other way around. The morality of our treatment of animals is used to support the doctrine of animal automatism.

Dilly's argument can be stated in terms of four premises:

(1) If God is just, then he does not give humans dominion over any being capable of enjoyment and suffering, unless humans are without sin.

(2) God is just.

(3) Humans are not without sin.

(4) God has given humans dominion over all animals.

From the first three premises, one can derive:

(5) God does not give humans dominion over any being capable of enjoyment and suffering.

This together with the fourth premise yields the conclusion:

(6) No animals are capable of enjoyment and suffering.

The notion of human sovereignty over animals comes from Genesis 1:26: "And God said, Let us make man in our image, after our likeness: and let them have dominion over the fish of the sea, and over the fowl of the air, and over the cattle, and over all the earth, and over every creeping thing that creepeth upon the earth." Man was still in the state of innocence when he was given dominion over the animals. The Bible nowhere says that this dominion was revoked after the Fall. In fact, the animals were "delivered" into Noah's hand after the Flood and proclaimed food for him (Gen. 9:2–3). At any rate, Dilly takes the original sovereignty to remain in effect as indicated in premise (4).

Some would simply dismiss Dilly's argument as a reductio ad absurdum of theology. This is the easy way out and not very illuminating. One of our fundamental working principles is that the most devastating way to criticize an argument is from within the arguer's own framework. Like Satan, we prefer to do battle in the theological context.

Saint Thomas Aquinas, noting that man was given mastership "over all the earth," distinguishes between two ways of being master: by commanding and by using. Commanding requires the capacity for obedience on the part of the subject; things that cannot obey commands cannot meaningfully be commanded to do anything. Plants and inanimate objects are by their nature incapable of obedience. Thus in the state of innocence man's mastership over them "consisted, not in commanding or in changing them, but in making use of them without hindrance" (*Summa Theologica* I, q.96, a.2). Over the animals he had the other sort of mastership. "All animals have by natural judgment a certain participation in prudence and reason," which makes them capable of obedience (I, q.96, a.1, *ad* 4). "So in the state of innocence man had mastership over the animals by commanding them" (I, q.96, a.2). That changed with the Fall. "For his disobedience to God, man was punished by the disobedience of those creatures which should be subject to him" (I, q.96, a.1).

The two kinds of mastership are by no means mutually exclusive. One can command a subject and also use it. On the question of whether innocent man used animals, Aquinas has this to say: "In the state of innocence man would not have had any bodily need of animals:—neither for clothing, since then they were naked and not ashamed, for there were no inordinate motions of concupiscence,—nor for food, since they fed on the trees of paradise,—nor to carry him about, for his body was strong enough for that purpose." He continues rather lamely: "But man needed animals in order to have experimental knowledge of their natures. This is signified by the fact that God led the animals to man, that he might give them names expressive of their respective natures" (I, q.96, a.1, *ad* 3). Though Aquinas probably had nothing gruesome in mind, one can imagine Adam, imbued with the wisdom of Cartesianism, performing vivisections on the animals in paradise in order to name them more exactly.

On Aquinas's interpretation of mastership as power to command, Dilly's argument fails to go through. It is essential to the argument that premise (4) apply to all humans irrespective of their state. In other words, the dominion that God gave to man in the state of innocence must remain essentially unchanged by the Fall. On Aquinas's analysis it does not; we no longer have command over the brutes. Moreover, there was no need for God to inform Adam and Eve that their mastership was rescinded. They would know soon enough when the animals ceased to obey them.

No defender of animal automatism would ever accept that dominion over the animals consists in commanding them. Machines do not participate in reason and cannot obey. Thus the Cartesian is obliged to go with Aquinas's other sense of mastership, which consists in using.

Dilly's first premise must refer to the right to use one's subjects however one wishes, to do to them whatever one pleases, without any restrictions. It must refer to a *right* and not just a power to use, for otherwise the infliction of suffering by human sinners would be no more problematic than suffering from natural causes. The premise must refer to an *unlimited* right, for it would be consistent with the divine justice to impose bounds on what may be done to sentient creatures. To be sure, sinners are likely to overstep any bounds placed upon their dominion, but so too do they disobey God's other injunctions. If "dominion" means "absolute dominion" in premise (1), it must mean the same in premise (4), or else the argument commits the fallacy of equivocation. Indeed that is how Dilly takes it, for he describes our dominion over the beasts as tyranny.

It says in Genesis that man in the state of innocence was given dominion over the animals. Let us grant the Cartesian that this dominion or mastership was a right to use animals rather than a power to command them. There are two questions: Was the dominion absolute? And did humans keep it after the Fall? The success of Dilly's argument depends upon answering yes to both questions. Our contention is that an affirmative answer to either one demands a negative answer to the other.

Suppose on the one hand that God gave human beings the unlimited right to use animals however they choose and that humans subsequently sinned, so that now they have disorderly desires and evil purposes. We submit that it is theological nonsense to say that God has given us the right to use certain objects to fulfil desires or to accomplish ends contrary to his own laws. Freedom, yes. As free agents it is within our power to sin, but not within our rights. One can commit murder by crushing the victim under a stone or under an elephant, but one does not have a God-given right to employ either as a tool for such a purpose. If man in the state of innocence was given absolute dominion over anything, sentient or not, that dominion would have to be restricted after the Fall.

On the other hand, suppose that the dominion given to man in the state of innocence is also in effect for sinners. In that case it cannot have been absolute in the first place. Man must have been granted the use of objects only to satisfy his just and orderly desires. Innocent man did not need to have restrictions placed upon his use of objects since he had no base desires and no inclination to abuse his subjects. Yet the restrictions must have already been there, for sinful man would need them. Again it makes no difference whether the objects being used have feelings or not. If dominion applies to all people, including sinners, it cannot be absolute.

5

A Debauchery of Reason

A Voyage to the World of Cartesius by the Jesuit Father Gabriel Daniel was first published in 1690. Cartesianism is the target of this satirical piece of seventeenth-century science fiction. Descartes, so the story goes, had found the secret of how to separate his soul from his body whenever he pleased. During the soul's extracorporeal sojourns, the body continued to display all those operations in which the soul plays no part. These included not only the purely physiological processes of respiration, blood circulation, and so on, but also reactions such as brushing a fly away from the nose and habitual actions in which the appropriate neurological and muscular associations had already been established.

A few months after his arrival in Sweden Descartes fell ill, as everyone knows. Contrary to popular belief, he recovered and is still alive! What happened was this. The night after the fever left him, his soul went on one of her rambles for diversion. Meanwhile Descartes's physician came in to check on his patient. When queried, the body responded with nonsense since the soul was not there to speak rationally. Believing Descartes was delirious, the doctor bled him and applied such violent remedies that the body could no longer maintain itself. It was pronounced dead and was buried with great pomp and solemnity. Descartes's soul, thus deprived of its lodgings, was condemned to wander the heavens. The disembodied philosopher traveled out beyond the stars, where there was matter aplenty but no motion and hence no diversity of forms. There he set about to construct a world according to the principles he had expounded in his writings. An old man privy to the secret shares it with the narrator, who leaves his body temporarily for a visit to the great philosopher.

The narrator is converted to Cartesianism. "My *Soul* thus seated on the *Pineal Gland* of my Brain, as a *Queen* upon her *Throne,* to conduct and govern all the Motions of the *Machine* of my Body, was extremely pleas'd with the change of her Ideas; and complimented her self with the honorable new Character of *Cartesian,* wherewith I began to be distinguisht amongst the Learned" (Daniel 1692, 240). He describes the change in his attitude toward animals:

> Before my Conversion to *Cartesianism,* I was so pitiful and Tender-hearted, that I could not so much as see a Chicken kill'd: But since I was once persuaded that Beasts were destitute both of Knowledg and Sense, scarce a Dog in all the Town, wherein I was, could escape me, for the making *Anatomical* Dissections, wherein I my self was *Operator,* without the least inkling of Compassion or Remorse; as also at the opening of the Disputes and Assemblies of the Learn'd, which I thought good to keep at my House, for the inhancing and propagating the Doctrine of my *Master* in the Country; the first Oration I made before them, was an Invective against the Ignorance and Injustice of that Senator, the *Areopagite,* that caus'd a *Noble Man's* Child to be declar'd for ever Incapacitated from entring on the Publick Government, whom he had observ'd take pleasure in pricking out the Eyes of Jack-Daws, that were given to him to play with. (241–42)

The image of the philosopher calmly committing atrocities to animals reappears in Nicolas Fontaine's history of Port-Royal: "They administered beatings to dogs with perfect indifference, and made fun of those who pitied the creatures as if they had felt pain. They said that the animals were clocks; that the cries they emitted when struck, were only the noise of a little spring which had been touched, but that the whole body was without feeling. They nailed poor animals up on boards by their four paws to vivisect them and see the circulation of the blood which was a great subject of conversation" (Fontaine 1738, 2:52–53; Rosenfield 1968, 54). Sainte-Beuve (1908, 2:316) adds that when observers protested the vivisections, Arnauld responded as Malebranche later would upon kicking his dog: "Well! Don't you know that it does not feel?"

In the *Discours sur la fable* of 1719 Antoine Houdar de la Motte ventures the opinion that it is "a debauchery of reason" to make animals machines (La Motte 1754, 9:27). Fontenelle found the phrase very apt, according to Trublet (1761). It conveys that the Cartesians were led to the doctrine by an inexorable chain of consequences drawn from their metaphysical principles. Trublet doubts whether Descartes himself held it sincerely, though he grants that Malebranche did, as the dog story plainly shows (Trublet 1761, 114–15).

The great skeptic Pierre Bayle offers a more cautious assessment of the beast-machine doctrine. We shall consider Bayle's verdict in light of what we have uncovered in the preceding chapters. Then we shall turn to Dilly's opponent Pardies as an ally on nonreflective consciousness and as inspiration for some methodological objections to animal automatism. The chapter ends with a discussion of the role of anecdotes in the beast-machine debate. Here we finally give Descartes the credit he is due.

BAYLE'S VERDICT

The "Rorarius" article of Bayle's *Historical and Critical Dictionary* deals with one Hieronymus Rorarius, a minor sixteenth-century figure who endeavored to show that animals are rational and that they make better use of their reason than people do. This goes against the Aristotelian view that animals have sensations, memory, and passions, but not reason. It also goes against Cartesian animal automatism. Bayle takes the opportunity to weigh these two opposing views.

The Aristotelians think they have avoided the distressing consequences of attributing a rational soul to beasts, but they haven't, says Bayle. They claim that animal souls differ in kind from human souls. But if the difference consists in the animals' failure to reason and to have knowledge of universals, then it is only accidental and not substantial. "Aristotle and Cicero at the age of one did not have more sublime thoughts than those of a dog" (Bayle 1965, 224). The human brain allows for greater development of thought than animal brains. "The soul of a dog in the organs of Aristotle and Cicero would have lacked nothing for acquiring all the knowledge of those two great men" (Bayle 1965, 224). If the souls of men and beasts are of the same species, then either both are material and mortal, or both are spiritual and immortal. Bayle considers both alternatives and finds them wanting:

> These are horrible consequences no matter which way one looks at them. For, if, in order to avoid the immortality of the soul of beasts, we suppose that the soul of man dies with the body, we thereby overthrow the doctrine of another life and undermine the foundations of religion. If, however, in order to preserve for our soul the privilege of immortality, we extend it also to the soul of beasts, then into what an abyss shall we fall? What will we do with

so many immortal souls? Will there also be a paradise and a hell for them? Will they migrate from one body to another? Will they be annihilated in proportion as beasts die? Will God incessantly create an infinitude of spirits, to plunge them back again so soon into a state of nothingness? (225)

The Cartesians should not gloat too much over the deficiencies in the Aristotelian doctrine, for they have a few of their own. Here Bayle's skepticism comes to the fore: "It seems that God . . . acts like a common father of all sects; that is, he will not allow one sect to triumph completely over the others and destroy them utterly. An overwhelmed sect, put to rout, and almost worn out, always finds the means to recover as soon as it gives up defending itself, creating a diversion by taking the offensive and retaliating" (231–32). The Cartesian view has two weaknesses. One is that it seems to prove too much. Could it not equally well be argued that other people are machines (231)? The other weakness is that it explains too little. "Everyone knows how difficult it is to explain how pure machines can accomplish what animals do" (214–15). The problem is not so much the variety of animal movements, "but that they exhibit many signs of friendship, hate, joy, jealousy, fear, suffering, and the like" (244). Bayle hands in his verdict on the beast-machine: "It is too bad that Descartes' view is so difficult to maintain and so far from being probable; for it is otherwise of very great advantage to the true faith, and this is the only reason that keeps some people from giving it up" (215–16).

The difficulty of explaining animal actions mechanistically is put more forcefully in Daniel's *Voyage*. There Aristotle presents a long list of objections to the new philosophy, including the following: "That the Promise the *Cartesians* had made, to explain all that we see admirable in Beasts, by the sole disposition of the *Machine* was whimsical, and not to be relied on, since it never had been put in Practice. That when they talked of these Matters in general, they sometimes spoke plausibly enough; but when they descended to Particulars, they were either much to be pitied or not endured" (Daniel 1692, 139).

Daniel's point is well taken. The hypothesis of animal automatism rests on a promissory note. There is nothing wrong with promissory notes in science so long as the issuers recognize the need to make good on them. It is easy to assure one's audience that all will be explained in the sweet bye and bye. To be taken seriously, however, one must provide examples of successful explanations in particular cases.

Descartes and his followers take great pains to show how mechanical principles govern relatively simple phenomena such as magnetism, but toward animal behavior their approach is strangely cavalier. Consider, for instance, Descartes's handling of the sheep's flight from the wolf: the light reflected from the body of the wolf onto the eyes of the sheep sends the animal spirits into the nerves in the manner necessary to produce the movements of flight (AT 7:230; CSM 2:161; HR 2:104). Now apart from the complexities of muscle physiology, which he recognizes and treats elsewhere, Descartes passes over another problem. Light can be reflected from the body of a wolf in innumerable ways: the wolf can appear head on, in profile, from the back, or at any angle in between, and in many different postures. Do all of these wolf images trigger flight or only some of them? Do they produce flight in some circumstances, but not in others? What at first glance seemed to be a standard response to a single stimulus comes dangerously close to being an appropriate response to a variety of stimuli—shades of the action test. The ideal of complete mechanistic explanation demands more than Cartesian hand waving in response. The physiological basis for recognition must be spelled out in detail.

The Cartesians berate the Aristotelians for their occult qualities, mere words without explanatory force. Yet when push comes to shove, the Cartesians, too, have recourse to pseudoexplanatory terms. Why does a sheep flee from a wolf and not from a dog? Dilly's answer is "instinct," which he defines as "certain actions performed naturally by all members of an animal species" (Dilly 1676, 231–32). Instinct always relates to the animals' preservation, for "it can only consist in the particular disposition of their brain when they are born. Thus a lamb flees the wolf, because the sight of this beast determines the animal spirits to produce this movement by the natural harmony of the lamb's brain, for nothing can be better ordained for its preservation" (232). The beauty of this account is that it can be expanded or contracted to fit virtually any state of affairs. If sheep fail to run from certain predators, it is because their brains are not "disposed" to produce a response to that particular type of danger. When they graze on poisonous plants, it is because their "instinct" leads them to eat but not necessarily to consume what is good for them. When they do refuse certain kinds of food, such as meat, it is by the "natural harmony" of their brain.

According to Bayle, the major weakness of the Cartesian theory is that it proves too much. The same reasons that the Cartesians bring against animal thought can also be used to deny thought to other people—an absurd consequence if ever there was one. "For where is the man who would dare to say that he is the only one who thinks and that everybody else is a machine?" (Bayle 1965, 232).

When faced with the threat of turning humans into machines along with the brutes, it will not do for the Cartesians to appeal to each individual's own subjective experience of thinking. Consider the following scenario. The anti-Cartesian says: "Once it is granted that all the actions of animals can be explained mechanically, there is nothing to prevent one from asserting the same about people." The Cartesian answers: "You know full well that you are not a machine, since you are aware of your own thinking." The anti-Cartesian can easily retort: "So *I* am not just a machine. But since I have no experience of anyone's thinking but my own, there is nothing to prevent me from holding that everyone else is a machine."

Is Cartesianism really caught in this bind? As Bayle presents it, the Cartesian case for distinguishing man from the beasts seems to rest primarily on the fact of human self-consciousness. Some Cartesians did reason in this way, Dilly being a prime example (Dilly 1676, 111–12). Indeed Descartes himself suggests something along these lines in the Fifth Replies: "Your questions about the brutes are not appropriate in this context since the mind, when engaged in private meditation, can experience its own thinking but cannot have any experience to establish whether the brutes think or not; it must tackle this question later on, by an *a posteriori* investigation of their behavior" (AT 7:357–58; CSM 2:247–48; HR 2:211).

The last clause shields Descartes from the full thrust of Bayle's attack. Descartes makes it perfectly clear in the *Discourse* that it is people's behavior, specifically their ability to pass the language and action tests, that prevents us from asserting that they are machines devoid of thought. Recall also that in the fable of the land with no animals, the man used the two tests to tell the difference between real people and automata in human form. It was the tests, not his awareness of thinking, that convinced him of the difference between real animals and people.

The major weakness of the Cartesian theory is not that it proves too much but that it proves too little. The trouble lies not in what it implies about people, but rather in what it fails to establish about animals. The main support for animal automatism comes from Descartes's two tests of thought. For this reason the Cartesians are by no means committed to the solipsistic conclusion Bayle tries to foist upon them. But for the same reason they have no metaphysical or behavioral justification for denying Cartesian thought to the beasts. Neither test leads to the conclusion that animals lack consciousness.

Either animals pass the language test or else it is not a test of thought in the Cartesian sense. If the language test consists simply in whether a creature gives appropriate responses or, more specifically, appropriate responses that at least sometimes express something besides passion, then some animals pass. If the appropriate responses must pertain to pure thought or pure intellect, then animals fail, but it is not a test of thought in the sense of anything of which the thinker is conscious.

The action test is set up on too narrow a conception of acting through reason. It therefore scores a hollow victory against the brutes. A being can act through reason in the sense of following limited and faulty principles, yet fail the action test. Even if we were to grant that the action test shows that animals fail to act through reason, it still does not establish that they lack all modes of Cartesian thought.

Another premise is needed for the beast-machine doctrine: that the possession of pure thought or reason is necessary for having thought at all. Not only is this premise unwarranted on Cartesian grounds, but it is contraindicated by the Cartesian view of human fetuses who, according to Descartes, have no acts of pure understanding but only confused sensations.

It is no great threat to Aristotelianism that animals should fail the language and action tests, thereby indicating their lack of pure intellect and reason. The Aristotelians never claimed that animals had those capacities in the first place, only that they had sensation, imagination, and memory. As Bayle observes, the traditional stories of animal sagacity, insofar as they impute reason to the beasts, work against the Peripatetics as much as against the Cartesians (Bayle 1965, 216).

In light of the Cartesian failure to link sensation with intellect, the Peripatetic account of sensation, or one version of it at any rate, deserves closer examination. Our aim is not to vindicate Aristotelianism but to discover what the Cartesian theory of mind really implies about animals. Surprisingly enough, the Jesuit Pardies, a Peripatetic, is in some respects closer to Descartes's view of consciousness than are some of the philosopher's own followers. Moreover, in Pardies's work lies the germ of a major challenge to the beast-machine doctrine. By playing sufficiently free with the text, we can do for Pardies what Montaigne did for Raymond Sebond.

APOLOGY FOR FATHER PARDIES

In the *Discours de la connoissance des bestes* Pardies considers the reasons that have led the Cartesians to deprive beasts of knowledge and sentiment, lest he be accused of dismissing their opinion without giving it a fair hearing. The first half of the book is taken up with presenting the Cartesian case. So well did Pardies succeed in this task that Daniel accused him of being a closet Cartesian (Rosenfield 1968, 85–86). Its eloquence notwithstanding, this half of the book does not concern us here. We are interested in the second half, which contains Pardies's own position on animal knowledge. This is the part that provoked the ire of Dilly and led him to write *De l'ame des bêtes* in reply.

Pardies distinguishes between two types of knowledge, intellectual and sensible. Intellectual or spiritual knowledge is "an intimate perception by which we perceive an object in such a way that we perceive ourselves as well; that is to say, a perception which essentially involves a kind of reflection that it indivisibly makes on itself, so that we know very well that we know" (Pardies 1672, 150). I have intellectual knowledge of an object when, in the very act of perceiving it, I know or perceive that I perceive it. There is no need for a separate act of understanding in order to accomplish the reflection. The act by which I perceive is the same act by which I perceive that I perceive. This is what Pardies means when he says that this sort of knowledge is "essentially and indivisibly reflective on itself" (152).

Sensible knowledge is "a simple perception of an object without this reflection" (150–51). Pardies gives two examples of human sensible knowledge. One is seeing a friend pass by while our mind is occupied with something else. We have indeed seen him, insists Pardies, for we are not blind, and this seeing is more than just light striking the retina. "Whence I conclude that one can see without this particular attention, I mean without perceiving that one perceives" (157). His other example is seeing the letters in a book. The reader is attentive to the meaning of the passage, not to the characters. Yet in order to read, one must notice the shape of the letters, distinguish them from one another, and consider how they are connected to form words. We perceive them, but not "with the reflective perception by which we can render an account to ourselves of what we perceive and which makes us perceive that we perceive" (160).

People have both intellectual and sensible knowledge. The beasts have only sensible knowledge. "Is it not true that a dog sees his master, and distinguishes him from all the other men in a crowd, in the same way that we see the letters in a book and in such a great multitude distinguish them one from another?" (175).

Dilly takes Pardies's definition of intellectual knowledge as reflective and applies it to thought in general. He writes in the second chapter of *De l'ame des bêtes:*

> To think is to have operations of the existence of which one is immediately certain by themselves in the moment one has them. Thus when I conceive a triangle, this knowledge makes itself perceived and assures me of its existence

at the very moment I form it. If I doubt, if I will, if I love, if I hate, if I hear, if I see, if I taste, and so on, it is certain that the same thing happens there, and that all these different modes of thinking inform me by themselves of their existence; so that I do not love without feeling that I love, I do not will without knowing it, I do not see without perceiving that I see, and so with all my other thoughts. (Dilly 1676, 8–9)

This perceiving that I see is not supposed to be a separate mental act from the seeing. In chapter 13, Dilly explains that although we sometimes do reflect upon our mental acts by means of other acts, such reiterated inspection is not involved in our immediate certainty of our thoughts. "Thus it is not necessary to believe that each thought is followed by a second which makes it known, for this latter would require a third, and so on to infinity; but we affirm only, being convinced by our own experience, that each thought makes itself felt to the soul, not by any real examination of itself, but directly and immediately by its sole presence" (117).

Dilly's definition of thought differs from Descartes's in an important respect: for "immediately conscious" Dilly substitutes "immediately certain." As we explained in our first chapter, Descartes's definition commits him neither to the evidence thesis (if I am in a certain state then I know I am in it) nor to the incorrigibility thesis (if I believe I am in a certain state then I am in that state). It is a short step from Dilly's definition to both theses, a step he gladly takes. Thus he asserts that "we know the nature of each thought in particular," that to know a thing is "to be able to distinguish it from every other thing without the possibility of our being mistaken," and that we do not make mistakes in identifying our own mental states. "Have we ever confused a thought of love with a thought of hate, or with a judgment?" (15)

Like Descartes's consciousness (C2) of thinking, Dilly's immediate certainty is supposed to be an ingredient of each act of thinking, thereby eliminating the need for a separate mental act to perceive the original act. As soon as I see an object or form a desire, my sensation or volition "makes itself felt" or "makes itself perceived" in such a way that I "perceive that I see" or "know that I will." The example of willing reveals that despite Dilly's protestations to the contrary, being immediately certain of one's thoughts involves reiterated inspection; for willing and perceiving are, by Cartesian classification, two distinct types of mental acts. Dilly cannot have it both ways. Either we experience thinking in the very act of thinking, in which case we cannot be said to "perceive" or "know" that we think, or we do perceive it, in which case we reflect upon our acts by means of other acts.

Pardies, too, tried to have it both ways: we perceive and perceive that we perceive, yet there is only one act. The virtue of Pardies, from our point of view, is that he confines the problematic "indivisible reflection" to intellectual knowledge and allows that there is another kind of knowledge that does not involve it. Insofar as he admits that one can perceive without perceiving that one perceives, he is closer to Descartes than Dilly is.

Unfortunately, Pardies does not develop the notion of nonreflective knowledge but falls back on examples. The examples are rich in suggestions, but instead of mining them, he merely states that animal perceptions are like that. As a Peripatetic priest he is more concerned with the materiality of animal soul than with the nature of animal cognition. Spiritual knowledge requires an indivisible principle whereas sensible knowledge does not. "Since there is no reflection in it whereby the animal can say to itself, I see, I touch, I sense, likewise it is by no means necessary that this principle which makes it see and feel thus should be indivisible. It can be diffused throughout the whole body, and it can even sometimes be divided, when the animal is cut into pieces" (Pardies 1672, 179). The difference between animal and human souls is thus assured.

In the final analysis Bayle is right: neither side could claim victory in the beast-machine debate. The Cartesians failed to come up with any sound metaphysical reason to deprive animals of Cartesian consciousness. Instead of pointing this out, the Peripatetics chose to fight the battle in terms of material substantial forms, where their defense was weakest.

Of all Pardies's reasons for rejecting animal automatism, the most interesting are two based on God's nature. The first is that it would ill suit the divine wisdom "to form eyes and ears which served only for external show and not to see or to hear" (148). The second reason involves divine veracity, an attribute dear to the heart of the Cartesians. We attribute soul to the beasts, maintains Pardies, because we observe in them organs and actions similar to ours. Now suppose God made a machine exactly like a beast, which did everything without knowledge and sentiment. We must admit that it is possible for God to do such a thing, for he is omnipotent. Were he to do it, "we would find no difference in this machine which enables us to distinguish it from animals; in short, we would take it for a true animal" (219). The question is, did God do this? According to Pardies, "unless we grant that God can deceive us, we must say that they are not pure natural machines but true animals, which have cognitions and sentiments" (224). He explains by way of an analogy. A skillful handler can make puppets act like humans. Watching the puppets, we are inclined to attribute knowledge and sentiment to them. The puppeteer engages in deception to the extent that he instills this false belief in us. Likewise, the similarities between animal and human actions incline us to attribute cognitions and sentiments to animals. If God made them as pure machines then he too would be guilty of deception (227–28).

Dilly finds both arguments ridiculous. The one from the divine veracity fails because God only guarantees the truth of our clear and distinct ideas. The belief in animal sentiment does not fall into this category. God "would deceive us if we knew clearly that beasts have a soul, after divesting ourselves of all our prejudices and having examined the matter seriously. But who can pride himself on having this knowledge?" (Dilly 1676, 93). The other argument fails because the sense organs have functions in the operation of the beast-machine. "It is no less false to say that the external senses serve only for show in beasts, supposing they do not know, than it would be to affirm that the spring of a watch or the counterweight of a clock are only external ornaments and useless to this machine." (107–8).

Taken at face value, Pardies's arguments are easy to demolish. Their real worth lies beneath the surface. The kinds of problems Pardies poses in theological terms can also be formulated in methodological and scientific terms.

As Pardies states the deception argument, God would deceive us if He created animals as pure machines, since we are inclined to attribute sensible knowledge to them. The deception consists in instilling in us the false belief that animals have sentiments. The analogy of puppets reveals the deficiency of the argument but also shows how to overcome it. Most people are not fooled by puppets, at least not for long, because there are plenty of ways in which puppets differ from real people. By the same token, God would be no deceiver if he provided the means to tell his beast-machines from beings with sensible knowledge. The crucial point for divine deception is not that "we would take it for a true animal" or, in other words, that we would form a false belief. It is rather that we would have no way to guard against such an error. In Pardies's words, "we would find no difference in this machine which enables us to distinguish it from animals." The latter point can be translated into methodological terms. If there is no observable difference between a beast-machine and a sentient animal, then there is no meaningful difference between the two. The Cartesians insist that there is a difference, to wit, that some entity (soul) or set of entities (sentiments) is present in one but not in the other. The onus is therefore upon them to come up with behavioral tests to distinguish between beast-machines and conscious animals, just as they have tests for telling mechanical people from real people. Otherwise the presence or absence of soul or sentiment is not a difference that makes a difference.

As Pardies states the argument from divine wisdom, the key issue is whether animals' sense organs are "only for external show." The phrase suggests that they are something like the button eyes on a teddy-bear. If this is all Pardies had in mind, then Dilly has amply refuted him by noting that animal eyes and ears are integral parts of a physiological network. Pardies could always come back with the retort that the network itself is just for show since no real seeing or hearing is going on. Dilly has a rejoinder ready. The sensory apparatus serves to initiate movements that are necessary to the maintenance of the organism. Through the sense organs external objects act upon the brain and determine the animal to approach or withdraw, according as they are beneficial or harmful (Dilly 1676, 108).

Pardies's argument works best when it is turned upside down. Instead of the sense organs of animals, let us apply it to the consciousness of humans. To make it even more interesting, let us follow the nineteenth-century precedent and replace the divine wisdom with natural selection. Now the question is this: Is human consciousness only for internal show? If eyes and ears can operate perfectly well without awareness—well enough for the organism to pursue what is beneficial and avoid what is harmful to it— then sense perceptions in humans are mere epiphenomena that have no use, in short, they are just for show. But if human sensory awareness serves no useful function, why did natural selection favor it?[1]

Nature teaches me by my sensations of pain, hunger, and so on, that I am not in my body like a pilot in a ship but joined with it in a union. So wrote Descartes in the Sixth Meditation (AT 7:81; CSM 2:56; HR 1:192). The pilot metaphor remains inappropriate on the present line of reasoning, but an even more dangerous metaphor emerges. So far as sentiment is concerned, it seems that I am in my body like a passenger in a ship. The bodily vessel would function just as well, if not better, without its epiphenomenal passenger. If the ship is in trouble, the pilot observes what is going on and acts accordingly. The passenger just gets in the way.

Descartes would never accept the metaphor of the passenger. Sensory awareness is supposed to have a function in the Cartesian scheme. Descartes states in the Sixth Meditation: "For the proper purpose of the sensory perceptions given me by nature is simply to inform the mind of what is beneficial or harmful for the composite of which the mind is a part" (AT 7:83; CSM 2:57; HR 1:194). And in Part Two of the *Principles:* "Sensory

---

1. Consciousness is the sort of complex phenomenon that one would expect to have a genuine biological function, which in turn is explained by natural selection. See the discussion of Romanes in chapter 6.

perception . . . merely shows us what is beneficial or harmful to man's composite nature" (AT 8A:41; CSM 1:224; HR 1:255). Sensory awareness appears to play the same role in human beings that physical sensations play in the beast-machine, but this is not really the case. In the beast-machine the physical sensations set the body in motion to pursue or avoid things in the environment. Human sensory perceptions "inform the mind" so that it can take part in the proceedings and direct the body in an apposite manner.

If there is this difference between animals and people, then explanations that work for animal behavior will not work for human behavior, and vice versa. It ought to be possible to explain all animal behavior in terms of simple attractive and repulsive principles. Only when it comes to human behavior should such explanatory tools prove inadequate. If it turns out that animals too engage in cognitive processing of sensory information, Cartesianism must give ground somewhere: either cognition can be accomplished physically or animals have awareness. Either alternative threatens the dichotomy between animal and human nature.

ANIMAL STORIES RETURN

When telling people about the Cartesian theory of animals, one is likely to hear this refrain: My dog/cat/horse/cow does such and such, which shows that it is thinking.

A charming instance from the seventeenth century is the story told to Arnauld by the Duc de Liancourt. Two dogs turned the spit in the duke's kitchen on alternate days. One hid when they went to fetch him on his appointed day, so they approached the other dog, intending to put him to work instead. The latter signaled that they should follow him. He routed his lazy comrade from his hiding place and rampaged at him. "Are they clocks?" asked the duke. Arnauld reportedly found the story so amusing that he could do nothing but laugh in reply (Fontaine 1738, 2:470).

The most surprising thing about this story is that so few like it were told in the course of the beast-machine debate. One expects the defenders of animal thinking to come forth with many such anecdotes, drawn either from their own observations or from those of their acquaintances. Michel de Montaigne, the bête noir of animal automatism, had plenty of tales in his arsenal. Not one of them was original; they were all in Aristotle, Aelian, Pliny, or Plutarch. The standard was thus set for animal stories in philosophy. One goes not to the bush or the barnyard but to the library for one's data on animal behavior. Tradition confers respectability, if not authenticity.

To his credit, Descartes insisted on treating the issue of animal thought in a theoretical way. He raised the discussion above the level of storytelling. The old saws about religious elephants and syllogistical foxes settle nothing. In order to determine whether a given action is performed mindfully or mindlessly, one needs to know what counts as mindful action and what the limits of mindless action are. These are theoretical questions.

The promise and the challenge of Cartesianism is to explain all animal actions in mechanistic terms. Particular instances of animal behavior can play two roles in such a research program. First, they can serve as illustrations of how the mechanical principles operate. Thus Descartes uses the sheep's flight from the wolf to demonstrate the link between corporeal seeing and the movement of the limbs. Second, they can be put forward as problem cases to be accommodated by the theory. The example of the parrot who says good day to its mistress serves this function in the letter to Newcastle (AT 4:574; K 207). The bird seems at first to be using speech, but it is really only giving a conditioned response.

Particular cases can be employed as weapons in the context of debate. The Cartesians claim that all animal behavior can be explained mechanistically, and that no set of animal actions counts as passing the language or action test. Hence the opposing side scores a point if it produces instances that either do not admit of mechanistic explanation or that pass one of the two tests. The Duc de Liancourt's dog story was obviously intended to serve as such an instance.

When faced with an alleged refuting instance, the defender of animal automatism has three alternatives: try to account for the action mechanically, question the quality of the evidence, or give up the beast-machine hypothesis. The last alternative is to be considered only if all else fails.

The first alternative has both an advantage and a pitfall. The advantage is that it can be kept alive almost indefinitely by pleading the need for more information. There is always more to be learned about the structure and functioning of the animal's brain. The pitfall comes from taking the description of the behavior at face value. If the claim is that an animal does x, where x counts as passing the language or action test, there is a danger that successful mechanical explanation of this behavior will undermine the tests as determiners of the presence of thought.

Let us illustrate with a story borrowed from Locke's *Essay Concerning Human Understanding*.[2] In the course of discussing personal identity, Locke

---

2. The parrot story was added in the fourth edition of 1700. It did not appear in the French translation. See Fraser's annotations of Locke's *Essay* in the Dover edition (1959) 1:466.

quotes a long passage from Sir William Temple's *Memoirs of what passed in Christendom from 1672 to 1679.* We abridge it slightly:

> "I had a mind to know, from Prince Maurice's own mouth, the account of a common, but much credited story, that I had heard so often from many others, of an old parrot he had in Brazil, during his government there, that spoke, and asked, and answered common questions, like a reasonable creature. . . . I had heard many particulars of this story, and assevered by people hard to be discredited, which made me ask Prince Maurice what there was of it. . . . He told me . . . that he had heard of such an old parrot when he had been at Brazil; and though he believed nothing of it, and it was a good way off, yet he had so much curiosity as to send for it: that it was a very great and a very old one; and when it came first into the room where the prince was, with a great many Dutchmen about him, it said presently, *What a company of white men are here!* They asked it, what it thought that man was, pointing to the prince. It answered, *Some General or other.* When they brought it close to him, he asked it, *D'où venez-vous?* It answered, *De Marinnan.* The Prince, *À qui estes-vous?* The parrot, *À un Portugais.* The Prince, *Que fais-tu là?* Parrot, *Je garde les poulles.* The Prince laughed, and said, *Vous gardez les poulles?* The parrot answered, *Oui, moi; et je sçai bien faire;* and made the chuck four or five times that people use to make to chickens when they call them. I set down the words of this worthy dialogue in French, just as Prince Maurice said them to me. I asked him in what language the parrot spoke, and he said in Brazilian. I asked whether he understood Brazilian; he said No, but he had taken care to have two interpreters by him, the one a Dutchman that spoke Brazilian, and the other a Brazilian that spoke Dutch; that he asked them separately and privately, and both of them agreed in telling him just the same thing that the parrot had said. I could not but tell this odd story . . . for I dare say this Prince at least believed himself in all he told me, having ever passed for a very honest and pious man: I leave it to naturalists to reason, and to other men to believe, as they please upon it. . . ." (Locke 1959, 1:446-47)[3]

Cartesian naturalists would be ill advised to accept this story as grist for the mechanistic mill. As soon as they grant that the parrot really said such things, they are faced with an animal that to all intents and purposes has passed the language test. The alleged responses show variety, relevance, and grammatical competence to boot. If the Cartesians try to concoct a

---

3. Fraser translates the dialogue between the prince and the parrot thus: The prince asks, "Whence come ye?" Parrot: "From Marinnan." "To whom do you belong?" "To a Portuguese." "What do you there?" "I look after the chickens." "*You* look after the chickens?" "Yes, I; and I know well enough how to do it" (447n).

mechanical account of how certain kinds of inputs trigger the brain to produce certain outputs, what is to stop their opponents from insisting on the same treatment for human linguistic behavior?

The second alternative, that of questioning the evidence, avoids this pitfall. Anecdotal evidence can be questioned on at least four levels. First and most obvious is the integrity of the source. Did the observer falsify or embellish the report? In the above passage Temple tries to allay any doubt on this score by noting the prince's integrity. The second level has to do with the accuracy of the observation. Here one might wonder whether Prince Maurice was the victim of a ventriloquist's hoax. Inaccurate observation need not be the result of a deliberate trick. It may just be that the observer has misperceived or overlooked some important details. For example, a cat may appear to reach up and lift the latch, whereas in fact it was batting a butterfly and opened the gate by accident. The third level somewhat overlaps with the second. It has to do with interpreting what is observed, and, as every philosopher of science knows, one's observations are colored by one's interpretations. We list them separately in order to emphasize that sometimes the problem is that we do not see all there is to see, and sometimes it is more that we do not know what to make of what we see. In the case of the cat opening the gate, closer examination would have revealed the butterfly and its role in the scene. By contrast, when we misdescribe animal expressions, for example, in attributing haughtiness to a llama, our error comes not from having missed some part of the display, but from our inclination to interpret it along human lines.

On the fourth level the particular instance is considered as part of a whole spectrum of cases, including the animal's past behavior and its behavior in other circumstances. The questions raised about the evidence depend on the type of behavior involved and the claims made for it. Here are two examples of questioning on the fourth level. The first comes from the comparative psychologist Conwy Lloyd Morgan, of whom more will be said later. Suppose you see a dog open a gate by pushing up the latch with its head. Before you take this as evidence of canine insight, you should ask about the history of the animal's behavior. Did the dog ever do this or something like it before, and in what context? What in the single instance appears to be insight may in fact have been the result of conditioning (Morgan 1894a, 287–90).

Our second example is drawn from research on the incubation behavior of gulls (Tinbergen 1953; Beer 1961; Baerends and Kruijt 1973). Suppose you observe a herring gull retrieve an egg that has rolled out of its nest. By experimentation you determine that egg models of various sizes and colors elicit this behavior although the bird shows certain preferences: larger eggs are preferred to smaller, speckled to plain, green over other colors. Before you conclude that the gull is using the concept of an egg, you should see how far the behavior extends. Are items besides eggs and egg-shaped dummies brought into the nest as well? It turns out that gulls will behave similarly toward blocks, cylinders, and prisms, especially those with rounded edges. Black-headed gulls have been known to sit on stones, small bottles, flashlight batteries, and rabbit skulls. Before you conclude from this additional data that the gull has a defective concept of an egg, you should ask whether it can distinguish eggs from nonegg-shaped objects under nonbrooding conditions. If it can, then it is implausible to attribute the gull's eclectic retrieval practices to an inadequate concept. A more cautious account is that the set of properties that enables it to discriminate eggs is more specific than the set that elicits egg retrieval (cf. Premack 1978).

The mantle of Aelian, Pliny, and Plutarch has passed on to the ethologists. Unlike behavioral psychologists, who seek universal laws of learning, ethologists explore the whole range of individual and group behaviors with a view to determining the characters of each species. In this respect the ethologists carry on the tradition of animal stories. Discipline and detailed observation have replaced legend and hearsay, but the aim remains to chronicle the diversity of natural behavior.

To the extent that the theory of animal automatism has behavioral consequences, the new animal stories can provide evidence for or against it. Should the ethologists come up with data that threaten the theory, its defenders must find some grounds on which to question the evidence, or they must try to accommodate it in their framework. A good fight is to be expected either way. It is hard to kill a beast-machine with evidence.

Part Two

Science and Animal Mind: Descartes's Legacy

Introduction

The animal consciousness issue is a mixture of philosophy and science. This is as true in the post-Darwinian era as it was in Descartes's time. The balance in the mixture has shifted to the advantage of science. One might think that in the modern age, scientists would be more competent than philosophers to settle questions about the nature of the world. On the level of detail this is undoubtedly true, but for an overall picture the scientist is at a disadvantage.

Science is a collection of special subjects—a kind of patchwork quilt. Biology and psychology are composed of smaller fields, each with its own orientation and conceptual arsenal. Paleontologists do not think like geneticists, who in turn do not see things the way taxonomists do. Physiological psychologists view organisms differently from the way cognitive psychologists view them.

In each field, research paradigms set the style of work and determine to a large extent what range of results is considered valid. Research paradigms must facilitate the obtaining of results and not get hung up on insoluble problems, whether conceptual or technical. At any given time, some concepts and questions will be bypassed because they do not fit conveniently into any specific research program.

When scientists extrapolate their specialized viewpoints into world views, the result is a diversity of philosophical orientations. Mostly these world views remain private. A few are highly publicized, as in the teachings of B. F. Skinner and E. O. Wilson. Scientists do not, by their professional training, aim at a balanced, interdisciplinary point of view. The limitations of the original paradigm color the global picture.

Nonscientific criteria can be imported into scientific work. Besides the

117

motivation to choose concepts amenable to measurement and calculation, the scientists' extrascientific biases—religious or political, say—can affect both how the research paradigm is formulated and how the results are interpreted. The history of evolutionary biology reveals a variety of post-Darwinian evolutionary theories proposed and promoted with obvious theistic, antitheistic, socialist, and capitalist inclinations (Bowler 1983). For example, the Russian naturalist and philosopher Peter Kropotkin wrote *Mutual Aid* in 1902 to counteract the rather violent version of animal competition promulgated by T. H. Huxley.

Consciousness is one of the contentious issues caught between the interests of the scientists and the philosophers. Animal consciousness is in a more awkward position than human consciousness. Anyone who tells average educated readers that they are not conscious or that consciousness is not important will be instantly disbelieved. This healthy skepticism about scientific reductionism does not seem to extend to animal consciousness. When it is written that animals and humans are just stimulus-response systems or computing devices or whatever, readers often react with a double standard. Of course, such reductionist theories don't apply to me. I know I am a conscious being. As for animals, though, maybe the scientists have a case. After all, how can anyone be sure that animals are conscious?

The double standard is especially apparent in the debate over the sociobiology of E. O. Wilson. Sociobiology is an alliance of evolutionary disciplines that manages to offend a great many people. The typical hostile response is not that Wilson's theory is illegitimately reductionist and over-simplified with respect to human and nonhuman animals alike. Rather, Wilson's opponents are quite willing to throw the brutes to him as long as they themselves can escape his clutches. Nowadays, of course, the defenders of a sublime human nature are as likely to be humanists as theists. Neither faction is interested in saving animal souls.

Consciousness functions in Descartes's natural philosophy like a *deus ex machina,* supernaturally introduced to meet the exigencies of the plot. Mind does not obey mechanical laws, yet it can influence mechanical processes by sending the animal spirits in different directions to move the limbs according to its will. When God put a mind into the human body-machine, he, as it were, threw a metaphysical monkey wrench into the works, profoundly altering the operation of the system. Backed up by the power of God, human uniqueness was secure—until the Darwinian revolution changed the rules.

The *deus ex machina* is no longer an accepted technique of biological explanation. Any monkey wrenches thrown into the works must have naturalistic origins, and their operation must be explainable by the same laws as the rest of the system. If consciousness exists in human beings, it must have evolved; and if human consciousness evolved, it must have had some precedent.

Darwin was far from Descartes on the question of the origin of human consciousness, but quite close to the Cartesian position on the expression of emotion. Descartes insisted that animal cries and gestures were merely expressions of passion and not at all akin to language. Darwin (1965) took similarities of expression between species, including man, to indicate descent from a common ancestor; yet the communicative function of emotional expression eluded him as surely as it had eluded Descartes (Burkhardt 1983; Richards 1987).

It was not until ethology emerged as a discipline that animal vocalizations and gestures came to be viewed as a form of communication. There are two traditions in ethology. One, typified by Konrad Lorenz, involves personal interactions between the ethologists and their subjects, and even hand rearing of animals. Insight is gained from the close contact, but at the cost of distorting animal social relationships (Durant 1981). The other tradition, represented by Niko Tinbergen, involves the observation of wild animals in their natural setting. Every effort is made to leave the animals to their own devices and to minimize contact with human observers. When experiments are performed, they are designed to be as nondisruptive as possible. The first tradition allows for more thorough observation; the second, for purer results. The greatest contributions to the study of animal communication come out of the latter tradition. Not surprisingly, animals communicate best when they communicate with one another, in situations where their signals have a definite biological use.

After Darwin and after the development of ethology, certain aspects of Cartesian natural philosophy seem hopelessly naive. Yet much of what Descartes said about animals and their difference from people is still widely considered to be obvious and right. Language constitutes an unbridgeable gap between mankind and the brutes. Animals exhibit a mindlessness that goes beyond anything encountered in the human species. You cannot answer questions about alleged conscious experiences of animals because you cannot see into their hearts. Such claims are the subject of this part of our work.

In chapter 6 we consider the career of consciousness in animal psychology following Darwin. Our interest is not in the history per se but in certain philosophical themes and arguments. Chapter 7 deals with various controversies in the general area of animal communication: whether apes show any evidence of ability to learn human language; whether animals ever communicate about their environment as opposed to their own internal states;

whether animal communication is merely a form of manipulation. In chapter 8 we examine some paradigm cases of animal mindlessness. We bring in the notion of intentional stance and show how the assessments of mindlessness arise from too narrow a view of intentional systems. In the ninth chapter we consider three common objections to the scientific investigation of animal consciousness and argue that they are ill-founded.

6

What Happened to Consciousness?

All living creatures are products of the same process of biological evolution. Humans are related to other present-day animals through common ancestors. A rich mental life is vital for human activities. The organs of human mental life are the brain and nervous system. Other animals have similar neurological apparatus. Hence it is plausible to conclude that they, too, have varied mental lives. This train of reasoning could only attain its full force in the years following the publication of the *Origin of Species* (1859).

Thomas Henry Huxley was a historian of ideas as well as a staunch defender of Darwin. He evaluated the status of the beast-machine under the new evolutionary regime in his 1874 address "On the Hypothesis That Animals Are Automata, and Its History." Huxley was strongly sympathetic to a mechanistic conception of life. He willingly conceded that the march of physiological science actually strengthened Descartes's hand. The nineteenth-century neurophysiological results on spinal reflexes and other topics "would have furnished [Descartes] with far more powerful arguments than he possessed in favor of his view of the automatism of brutes" (Huxley 1896, 1:225). Further, Huxley's epistemology retained a Cartesian flavor. "It is wholly impossible absolutely to prove the presence or absence of consciousness in anything but one's own brain, though, by analogy, we are justified in assuming its existence in other men" (1:219). Nevertheless, evolution tips the scales against Descartes. "But though I do not think that Descartes' hypothesis can be positively refuted, I am not disposed to accept it. The doctrine of continuity is too well established for it to be permissible to me to suppose that any complex natural phenomenon comes into existence

121

suddenly, and without being preceded by simpler modifications; and very strong arguments would be needed to prove that such complex phenomena as those of consciousness, first make their appearance in man" (1:236).

In his 1871 essay "Mr. Darwin's Critics," Huxley points out that evolutionary continuity places the analogical argument for animal consciousness on a new footing. "Descartes' position is open to very serious objections if the evidence that animals feel is insufficient to prove that they really do so." If the only evidence for consciousness in another person is "the similarity of his structure and of his action to one's own," and if this sort of evidence "is good enough to prove that one's fellow-man feels, surely it is good enough to prove that an ape feels. For the differences of structure and function between men and apes are utterly insufficient to warrant the assumption that while men have those states of consciousness we call sensations apes have nothing of the kind" (1896, 2:160–61).

The straightforward evolutionary argument for animal minds led to a new discipline—comparative psychology. George John Romanes and Conwy Lloyd Morgan were among its first practitioners. Today, despite the intervening century of research in experimental psychology and evolutionary biology, arguably there is more ambivalence about animal consciousness than there was in Darwin's time. The evolutionary arguments are just as good or even better now, but the issue is confused and is fragmented among psychological and biological specialties. There is not so much an open defense of animal automatism—quotations in direct support of it are hard to find—as a reluctance to admit any doctrines alternative to the beast-machine.

The situation in Darwin's time was different. Then it was generally assumed that animals were conscious. Romanes summed up the prevailing view in 1884: "The theory that animals are unconscious machines need not detain us, for no one at the present day is likely to defend it" (Romanes 1897, 64). Comparative psychology was supposed to answer questions about kinds of animal consciousness, leading up to the human brand of consciousness as the culmination of the evolutionary story.

This chapter explores some of the consequences of the Darwinian revolution for the animal consciousness issue. Animal psychology or comparative psychology, to which the topic naturally belongs, has had an unsteady career since Darwin's time. We consider some of the philosophical aspects of that career, beginning with the cornerstone of the subject—evolutionary continuity. We examine the metaphysical background and its relation to the methodological topics of Morgan's canon and anthropomorphism. Finally we return to evolutionary biology to see how animal mind fits into the framework of it. Psychologists still need to learn the lessons taught by Darwin and the later evolutionists. As Edward A. Wasserman observes, "the hypothesis that man and animal share common cognitive capabilities is simply the single most important idea of comparative psychology. Darwin's thesis will just not fade away no matter how many generations of experimental psychologists choose to ignore it" (1981, 246).

EVOLUTIONARY CONTINUITY

The *Origin of Species* stops short of the human species. To establish that evolution applies to human as well as nonhuman animals, Darwin must show that people are not radically different from other biological organisms. This he does in *The Descent of Man,* first published in 1871.

Darwin enlists the aid of T. H. Huxley, whose book *Evidences as to Man's Place in Nature* (1863) provided evidence that man belongs to the same order as the great apes. Huxley reviewed the proportions of limbs, numbers of ribs and vertebrae, dentition, and cranial capacity. He also compared human hands and feet with those of the gorilla, finding that gorillas possess a true foot as humans do. He concludes that "whatever system of organs be studied, the comparison of their modifications in the ape series leads to one and the same result—that the structural differences which separate Man from the Gorilla and the Chimpanzee are not so great as those which separate the Gorilla from the lower apes" (103).

Darwin's review of the evidence is wide-ranging and not restricted to comparisons with apes. He notes extensive similarities between humans and animals with regard to bones, muscles, blood vessels, and viscera. Humans have many diseases in common with animals, and medicines produce the same effect on animals as on people. Monkeys "have a strong taste for tea, coffee, and spirituous liquors: they will also, as I have myself seen, smoke tobacco with pleasure" (Darwin 1871, 1:12). Wild baboons, drunk on beer, have classic hangovers the next morning. These facts testify to similar physiologies. Embryology supplies further evidence. The human embryo "at a very early period can hardly be distinguished from that of other members of the vertebrate kingdom" (1:14).

Darwin concludes that human beings must be classed among creatures that have evolved into their present forms.[1] Mankind and animals share

---

1. Stronger evidence of common descent has, of course, accumulated since the time of Darwin. A new chapter in evolutionary biology opened wtih the molecular biology of the gene. For discussion of similarities between human and animal neurologies, see Changeux 1985.

a common descent. "It is only our natural prejudice, and that arrogance which made our forefathers declare that they were descended from demigods, which leads us to demur to this conclusion" (1:32–33).

The human species did not come into being by special creation, and mind did not arise in it suddenly, for the first time. Mind, a complex of functions dependent on the appropriate physiological apparatus, evolved from more primitive stages to its present level in humans and animals. The more primitive forms of mentality are still present in the "lower" animals.

Once it is accepted that man is part of the evolutionary scheme, the complexity of human mental functions, plus similarities between human and animal neurologies, can be used to argue claims about animal minds and consciousness. But Darwin needed to convince his contemporaries that man belongs in the evolutionary scheme. To do this, he had to undermine any claim that a particular human trait, mental or otherwise, did not evolve but arose suddenly by special creation. He had to make plausible that every characteristic of man evolved from more rudimentary characters in nonhuman ancestors. For every significant human trait, he had to locate corresponding precursor traits in animals. If he left out just one significant trait, his opponents could seize on it and use it as an opening wedge for a whole host of nonnatural properties. Religious feeling, altruism, shame, humor—any of these could represent a break in the evolutionary continuum. For this reason Darwin covers as wide a variety of mental traits as he can, using whatever data and reports he can find. He utilizes a whole spectrum of information, from the rigorously scientific to secondhand tales.

Darwin is on comparatively solid ground when he can connect his claims with physiology. Sense experiences are physiologically grounded: "As man possesses the same senses with the lower animals, his fundamental intuitions must be the same" (1:36). So are basic emotions: "Terror acts in the same manner on them as on us, causing the muscles to tremble, the heart to palpitate, the sphincters to be relaxed, and the hair to stand on end" (1:39). No such careful delineation of responses accompanies his assertions that dogs express jealousy, pride, shame, modesty, and magnanimity (1:42).

For some traits Darwin relies upon eminent writers on animal behavior. Revenge is the subject of this story told to Darwin by the zoologist Sir Andrew Smith. A baboon, persecuted by a certain British officer, took revenge by spattering the man's dress uniform with mud. "For long afterward the baboon rejoiced and triumphed whenever he saw his victim" (Darwin 1874, 78).

Beyond the senses and emotions, Darwin discusses curiosity, imitation, attention, memory, imagination, and reason. He mixes his scientific sources of information with less reliable reports and stories.

Darwin does not claim that animals possess mental faculties in the same degree as man. It is enough that the difference is *only* one of degree. So long as he can identify some animal as having a given mental trait, he can conclude that there is no absolute gap with respect to the trait. Like Huxley, Darwin draws further support from the narrowness of the difference between man and the creatures closest to him: "We must also admit that there is a much wider interval in mental power between one of the lowest fishes, as a lamprey or lancelet, and one of the higher apes, than between an ape and man; yet this immense interval is filled up by numberless gradations" (1871, 1:35).

Proponents of human uniqueness claim that only man has the capability of progressive improvement, tool use, the ability to form general concepts, language, self-consciousness, a sense of beauty, and a conscience. Darwin counters that birds have a sense of beauty, as evidenced by their displays of colorful plumage; that chimpanzees, monkeys, and elephants use tools. When a given trait is not observed in animals, Darwin has two more tricks up his sleeve. The first is to argue that some qualities are derived from others that can be more easily established for animals. Thus he says of conscience: "Any animal whatever, endowed with well-marked social instincts, would inevitably acquire a moral sense or conscience, as soon as its intellectual powers had become as well developed, or nearly as well developed, as in man" (1:71–72). His evidence of social instinct includes Brehm's reports of animal rescues. A young monkey is saved from the eagle's talons by its comrades, who pluck many feathers from the bird. A large male baboon, "a true hero," goes back down into a valley and leads a young baboon away from fierce dogs (1:76). Darwin's second tactic is to point out that humans themselves exhibit the traits in a considerable spectrum. Part of the apparent gap for qualities such as moral sense can be filled within the scope of human societal variations and historical development.

Having told more or less questionable stories in the *Descent*, Darwin passed his collection on to Romanes, who told the stories again. It is easy to dismiss the use of anecdotes in the evolutionary debate as not being up to our present standards of rigor. In doing so one runs the risk of underrating Darwin and his contemporaries. Granted, some of the stories are doubtful, but what does this tell us about Darwin? Do the animal stories convict him of a bad grasp of scientific method? If he had a sound grasp of methodology, why did he mix reliable and questionable reports?

Two factors indicate that good, though not necessarily widespread, standards of rigor existed at the time. First, a contemporary critic, St. George Mivart, took Darwin to task on the reliability of his animal reports, even when derived from famous authors such as Brehm. Did Darwin actually see any incidents like the monkeys saving their infant from eagles, the baboon biting off the kitten's claws, or the troop of baboons rolling stones down on their attackers (Mivart 1871)? Second, Darwin held himself to high scientific standards in his own research. Michael Ghiselin argues at length in *The Triumph of the Darwinian Method* (1969) for the unity and rigor of Darwin's scientific practice. In his chapter on psychology, Ghiselin stresses Darwin's observations on the behavior of organisms including earthworms and climbing plants. Darwin performed experiments on the plants to determine the cellular mechanism that caused their movements. He investigated the ability of worms to learn how to drag leaves into their burrows. Darwin's work *The Expression of Emotions in Man and Animals,* published in 1872, is devoted to the careful analysis of bodily states, especially the patterns of muscle contractions, corresponding to various emotions.

From Darwin's own research practice and from the response of critics such as Mivart, it can be concluded that Darwin likely recognized the risks inherent in reporting the results of such a diverse group of observers. But he had to work with whatever information he could garner. The marshaling of available data and arguments in support of a scientific thesis of such scope is a far more untidy business than performing a few isolated experiments. We concur with Robert M. Young's summary of how Darwin supported the evolutionary continuity of mind in the *Descent:* "Darwin's strategy is the same as it is in the *Origin*—to explain away apparent discontinuities by a judicious mixture of anecdotage, rhetorical questions, and appeals to the uniformity of nature. This approach on Darwin's part was not unusual in the nineteenth century; nor, for that matter, are current writings in biology and psychology fundamentally different. It is difficult to see how they could be" (Young 1985, 102).

DARWIN'S CRITICS

Richard Owen alleged in 1858 that the human brain, by its possession of a hippocampus minor, differed importantly from ape brains. T. H. Huxley seized the opportunity to attack Owen, with whom he was already on bad terms. Owen was one of the great comparative anatomists of the nineteenth century, but, to put it kindly, he had no skill at public relations. The anatomical facts supported Huxley: the organ in question occurs in both apes and humans. Owen steadfastly refused to retract his claims.[2] The incident is satirized in *The Water Babies* by Charles Kingsley, a friend of Huxley.

---

2. For discussion of Owen and the Darwinians see Desmond 1982, 72–83.

Nothing is to be depended on but the great hippopotamus test. If you have an hippopotamus major in your brain, you are no ape, though you had four hands, no feet, and were more apish than the apes of all aperies. But, if a hippopotamus major is ever discovered in one single ape's brain, nothing will save your great-great-great-great-great-great-great-great-great-great-great-greater-greatest-grandmother from having been an ape too. No, my dear little man; always remember that the one true, certain, final, and all important difference between you and an ape is, that you have a hippopotamus major in your brain, and it has none; and that, therefore, to discover one in its brain will be a very wrong and dangerous thing, at which every one will be very much shocked. . . . Though really, after all, it don't much matter: because— as Lord Dundreary and others would put it—nobody but men have hippo-potamuses in their brains; so, if a hippopotamus was discovered in an ape's brain, why it would not be one, you know, but something else. (Kingsley 1869, 173–74)

Owen uncovered one of the risks of arguing from anatomy to mental powers. The risks were present for both evolutionist and antievolutionist, because science knew so little about how brains work. The risk is still there. For a long time the mental powers of birds were disparaged on the basis of observed differences between avian and mammalian brain structure. As more was learned about the "wiring" of brains, the picture changed. Cohen and Karten (1974) state: "Though the gross morphology of the telencephalic projection field differs markedly between birds and mammals, there is sur-prisingly little difference in the sequence of anatomical projections, electro-physiology or behavioral functions of these systems" (48).

Apart from access to minds via neurological hardware, Darwin's op-ponents could argue on the basis of mental performance and behavior. Ironically, one of the chief opponents of Darwin's evolutionary theory of mind was his colleague Alfred Russel Wallace, the co-inventor of the natural selection doctrine. Wallace reasoned that since natural selection fails to account for all aspects of the human mind, another kind of factor—"a superior intelligence"—must have guided the development of man (Wallace 1870, 359). This factor affects Wallace's whole conception of evolution and makes it man-centered, in contrast to Darwin's view.

Wallace's objections to continuity focus on the limits of explanation by natural selection. Whereas Darwin was flexible on the sorts of mechanisms that might be needed to supplement natural selection, Wallace was rigidly committed to natural selection. Once Wallace concluded that aspects of hu-manity transcended the bonds of natural selection, he adverted to causes which Darwin would consider to be outside of natural science.

The basic principle of natural selection, according to Wallace, is "that all changes of form or structure . . . can only be brought about, in as much as it is for the good of the being so modified" (1870, 333). Natural selection has no "power to produce modifications which are in any degree injurious to its possessor." The presence of injurious or useless modifications "would prove, that some other law, or some other power, than 'natural selection' had been at work." This is true even though the modifications become useful at a later period. If there are any such human faculties, useless at first but now useful and "essential to the full moral and intellectual development of human nature, we should then infer the action of mind, foreseeing the future and preparing for it, just as surely as we do, when we see the breeder set himself to work with the determination to produce a definite improvement in some cultivated plant or domestic animal" (334).

Wallace, like Darwin, viewed natural selection as a blind process. Indeed, Wallace disapproved of Darwin's analogy between artificial and natural selection on the ground that it, together with the sometimes metaphorical language of the *Origin,* was an open invitation to irrelevant criticism. Darwin's use of the breeder analogy suggested that natural selection is guided by an intelligence (Wallace 1870, 269; cf. Young 1985). Darwin, mindful of the imperfections of the analogy, persisted in using it as a stepping-stone to natural selection. Wallace uses the breeder analogy to set limits on natural selection. If foresight is necessarily involved in the production of a given biological structure or function, then natural selection cannot be the sole power operating. There must be a breeder for people, just as people are breeders for domestic animals and plants. Darwin's analogy, turned upside down, yields an argument for a governing intelligence—a variation on the argument from design.

What aspects of the human species are inexplicable by natural selection? One physical characteristic proposed by Wallace is the paucity of hair. How could natural selection favor a change from our presumably hairy ancestors to our comparative lack of protection and insulation? Wallace also finds anomalous the loss of prehensile power in the human foot. These are just indicators that humans do not fit neatly into the evolutionary scheme based on natural selection alone. The most crucial considerations, and those on which he later relied exclusively, have to do with the brain and mind.

It is generally agreed, says Wallace, that the brain is the organ of the mind and that "the size of brain is one of the most important of the elements which determine mental power or capacity" (335). The brains of savages are comparable in size to those of civilized people. It may be concluded that their mental capacities are on a par with those displayed in civilization.

Yet savages "pass their lives so as to require the exercise of few faculties not possessed in an equal degree by many animals. . . . What is there in the life of the savage, but the satisfying of the cravings of appetite in the simplest and easiest way? What thoughts, ideas, or actions are there, that raise him many grades above the elephant or the ape?" (342). How much more true this must have been of the earliest people, whose cultures were even more primitive than those of savages, yet whose brain capacity was up to the average of "the lower savage races" (343). This excess brain and mental capacity could not have come about by natural selection, for this process "has no power to produce absolute perfection but only relative perfection, no power to advance any being much beyond his fellow beings, but only just so much beyond them as to enable it to survive them in the struggle for existence" (334). The extraordinary mathematical and artistic powers of the human mind are exercised in a nontrivial manner only in civilized societies, although their biological basis was laid down much earlier. They must therefore have been conferred on humans in the knowledge that they would eventually play a role in human existence.

In a later work Wallace offers another proof that special talents such as the mathematical do not conform to the principles of natural selection. The characters developed by natural selection "will be present in all the individuals of a species, and, though varying, will not vary very widely from a common standard. The amount of variation we found . . . to be about one-fifth or one-sixth of the mean value" (Wallace 1897, 469). The range of mathematical ability across the population is far greater than this. A first-class mathematician has at least a hundred, and possibly a thousand, times the ability of a person with little mathematical aptitude or interest. Great mathematicians are not only far above the average in ability, but they are also rare—another sign that human mental powers fall outside the scope of natural selection (1897, 470).

Wallace does not hold that the human species arose by special creation. Far from it. He uses the Darwinian arguments from embryonic development, rudiments of animal organs in humans, diseases common to animals and humans, to support the conclusion that man evolved from other life forms. Nor does he dispute Darwin's claim that human mental traits such as moral sense have precursors in the brutes. He does not question Darwin's evidence, only the conclusion Darwin draws from it. "To prove continuity and the progressive development of the intellectual and moral faculties from animals to man, is not the same as proving that these faculties have been developed by natural selection; and this last is what Mr. Darwin has hardly attempted, although to support his theory it was absolutely essential to prove it" (1897, 463).

Wallace is asking a lot of Darwin. Darwin's task in the *Descent* was to bring human beings within the scope of the evolutionary process. He supports his thesis by demonstrating the relatedness and continuity between humans and animals, thereby making it highly plausible that man is a viable candidate for subsumption under evolutionary theory. Darwin is in no position to rule out theistic explanations of man's origin. Supernatural powers can always be invoked by those who are not committed to a purely naturalistic framework. Wallace was such a person.[3] He saw only two alternatives—natural selection and guidance by divine intelligence—and considered both to be legitimate forms of scientific explanation. Having identified natural selection with the theory of evolution, and having demonstrated to his own satisfaction the failure of this particular mechanism to account for the intellectual and moral nature of man, he resorted to the supernatural as the only other viable alternative.

Wallace is open to attack on two fronts: his reliance on strict selectionism, and his argument that natural selection fails when applied to human traits. The first strategy would take us far from our topic, so we will not pursue it but will confine ourselves to the second.

Wallace's argument rests heavily on the assumption that the mental performance of savages is not much above that of animals. Without this assumption, he would leave open the possibility that human mental powers first appeared when they were useful to the organism, that is, they came into being by natural selection. Huxley chides Wallace for his failure to heed his own account of the great navigational skills required by savages.

> Add to all this the knowledge which a savage is obliged to gain of the properties of plants, of the characters and habits of animals, and of the minute indications by which their course is discoverable . . . consider that every time a savage tracks his game he employs a minuteness of observation, and an accuracy of inductive and deductive reasoning which, applied to other matters, would assure some reputation to a man of science, and I think we need ask no further why he possesses such a fair supply of brains. In complexity and difficulty, I should say that the intellectual labor of a "good hunter or warrior" considerably exceeds that of an ordinary Englishman. (Huxley 1896, 2:175–76)

The other side of the coin to Wallace's reasoning is that if any animal is in the same position as Wallace's savage, there are equal grounds for

---

3. We dismiss Wallace's attempt to incorporate the supernatural into the natural by positing "will-forces" (1870, 368–70). For Wallace's relation to nineteenth-century spiritualism see Kottler 1974 and Oppenheim 1985.

abandoning natural selection in favor of the supernatural. If any animal is found, either by subsequent education or by considerations of brain size and complexity, to have more mental equipment than it needs for its survival and well-being, it must be that, as Wallace says of man, "a superior intelligence has guided the development . . . in a definite direction, and for a special purpose" (Wallace 1870, 359). Huxley proposes some examples of animals whose mental organs are greater than their requirements. "The brain of a porpoise is quite wonderful for its mass, and for the development of the cerebral convolutions." Is this "a preparation for the advent of some accomplished cetacean of the future" (Huxley 1896, 2:176)? Moreover, the wolf displays much less intelligence than the dog, though its brain has the same size and form. "The wolf stands to the dog in the same relation as the savage to the man; and, therefore, if Mr. Wallace's doctrine holds good, a higher power must have superintended the breeding up of wolves from some inferior stock, in order to prepare them to become dogs" (2:177). The uniqueness of human mentality in being exempt from the evolutionary process is threatened by an argument that proves too much.

METAPHYSICS OF THE EVOLUTION OF MIND

T. H. Huxley, Herbert Spencer, the physicist John Tyndall, and the mathematician W. K. Clifford were part of a loose coalition of Victorian scientists and men of letters committed to the world view of scientific naturalism (Turner 1974). World views involve metaphysical preconceptions, and this one was no exception. Metaphysical preconceptions can affect the content of and support for scientific theories. We bring up Victorian scientific naturalism in order to show how the progress of evolutionary or comparative psychology was hindered by an inappropriate metaphysics.

In 1874 John Tyndall presented his notorious Belfast Address to the British Association for the Advancement of Science. In it he traces the tradition of naturalism from Greek atomism to the present. Tyndall notes with satisfaction the recent advances of science. The origin of the stars and planets, the structure of the earth's surface, the sources of the order and diversity of organic life—all these had once seemed impervious to naturalistic explanation. Yet within a small compass of time, modern science discovered how to investigate these problems.

Darwin engineered the latest victory for naturalism. His achievement in explaining organic design on nontheological grounds allows scientists to put matter and life in the same intellectual framework. Both the organic realm and the realm of physical astronomy operate by "evolution"—the one by natural selection, the other by continuous alterations in clusters of atoms in accordance with the laws of mechanics. Two other breakthroughs forged the links between matter and life. First, the principle of the conservation of energy, developed by Helmholtz and Mayer, encompasses both mechanical and physiological processes. Second, chemists can now make organic compounds; the distinction between living and nonliving matter has become blurred. Nature does not consist of isolated domains but possesses an essential continuity. There is only one causal network at bottom obeying a unified set of laws.

Tyndall recognized that many phenomena of physics and organic life so far escaped detailed explanation, but he was willing to bet on the eventual success of natural science. At least there was now a unified conceptual scheme which he and others in the naturalistic movement could pit against their opponents.

One problem still blocked the progress of scientific naturalism, namely, the relation of mind to matter. Tyndall sums up the problem in the Belfast Address: "We can trace the development of a nervous system, and correlate with it the parallel phenomena of sensation and thought. We see with undoubting certainty that they go hand in hand. But we try to soar in a vacuum the moment we seek to comprehend the connection between them" (Tyndall 1889, 2:194). Half a dozen years earlier he had expressed the same problem in his president's address to the Mathematical and Physical Section of the British Association at Norwich: "Were our minds and senses so expanded, strengthened, and illuminated, as to enable us to see and feel the very molecules of the brain; were we capable of following all their motions, all their groupings, all their electric discharges, if such there be; and were we intimately acquainted with the corresponding states of thought and feeling, we should be as far as ever from the solution of the problem, 'How are these physical processes connected with the facts of consciousness?' " (1889, 2:87).

Huxley took a bolder approach than Tyndall to the status of mind. His conscious-automaton theory appeared in the essay about the beast-machine.[4] This essay was originally presented at the same British Association meeting at which Tyndall gave his Belfast Address. Huxley saw a trend

---

4. The scientist and historian Philip Howard Gray (1968) has shown that the real originator of the conscious automatism theory was Douglas Spalding, a student of Alexander Bain, a friend of Tyndall, and later tutor to the young Bertrand Russell. Although Spalding's thought was far more careful than Huxley's, we limit ourselves to the more highly publicized writings of Huxley. Both versions of the theory share the principal defect that concerns us.

in brain and behavioral research. Scientists were learning that a considerable range of behavior is controlled by neurological processes apart from the conscious centers of the brain. In some cases of brain injury, whole episodes of behavior occur that are apparently inaccessible to normal consciousness. Huxley carries the results to their logical extreme. All animal and human actions are determined by bodily mechanisms. Conscious states have no causal efficacy. Consciousness is simply "a collateral product" of the working of the body, "as completely without any power of modifying that working as the steam-whistle which accompanies the work of a locomotive engine is without influence upon its machinery" (Huxley 1896, 1:240) This remark is made specifically about animals, but a few pages later Huxley extends the theory of conscious automatism to human beings: "It seems to me that in men, as in brutes, there is no proof that any state of consciousness is the cause of change in the motion of the matter of the organism. . . . We are conscious automata" (1:244).

Huxley sees the mind-body gap as bridgeable. "All but the adherents of 'Occasionalism,' or of the doctrine of 'Pre-established Harmony' (if any such now exist), must admit that we have as much reason for regarding the mode of motion of the nervous system as the cause of the state of consciousness, as we have for regarding any event as the cause of another" (1:238–39). Science has little insight into this connection, but the same is true of other cases of physical causation. There is a causal tie between mind and matter, but it only goes one way: volition, as a conscious state, cannot act upon matter and plays no causal role in action (1:241, 244).

Tyndall objected to this double standard for body-mind and mind-body interaction. "This production of consciousness by molecular motion is to me quite as unpresentable to the mental vision as the production of molecular motion by consciousness. If I reject one result I must reject both. *I, however, reject neither,* and thus stand in the presence of two Incomprehensibles, instead of one Incomprehensible" (Tyndall 1889, 2:407). Tyndall's picture of nature really has no place for mind. The principle of the conservation of energy requires that any interaction of mind with matter affect the energy bookkeeping of the material system. Either mind must be kept out of the picture, or one must be prepared to apply energy considerations to it. Tyndall could accept neither alternative. Huxley opted for materialism: "I believe that we shall, sooner or later, arrive at a mechanical equivalent of consciousness, just as we have arrived at a mechanical equivalent of heat. If a pound weight falling through a distance of a foot gives rise to a definite amount of heat, which may properly be said to be its equivalent; the same pound weight falling through a foot on a man's hand gives rise to a definite amount of feeling, which might with equal propriety be said to be its equivalent in consciousness" (Huxley 1896, 1:191).

The critics of naturalism did not remain silent on these issues. The line-up includes Romanes, Wallace, the philosopher and psychologist James Ward, and, in America, William James. Romanes (1882) argued that the idea of an energy exchange between matter and thought was absurd. Wallace (1870), defending a spiritualist position, held that the physics of atoms rests on the calculation of forces, which in turn are probably mental in nature. We are more interested in the consequences of the theory vis-à-vis evolution. The critics pointed out that Huxley's position did not make much sense from the evolutionary point of view. It may seem strange to charge Huxley, who called himself "Darwin's bull-dog," with being un-Darwinian, but the charge has merit.

Romanes states the criticism thus: "Assuredly, on the principles of evolution, which materialists at least cannot afford to disregard, it would be a wholly anomalous fact that so wide and general a class of phenomena as those of mind should have become developed in constantly ascending degrees throughout the animal kingdom, if they are entirely without use to animals" (1882, 880). The correct evolutionary conclusion is "that consciousness and volition are functions of nerve-tissue superadded to its previous functions, in order to meet new and more complex demands on its powers of adaptation" (881).

One might think that Romanes's argument is based on the same strict selectionist principle that Wallace held: natural selection can produce nothing useless. But Romanes's reasoning follows a different path. He is arguing that mind is an adaptation, that is, a mechanism produced by natural selection to fulfil a definite function. The evolutionary scientist George Williams describes the same strategy in his influential book *Adaptation and Natural Selection* (1966). The purpose of some biological mechanisms, such as bird wings, is evident. "At other times the purpose of a mechanism may not be apparent initially, and the search for the goal becomes a motivation for further study. Adaptation is assumed in such cases, not on the basis of a demonstrable appropriateness of the means to the end but on the indirect evidence of complexity and constancy" (10).

If consciousness is complex and widespread through the animal kingdom, then it is likely to be an adaptation and unlikely to be a "free rider" on the natural selection of other characters. Elliott Sober introduced terminology which makes the distinction clear. " 'Selection of' pertains to the *effects* of a selection process, whereas 'selection for' describes its *causes*. To say that there is a selection for a given property means that having that property *causes* success in survival and reproduction. But to say that a given sort of object was selected is merely to say that the result of the selection process was to increase the representation of that kind of object" (1985, 100). Consciousness has been selected for and not merely selected. That is the upshot of Romanes's and Williams's arguments.

William James (1890) argues from the progressive complexity of consciousness through the animal kingdom—a point "generally admitted" though "hard to prove." Organs are superadded that help the organism in the struggle for existence. An organ cannot help man unless it is "in some way efficacious and influencing the course of his bodily history. If now it could be shown in what way consciousness *might* help him, and if, moreover, the defects of his other organs . . . are such as to make them need just the kind of help that consciousness would bring provided it *were* efficacious; why, then the plausible inference would be that it came just *because* of its efficacy—in other words, its efficacy would be inductively proved" (138–39).

James Ward, in his Gifford Lectures of 1896–98, states that "the most serious point in this doctrine of conscious automatism is that which is also its cardinal point, the impotence of mind to influence matter." He reminds his audience that "in the theory of natural selection it is everywhere taken for granted that instincts, habits, and inclinations are factors equally as potent as anatomical structure or physiological process. Thus Darwin speaks of the sense of hunger and the pleasure of eating as 'no doubt, first acquired in order to induce animals to eat' "(Ward 1899, 2:38–39). Ward assumes, as the naturalists also do, that these factors are mental (and conscious) aspects of the organism.

Huxley's conscious-automaton theory illustrates a crucial point in the metaphysics of evolutionary psychology. The scientific naturalist must either get rid of consciousness altogether, or else concede it a significant role in the evolutionary process. Modern naturalism does not always recognize that a choice must be made. The impotent-consciousness theory still creeps into behaviorism and cognitive psychology, where the controlling factors of behavior are removed ever further from conscious control.

Spencer and Clifford saw the need for scientific naturalism to integrate consciousness into evolutionary theory. Of the two alternatives above, they pretended to opt for the second, that of allowing consciousness a role in the evolutionary process; but their way of explaining the evolution of consciousness effectively blocked consciousness from playing any significant role in the evolution of the organism. We will concentrate on Clifford since his position is the more clear-cut of the two.[5]

---

5. According to the critics, Spencer, aided by his notoriously vague language, sneaks consciousness into evolution. See James 1890, 1:148.

Clifford denies any form of mind-body interaction. "The physical facts go along by themselves, and the mental facts go along by themselves. There is a parallelism between them, but there is no interference of one with the other" (Clifford 1879, 2:56). Given this radical distinction between mind and matter, and given that the evolutionary process does not allow for real discontinuities or novelties, it follows that consciousness cannot have evolved from matter but must have developed from something proto-mental. Clifford calls it "mind-stuff"; William James (1890, 1:146) satirizes it as "mind-dust." Clifford writes in his article "On the Nature of Things-in-themselves":

> That element of which . . . even the simplest feeling is a complex, I shall call *Mind-stuff*. A moving molecule of inorganic matter does not possess mind or consciousness; but it possesses a small piece of mind-stuff. When molecules are so combined together as to form the film on the under side of a jelly-fish, the elements of mind-stuff which go along with them are so combined as to form the faint beginnings of Sentience. When the molecules are so combined as to form the brain and nervous system of a vertebrate, the corresponding elements of mind-stuff are so combined as to form some kind of consciousness. . . . When matter takes the complex form of a living human brain, the corresponding mind-stuff takes the form of a human consciousness, having intelligence and volition. (1879, 2:85)

To the question "How did consciousness evolve?" Clifford gives an answer of sorts, vague though it be. Yet the answer has nothing to do with the answer to the corresponding question about the organism. Natural selection influenced the form and function of the brain and nervous system; but since the mental exerts no influence on the physical or vice versa, there is no reason to suppose that natural selection played any role in the development of sentience or the higher mental faculties. Consciousness has been banished to a metaphysical limbo.

COMPARATIVE PSYCHOLOGY

Comparative psychology has been defined in various ways (Dewsbury 1984). Schneirla (1972, 30) defines it as "the study of similarities and differences in capacities for environmental adjustment and for behavioral organization among the important types of living beings, from plants and unicellular organisms to the primates including man."

Comparative psychology as a historical movement of the late nineteenth and early twentieth centuries sought to devise a research program for tracing mental and behavioral similarities between animals and humans within an evolutionary framework. Conwy Lloyd Morgan was the most influential figure in this movement. His approach, continued by psychologists such as Margaret Floy Washburn, came to be identified with the project as a whole. That is why it is important to understand its presuppositions and defects.

Lloyd Morgan declares his philosophical position in the Prolegomena to his *Introduction to Comparative Psychology* (1894a) and in a *Monist* article of the same year (1894b). Attempting to keep mind-body dualism at arm's length, he embraces a threefold "monism." Its first principle is that naive experience is basically unitary and only secondarily divided into subjective and objective parts. The second is that man as an organism is one and indivisible, not a body with a mind superadded. The third principle is that the two aspects into which the organism can be analyzed, body and mind, "are strictly co-ordinate: each is as real as the other. The true reality is the man with which the analysis starts" (1894a, 7–8; 1894b, 330). The evolution of the bodily aspect can be traced back through simpler organisms to the inorganic. Likewise, it is not "illogical" to speculate that "with the simpler modes of nerve-energy there would go simpler modes of consciousness, and that with infra-neural modes of energy there would be infra-consciousness, or that from which consciousness as we know it has arisen in process of evolution" (1894a, 8; 1894b, 331). Thus Morgan aptly describes his view as a "modification of Clifford's mind-stuff hypothesis" (1894b, 323).

The consequences of this metaphysics are clearly drawn by the American psychologist Margaret Floy Washburn in her textbook *The Animal Mind,* first published in 1908. She accepts Morgan's philosophy in which every organism has at least infra-consciousness. She combines that premise with the fact that no one has yet been able to establish satisfactory criteria for mind. She concludes "that there exists no evidence for denying mind to any animals, if we do not deny it to all; in other words, that there is no such thing as an objective proof of the presence of mind, whose absence may be regarded as proof of the absence of mind" (1917, 27). So she treats the problem hypothetically. The psychologist abandons the ontological question of where consciousness resides in the world, and says instead: *if* a given animal has consciousness, then it would be of such and such a kind.

The trouble with this approach is that the results fail to shed any light on the objective part of experience, the physical and behavioral aspects of the organism. John B. Watson (1913), himself originally a comparative psychologist, put the difficulty in these words: "One can assume either the presence or absence of consciousness anywhere in the phylogenetic scale without affecting the problems of behavior by one jot or one tittle; and without influencing in any way the mode of experimental attack upon them" (161). In banishing consciousness to the nebulous realm of mind-stuff, the Clifford-Morgan-Washburn metaphysics left the door open for behaviorism. Watson was merely clearing away a concept which had already been rendered biologically useless by its own defenders.

Two methodological issues in early comparative psychology take on new significance once the philosophical assumptions of the movement are laid bare. One issue has to do with Morgan's canon, the other, with Washburn's anthropomorphism. Current opinion tends to be kind to Morgan and harsh on Washburn. Morgan's canon is often cited in support of simpler models of animal minds. But Morgan had quite another use for the canon—a use which essentially depended on assumptions unacceptable to present-day psychologists. Washburn's anthropomorphic reading of animal minds is held up nowadays as an example of how not to do science. Yet her methodology is a logical outcome of the philosophical premises from which she and Morgan began.

Morgan's canon is given in the third chapter of the *Introduction to Comparative Psychology*: *"In no case may we interpret an action as the outcome of the exercise of a higher psychical faculty, if it can be interpreted as the outcome of the exercise of one which stands lower in the psychological scale"* (1894a, 53). Psychologists frequently assert that the canon reduces to a version of the principle of parsimony, or Ockham's razor (e.g., Schneirla 1972, 34; Wasserman 1981, 244). Morgan, however, discusses objections to the canon, and the second objection is that the canon may *violate* parsimony. He admits that it may do so and adds: "But surely the simplicity of an explanation is no necessary criterion of its truth" (1894a, 54). Parsimony, then, is not really the aim of the canon.

D. K. Adams, writing in the *Psychological Review* (1928), is aware of Morgan's disclaimer. Still, he insists that the canon was *intended* as a principle of parsimony but that Morgan botched the job. We maintain that Adams was wrong about Morgan's intentions. One must take a closer look at Morgan's evolutionary theory to determine the meaning of his canon.

Morgan's canon is designed to operate in the context of the evolution of mind, where a hierarchy of mental functions is assumed. Man stands at the top of the hierarchy and constitutes the standard to which other organisms must be compared. Morgan carefully analyzes the kinds of relationships animal minds might have to human minds. He distinguishes three relations: (1) adding a series of new faculties as one proceeds up the evolutionary scale; (2) having the same faculties, but increased in power; and (3) adding new faculties or increasing their power, combined with a possible diminution of other faculties. Morgan states that the problem is "to gauge the psychical level to which any organism has been evolved" (1894a, 55). To accomplish that end, however, he must rigorously establish an evolutionary chain leading through various kinds of animals to man. The role of the canon is to ensure that the chain is soldered together by necessary inferences. The psychologist should move up to the next more complex stage only when the transition is made unavoidable by the data. Otherwise there is an arbitrary importation of higher faculties and a break in the necessary connections. If the series of inferences leads all the way to human minds, the psychologist is justified in asserting that complex minds, including the human mind, arose through a process of evolution.

The thesis of the evolutionary continuity of mind is in deep trouble if no animals are found to occupy the higher levels on the mental scale. One of the basic functions of the canon in Morgan's system is to ensure that higher mental processes can legitimately be attributed to selected animals, that such attributions are not just gratuitous extrapolations fostered by sentimentalists. Morgan needs to raise some animals up and make sure they stay raised. Thus he has a vested interest in failing to explain at least some animals' actions in terms of lower faculties. This interest is not shared by the modern advocates of "Morgan's canon," who see the principle primarily as a way of pushing animals down the mental scale and making sure they stay at the lower levels.[6]

The second methodological issue in early comparative psychology is anthropomorphism. Washburn begins her textbook with the "commonplace of reflection" that "the mind of each human being forms a region inaccessible to all save its possessor." Knowledge of minds other than one's own "must always be indirect, a matter of inference" from behavior (1917, 1). This holds for knowledge of animal as well as human minds. "*All psychic interpretation of animal behavior must be on the analogy of human experience. We do not know the meaning of such terms as perception, pleasure, fear, anger, visual sensation, etc., except as these processes form a part of the contents of our own minds. Whether we will or no, we must be anthro-*

---

6. Kluender, Diehl, and Killeen (1987) provide a recent counterinstance to that trend. They demolish one of the bastions of human uniqueness in their demonstration that Japanese quail can discriminate human phonetic categories. Invoking Morgan's canon, they conclude that "a theory of human phonetic categorization may need to be no more (and no less) complex than that required to explain the behavior of these quail."

pomorphic in the notions we form of what takes place in the mind of an animal" (13).

Washburn's admitted anthropomorphism is a consequence of her philosophy of psychology. The mental aspect is distinct from the physical aspect of an organism. Psychic building blocks, like biochemical components, are standard across species and can combine in different ways. Since mental properties such as pleasure and fear are directly accessible only in one's own (human) experience, the psychologist cannot be absolutely sure that they are the same across species, but it is a convenient and useful working assumption. If one subtracts enough components from human experience, one can imagine what the experience of a lower organism might be.

It is widely believed that anthropomorphism in general is a fallacy. On this view, Washburn is guilty of a cardinal methodological sin even before she launches into her discourse on the mind of the amoeba (44–52). Yet when it comes to stating precisely in what the fallacy consists, or explaining why it is a fallacy, the antianthropomorphic forces are strangely silent. As the geneticist A. D. Darbishire noted, the word originally meant "the endowing of God with the form and habits of man," which was certainly "a grave intellectual misdemeanor." Darbishire continues: "But those who were responsible . . . for applying the word anthropomorphic to an entirely different thing—the granting of intelligence, purpose, design, and human attributes in general to non-human animals, in order to stigmatize a concession to the 'lower animals' which was repugnant to them—were the unconscious perpetrators of a successful fraud" (quoted in Wheeler 1939, 47–48). There is nothing wrong with giving an old word a new meaning. The fraud lies not in extending the term to animals, but in retaining the negative connotation without giving any justification for doing so.

Given the framework of evolutionary biology, it is difficult to see what justification there can be for a general indictment of anthropomorphism. Darwin argued persistently and forcefully that humans are animals, a position that can be called zoomorphic (Durant 1985). Evolutionary biology licenses the search for similarities between animals and people. The search can proceed either up or down the phylogenetic scale. That is, one can either take characteristics observed in lower forms and see whether they persist on the higher levels, or start with features of higher organisms and look for their precursors on lower levels, as Darwin did with the emotions. The latter approach is most useful when one is dealing with features difficult to detect in lower organisms, or when more research has already been done on higher organisms.

One can deny that there is a general fallacy of anthropomorphism while conceding that there are genuine controversies about cross-species applications of particular terms. Some comparisons are valid, some are not. For example, sociobiologists and their critics debate the legitimacy of applying words such as "slavery" and "rape" to animals and then reapplying them to humans. Scientists studying animal behavior are free to introduce whatever terminology they find useful, so long as they are willing to defend it. Our only advice is to watch out for ideologies on both sides of the dispute.

The precept of human uniqueness is easy to uphold if one gets to cry "anthropomorphic fallacy" whenever a favorite human term is applied to animals. We choose a particularly egregious example of this use of anti-anthropomorphism. Joseph Le Conte, a professor at the University of California in the late nineteenth century, was the author of a well-known book blending theology and evolutionary science (Bowler 1983). In an article in the *Monist* (1896), Le Conte argued, among other things, that birds do not produce genuine music. Civilized man's aesthetic sense has long been considered one of his highest spiritual qualities. Why let mere birds share it? Le Conte tips his ideological hand in the following remarks: "Who has not been charmed by these songsters of nature? Who will deny that the pleasure we thus derive is really of a very high order? But the very fact that it is of a very high order ought to make us suspect that its source is all other than is usually supposed" (362).

Wallace had argued that the aesthetic sense is not explicable by natural selection and hence falls outside of Darwin's naturalistic framework. Le Conte does not appeal to evolution. Instead, he uses a form of antianthropomorphism. According to Le Conte's carefully chosen meaning of the word "music," the production of music requires stage-by-stage deliberation, and the appreciation of it requires intellectual perception of complex relations. Birds do not have the intellectual grasp of their tonal material needed to make and to appreciate real music. Le Conte judges birds against the standard of nineteenth-century Western classical music and finds them wanting: "Although I have a very keen appreciation of harmony—and perhaps for that very reason—I have never been able to assure myself of any true purposive harmonic relation among the consecutive notes of bird-song. Sometimes there seem to be, and sometimes not. When there is, it seems to be accidental and unintentional" (365).

Le Conte was aware that many of his contemporaries dissented from his opinion on bird song. He was not just following a fashion of his time. In more recent times, Charles Hartshorne (1973) has eloquently made the case for avian aesthetics. Le Conte's argument is a sample of the kind of simpleminded linguistic routine that antianthropomorphists are apt to fall into. Le Conte had no real interest in the question of what music is or how it should be defined. He was only interested in keeping birds out of the hallowed realm of spiritual life. The caveat against anthropomorphism becomes an easy way of retaining cherished dogmas about human nature while relegating all other creatures to a "lower" status.

What became of comparative psychology, the discipline which was supposed to implement an evolutionary psychology of animals? An adequate history would have to cover British and American researchers as well as those on the Continent. The development of ethology is relevant to the story. We will only briefly indicate some of the factors and trends.

The school of mechanists (J. Loeb, A. Bethe, T. Beer, J. von Uexküll) sought to reduce all biological processes, including animal behavior, to physicochemical laws. There was no room for consciousness in their scheme (O'Donnell 1985). Within psychology, twentieth-century behaviorists of various stripes formulated laws that avoided reference to central nervous system processes and to consciousness.

The American behaviorist and neobehaviorist schools eventually ran into difficulties in carrying out their research programs. The behaviorists advocated "general process" accounts of learning: a small set of laws was supposed to be sufficient to explain learning in all organisms. For instance, classical conditioning and instrumental conditioning together were once thought to be adequate. Two types of criticism of the program are especially worthy of note. First, E. C. Tolman (1948) and others developed the idea of a cognitive map, a mental representation the animal is said to need in order to perform certain tasks such as maze learning. Olton and Samuelson (1976) demonstrated spatial memory in rats, indicating a form of mental representation. Second, experiments by John Garcia and his colleagues showed learning theorists that they had to take into account the specialized tendencies of different animal species (Jenkins 1979).

General-process learning theory, from the time of its inception in America with E. L. Thorndike and others, separated instinct from learning and focused on learning alone. Instinct merely provided the raw material on which the laws of stimulus and response operated (Jenkins 1979, 183). The issue of specialization was not confronted until learning theory had existed for a number of decades. Early practitioners figured that the tasks they chose for the animals were neutral for them, or were artificial enough that instincts would be irrelevant in performing them (Dewsbury 1984). The assumption that experiment could divorce learning from instinct was only questioned much later in controversies about the biological boundaries of learning. Seligman and Hager (1972) call it the Equipotentiality premise: "In laboratory experiments, the very arbitrariness and unnaturalness of the experiment was assumed to guarantee generality, since the situation would be uncontaminated by past experiences the organism might have had and by special biological propensities that he might bring to it" (2).

Although overshadowed by the general learning theorists, a small number of comparative psychologists attempted to preserve the biological aspect of their discipline (Dewsbury 1984). In recent years they have been especially concerned with the methodology of their field and with relations to neighboring disciplines (Gottlieb 1979; Glickman 1985). In the meantime, evolutionary theory has not stood still. So comparative psychologists of the present day must contend with an intellectual landscape quite different from the one faced by Lloyd Morgan.

UPDATING EVOLUTIONARY PSYCHOLOGY

For the scientific naturalists Tyndall and Clifford, as well as for Morgan, the connection between consciousness and physical processes remained the unanswerable question. The incomprehensibility of the connection was not merely a function of the state of neurophysiology at the time. Enough was known about the brain to convince many people, including Wallace, who was a spiritualist, that the brain was the organ of the mind (Young 1970). Yet consciousness seemed somehow too different to fit into the same causal network with matter.

The seventeenth-century philosophers who sought ways out of the Cartesian mind-body problem realized that the problem was not a consequence of dualism alone but depended upon a particular causal theory (Radner 1985). One can get rid of the problem either by eliminating the dualism, by changing the causal theory, or by some combination of the two. The same options were open in the nineteenth century, and they are still open. Reductive materialism gets rid of the problem by defining away the mental. Functionalism handles it by keeping the mental but defining it independently of any particular physical embodiment. The approach we favor follows Mario Bunge (1980) and Jean-Pierre Changeux (1985). The only entities one has reason to believe have consciousness are biological organisms equipped with specific kinds of neurological structures. Moreover, there is no reason why conscious states—states subjectively experienced by the organism—cannot be part of the causal network of brain processes.

Biologists have long been suspicious of the introduction of conscious activity into evolution, because it smacks of Lamarckism. According to the popular conception, Lamarck had the animals desiring or willing bodily changes to suit their new habits.[7] It seemed a resurrection of the concept of design; the animals, directing the course of evolution, took over God's old role. Of course the mechanism by which the changes were preserved in the next generation, the inheritance of acquired character, was rejected by Darwinians in the post-August Weismann era.

Yet the sorts of problems raised by Lamarckians had to be confronted. Animals can change their life styles rapidly, too rapidly to be explained by natural selection. Environments can become hostile in short order due to atmospheric and geological events, sometimes of large magnitude. Also, animals emigrate or are introduced into new settings where they must adapt rapidly to novel terrain, food sources, and enemies.

One of the major figures of the evolutionary synthesis, Ernst Mayr, repeatedly pointed to the importance of behavioral initiative, but he did not systematically develop the theme. Mayr declared that "a shift into a new niche or adaptive zone requires, almost without exception, a change in behavior. . . . It is now quite evident that every habit and behavior has some structural basis but that the evolutionary changes that result from adaptive shifts are often initiated by a change in behavior, to be followed secondarily by a change in structure" (1960, 371).

How would mentality show up in the evolutionary process, given that the focus of evolutionary biology is on species and higher taxa rather than on the actions of individual animals? One answer lies in animal culture and tradition. Novel behavior initiated by an individual spreads through the community by imitation and in the next generation by parental instruction of the young. The most often cited examples are the British tits opening milk bottles (Fisher and Hinde 1949) and the Japanese monkeys washing sweet potatoes and grain (Kawai 1965). Bonner (1980) gives additional examples. The pattern of transmission from generation to generation mimics the pattern of transmission of characters by genetic mutation and inheritance (Endler 1986).

Attempts have been made in recent years to fit culture into mainstream Darwinian evolution. J. S. Wyles, J. G. Kunkel, and A. C. Wilson (1983) connect cultural and behavioral evolution with research on relative brain size and on rates of anatomical evolution. Jerison (1973) and others established mathematical relationships between brain size and body weight. The results demonstrate a characteristic brain size for various groups of animals. Birds and mammals fall into the same category by these measures, whereas fishes

---

7. For Lamarck's theory and its misinterpretations, see Burkhardt 1977 and Richards 1987.

and reptiles have a smaller relative brain size. What caused certain subgroups to evolve larger than average brains? Wyles, Kunkel, and Wilson bypass this question and focus on an interesting related phenomenon. There is a correlation between large brains and a rapid rate of anatomical evolution. This effect is notable in songbirds and higher primates. What is responsible for it?

Wyles et al. propose the hypothesis of "behavioral drive" or "behavioral selection." Briefly, it is that changes in behavior initiated by the animals introduce new selection pressures. The resulting genetic changes are fixed more rapidly than in environmentally driven evolution. For example, the adoption of cattle raising among some human populations probably led to the rapid spread of a lactose-splitting enzyme in the human digestive tract. Similarly, the habit of opening milk bottles and drinking cream exposed British tits to new selection pressures. One would have expected changes in their digestive chemistry to cope with the cream and anatomical changes to improve their bottle-opening ability.[8] Behavioral drive explains how culture is not an opting out of evolution, as is often believed, but an effective part of the process.

Thus one major defect in the old style of comparative psychology, the isolation of the mental sphere from a causal role in evolution, can be remedied.

Traditional comparative psychology has other flaws besides the one just mentioned. William Hodos and C. B. G. Campbell (1969) challenged its conception of the evolutionary hierarchy of animals. When psychologists compare the mental level of one living animal with that of another, the two creatures do not stand in the relation of ancestor and descendant. Often they are located on divergent branches of the phylogenetic tree. "Unless comparisons are made between organisms of a common evolutionary lineage, the relationship between the evolution of structure and the evolution of behavior will never become discernible. . . . many comparative psychologists, neuroanatomists, physiologists, etc., have applied the inappropriate phylogenetic scale model rather than the appropriate phylogenetic tree model" (348). The scale concept, they say, is really the old Great Chain of Being reappearing in modern dress. A proper comparative psychology should operate on the model of a genuinely evolutionary discipline such as comparative anatomy. There one distinguishes between similarities due to common descent (homology) and similarities due to other circumstances such as convergence and mimicry.

---

8. Unfortunately, this speculation cannot function as a prediction. The natural experiment came to an end when people put milk bottles in crates (A. C. Wilson 1985).

The most direct answer to Hodos and Campbell is to defend the progressive or "upward" conception of evolution while carefully distinguishing it from the phylogenetic tree. Bernhard Rensch and Julian Huxley introduced the term "anagenesis" for progressive evolution, with each stage being termed a "grade." Branching evolution is "cladogenesis" and its stages are "clades." Gilbert Gottlieb (1985) explains how comparative psychologists can utilize the grade concept and avoid confusing it with the branching concept of clade. They can catalogue cross-species relationships in behavior or mentality without treating them as homologies. He cites the example of Hölldobler and Wilson (1983), who identified progressive grades of social cooperation in the communal nest weaving of different species of formicine ants. These authors do not believe that the grades are clades, since the species do not lie along a common line of descent.

Gottlieb rescues comparative psychology from one difficulty only to uncover another more serious problem. Levels of behavioral complexity can readily be compared when the species in question share the same life style or, in ecological terms, occupy the same niche. When the niches are widely diverse, comparison becomes less straightforward. This severely limits the validity of the old Morgan-Washburn paradigm, where all animals are judged by the same criteria of intelligence.

The ecological point of view offers a more reliable route to animal minds. Each species has a role in the system of living things. Each species has evolved mental equipment suitable for its niche. The psychologist or biologist does well to look for abilities keyed to the particular occupation and life style of the animal. Rats and food-storing birds are found to have remarkable memory capacities, as would be expected for creatures who are required to retrieve food from diverse locations after long intervals. Pigeons, who need to recognize species of seeds and predators, as opposed to individual grains of corn or individual cats, show an impressive ability to generalize from particular instances and form natural categories (Herrnstein 1980).

The switch to an ecologically oriented approach to animal minds is a turn away from the built-in anthropomorphism of the Morgan-Washburn method. Instead of a hierarchy topped by the human mind, there is diversity, and a multitude of interesting talents that some creatures have and others do not. With the swing toward more biological content in comparative psychology, however, comes a threat from the opposite direction. Sociobiology threatens to absorb comparative psychology within its research program (E. O. Wilson 1975).

The sociobiologist identifies or postulates units of selection and argues that the actual outcome, the animal as now existing and behaving, is the result of selection pressures. Lumsden and Wilson (1983) apply this pattern of reasoning to units of culture, and behavioral ecologists such as Krebs and Davies (1981) apply it to strategies of foraging and defense.

Comparative psychologists can counter the sociobiology approach by explaining the relation of their discipline to the natural selection paradigm. In a 1978 symposium at the American Psychological Association, some eminent comparative psychologists offered their rebuttals to E. O. Wilson's challenge. Everett Wyers and Emil Menzel (1980) listed four basic ways in which the interests of comparative psychologists differ from those of sociobiologists. First, sociobiologists view the behavior of an individual animal only as an extension of its genetic constitution. Comparative psychologists, by contrast, are concerned with the individual as a product of the interplay between genetic constitution and other factors that influence development. Second, sociobiologists aim at comprehending behavior at the level of strategy, whereas comparative psychologists look at how the animal makes its decisions. An example will help make this clear. Great tits adopt an efficient strategy in selecting mealworm pieces from a conveyor belt (Krebs et al. 1977). The sociobiologist demonstrates that the strategy is a good one in relation to a set of postulated alternative strategies. The psychologist wants to know what kind of mental operation the bird actually performs in order to obtain this result. Third, sociobiology is concerned with the ecological niche in which a given species is situated. The comparative psychologist uses that niche as a means to get at the animal's *Umwelt*—the layout of the animal's world from its point of view, with its interests, needs, cognitive capacities, and perceptual abilities. Fourth, sociobiology focuses on fitness of populations, whereas comparative psychology explores how individual animals manage to cope with their surroundings and survive.

These differences should dispel any idea that sociobiology can supplant comparative psychology. The study of animal minds in the proper biological setting still belongs to the evolutionary psychologist, just as it did in Darwin's day.

7

Animal Communication

Once upon a time there was a land with an advanced computer technology. The inhabitants often played a game similar to that described by A. M. Turing (1950). The game required two people and a computer programmed to engage in conversation. One person asked questions. The other person and the computer responded over the terminal. The interrogator could ask them anything he wished. The object for him was to determine from their responses which was the machine and which was the person. The human respondent was supposed to try to help him make the right choice. The interrogators gave much thought to their questioning strategies. The programmers in turn worked hard to devise programs that could consistently pass for human.

There were no animals in this land. The people did not even know that such beings ever existed. Their old books contained detailed descriptions of various species, but the people thought they were just works of fantasy. The stories captivated them, however, and they built robots in imitation of these creatures. One robot, for instance, would come up to you and wag its tail. It could be taught to bring your slippers, but it had to be walked every day or it would soil the carpet.

An inhabitant of this land, a builder of robots, sees real animals for the first time. He wonders whether the Turing game can be adapted to these creatures. Obviously it will not do simply to ask questions and have the dog and the robot bark their replies, let alone type "woof" on a keyboard. Nor would it be fair to examine their internal construction, since this is

149

not done in the human imitation game. He decides that the only way to conduct the game is to observe the behavior of the animal and the robot. One must try to find subtleties in canine behavior just as one tries to find subtleties in human linguistic response.

A story should have a denouement. Four alternatives are open to us: (1) The man finds that he cannot tell the real dog from the robot on the basis of behavior, whereas he can tell a human from a computer on the basis of linguistic reponse. (2) He can distinguish the dog from the robot, but not the person from the computer. (3) He can tell neither the dog nor the person from their mechanical counterparts. (4) He can distinguish both from machines.

Which alternative is the most plausible? Descartes, of course, would vote for the first since it parallels his own story in the letter to Reneri for Pollot (April 1638) and preserves the uniqueness of human nature. Modern-day optimists in the field of artificial intelligence favor the third, whereas old-fashioned vitalists would prefer the fourth. The one that best reflects actual achievements, however, is the second.

Descartes believed that those actions we have in common with the beasts were amenable to machine simulation, whereas those involving pure understanding would resist any such attempt. Computer technology has not borne this out. At this point our machines are closer to the angels than to the brutes. From the point of view of artificial intelligence, the task of making one's way in the ordinary world, which animals do so proficiently, is harder than proving theorems and harder than conducting a conversation on a given limited topic (Heppenheimer 1985).

No longer is it taken for granted that human beings have an inner spark—call it soul or thought or consciousness—that can never be ignited in a mere machine. Some researchers are as eager to deny consciousness to human mental processes as they are to attribute mentality to computers. Because we now draw the line between the human and the mechanical differently from the way Descartes drew it, any similarities we find between animals and machines can no longer serve to drive a wedge between animals and people. For Descartes, a thinking being was fundamentally different from a machine, and this difference showed up in behavior. Consequently, if all animal behavior could be simulated by a machine, this would have provided strong evidence that animals do not think. In the modern context, since thinking behavior can be simulated by a machine, machine simulation of animal behavior provides no grounds for denying thought to animals.

Descartes used the language and action tests first to establish a difference between humans and machines, then to lump animals with machines. As tests of the presence of thought or reason, their role in securing human uniqueness has been undermined by modern computer science. But not their role in the debate on animal thought. A perusal of the literature on animal behavior reveals that Descartes's two tests are still very much alive, albeit in altered form. The present chapter considers how animals have fared with respect to the language test. The next chapter deals with the action test in its new garb.

As Descartes sets up the language test, there are two possible ways for animals to pass it: by using human language or by employing their own natural communication systems. Animals fail on both counts, according to Descartes. They are incapable of putting words together to form a relevant utterance, and incapable of expressing anything except their passions by their natural cries and movements.

The two ways of passing the language test suggest two different research programs. One consists in teaching a human language to animals, the most promising candidates being the great apes. The other examines the natural communicative behaviors of animals for possible similarities to human language, such as syntax and representative function. With Descartes's original language test we had to ask what it was supposed to test. The two research programs raise a parallel question. Evidence has been gathered, but evidence of what?

TEACHING LANGUAGE TO APES

In the middle of the eighteenth century, Julien Offray de La Mettrie, noting the structural similarity between apes and humans and the ape's skill at imitation, wrote: "I have very little doubt that if this animal were properly trained he might at last be taught to pronounce, and consequently to know, a language. Then he would no longer be a wild man, nor a defective man, but he would be a perfect man, a little gentleman, with as much matter or muscle as we have, for thinking and profiting by his education" (1961, 103).[1] In the twentieth century the task was undertaken in earnest. Attempts to teach spoken words to apes proved disappointing (e.g., Hayes and Hayes 1951), so researchers shifted their efforts to nonvocal languages.

The 1970s were the heyday of ape language research. R. Allen Gardner and Beatrice T. Gardner (1969, 1971) set the stage with their project to

---

1. For discussion of the relation between La Mettrie's man-machine and the Cartesian beast-machine see Gunderson 1964 and Rosenfield 1968.

teach American Sign Language (Ameslan) to a young female chimpanzee named Washoe. When Washoe signed "water bird" upon seeing a swan (Fouts 1974), she seemed to strike a blow at Descartes's theory. Did she not creatively combine words to describe something novel in her environment? Or did she, as the skeptics claimed, merely sign "water" at the sight of water and "bird" for the bird, as she had been taught to do (Marx 1980; M. Gardner 1981)?

As the controversy raged, the research went on. Francine Patterson taught Ameslan to Koko, a female lowland gorilla. When asked whether she was an animal or a person, Koko signed "Fine animal gorilla" (Patterson 1978). On another occasion she was asked where gorillas go when they die. Her reply was: "Comfortable hole bye" (Patterson and Linden 1981, 191).

Some researchers devised artificial visual languages. One such language is Yerkish, in which the words are geometrical configurations on colored backgrounds. The ape subject produces the word by pressing a key on a console; the configuration is displayed above the keyboard. In the LANA Project (Rumbaugh, Gill, and von Glasersfeld 1973; Gill and Rumbaugh 1974; Rumbaugh and Gill 1976a, b; Rumbaugh 1977), the chimpanzee Lana pushed keys to produce sequences such as "Please machine give piece of apple." Lacking a word for the orange, one of her favorite foods, Lana came up with "the apple which-is orange." When she saw a technician drinking an orange soft drink, she asked for "the coke which-is orange" (Rumbaugh and Gill 1976a, 110; 1976b, 564–65). In an experiment by Savage-Rumbaugh, Rumbaugh, and Boysen (1978) two chimps named Sherman and Austin used keyboards to request tools from each other in order to retrieve food.

David Premack (1971, 1976) devised a system of plastic chips that could be arranged to form statements, commands, and questions. His main subject, a gifted chimp named Sarah, evidenced mastery of symbols such as "color of," "not-color of," "name of," "not-name of," "same," and "different." What is more, she ascribed the same properties (red, round, stemmed) to the symbol for apple (a blue triangle) that she applied to the actual apple. This was taken to indicate that she analyzed the word in terms of what it represents.

One of the most influential of the ape language experiments was Project Nim. The principal investigator was Herbert S. Terrace. The subject was named Nim Chimpsky in obvious allusion to Noam Chomsky, the chief defender of human linguistic uniqueness. The major goal of the project was to determine whether a chimpanzee could use grammatical rules. In the end Nim vindicated his namesake. He never learned to create a sentence.

Like Washoe and Koko, Nim was raised in a human setting and instructed in Ameslan. The collection of his utterances was carefully examined for regularities of sign order. When videotapes of Nim's utterances were analyzed, it became apparent that most of his signing was prompted by his teachers. The pattern of discourse was quite different from that of a human child. The mean length of Nim's utterances failed to increase as he learned more words. His longer sequences were usually repetitive; typical four-sign utterances were "eat drink eat drink" and "banana me Nim me." Relatively few of his utterances were spontaneous; most were preceded by a teacher's utterance. His utterances tended to be more imitative—repeating some or all of the teacher's prior signs—than those of children at the first stage of language learning. The percentage of expansions, which include some of the teacher's signs plus new signs, was lower than for children. It did not increase with age as it does in children. The percentage of novel utterances (responses containing none of the teacher's prior signs) was also lower. Nim interrupted during conversation far more than children do (Terrace 1979, 1983; Terrace, Petitto, Sanders, and Bever 1979).

The various experiments have been the target of criticism both from without and from within the field of ape language research. Experimenters' criticisms of one another cover everything from experimental design to interpretation of results. Terrace, Petitto, Sanders, and Bever (1979) argue that specific sequences produced by Sarah and Lana are the result of rote training and that the available data on Washoe and Koko reveal a lack of spontaneity and creativeness. Patterson (1981) faults Terrace for having exposed Nim to sixty different teachers, most of whom lacked fluency in Ameslan. Terrace (1983) counters that Nim spent most of his time with a core group of eight teachers. He in turn questions the reliability of Patterson's interpretation of Koko's utterances and the Gardners' of Washoe's. Savage-Rumbaugh, Rumbaugh, and Boysen (1980) accuse the Gardners of equating production with comprehension, and Premack of confusing association and ordering strategies with representational and syntactical skills. Premack also comes under fire for failing to reveal crucial details of his experiments.

The most vociferous outside critics are Thomas Sebeok, a linguist, and Jean Umiker-Sebeok, an anthropologist. Their oft-repeated objection is that most of the results can be explained as instances of the Clever-Hans phenomenon (Sebeok 1980; Umiker-Sebeok and Sebeok 1980; Sebeok and Umiker-Sebeok 1981–82). Clever Hans was a horse that amazed audiences at the beginning of the twentieth century by tapping his hoof in answer to arithmetical and other questions. The German psychologist Oskar Pfungst discovered that the horse was responding to unintentional cues from his questioners. When the horse tapped the correct number of times, the observers relaxed, and Hans, detecting subtle movements, changes in posture, breathing, and so on, stopped tapping.

Premack's (1986) reply is that the Clever-Hans objection is a red herring. Pfungst saw the need to demonstrate that the horse's performance was causally dependent upon the detection of cues, and he proposed a control for this effect. In the ape language controversy, by contrast, "no critic ever undertook to say what a proper clever-Hans control would look like" (12). Premack proposes the following experimental design to determine whether an animal's performance involves unintentional cueing. Select two types of problems, one an easy match-to-sample, and one for which failure is virtually certain, for example, matching Roman and arabic numerals. Install "your best clever-Hans control procedures" and test the subject, counterbalancing the two kinds of problems. Then test the subject again, this time without the control procedures. If the results of the two test sessions are significantly different, then the control makes a difference. If there is no significant difference in the results, then the control is inefficacious. Premack did just such an experiment with Sarah. He does not describe the control procedures, but he reports that the results with and without control were indistinguishable (13). With each of two trainers, Sarah did better on object matching than on number matching, whether the control was present or not (156). Either Premack's best control procedures were not good enough, or the Clever-Hans effect is not a significant factor in Sarah's performance.

Umiker-Sebeok and Sebeok (1980, 31–32) applaud Terrace's discovery of cueing. The sort of cueing described by Terrace goes far beyond the capacities displayed by Clever Hans, however. It is verbal prompting. Analysis of the videotape of Nim's "me hug cat" shows the teacher signing "you" while Nim signs "me" and "who?" while he signs "cat" (Terrace, Petitto, Sanders, and Bever 1979). The cues do not account for Nim's choice of the appropriate individual signs—the teacher did not cue him to sign "cat" as opposed to "dog"—but only for their apparent grammatical order.

There is an important dissimilarity between Clever Hans's performance and the achievements of the apes. Whatever problem-solving abilities the horse may have had, there was no way he could have brought them to bear on the questions put to him. Social cues were all he had to go on. With Washoe, Koko, Sarah, and Lana, it is otherwise. There are associations to be learned. Certain words may be used to obtain particular foods or favors. Some sequences ("please machine give milk") work better than others ("give milk machine"). Once the animal has learned these associations, it can give the appearance of understanding without having to detect involuntary head movements and the like, as Clever Hans did. The apes have more sophisticated ways to cheat.

Take Sarah. Premack credits her with having grasped the concepts "color of" and "name of." He describes one of her lessons in *Intelligence in Ape and Man* (1976). Sarah was given questions—sequences of symbols in which she was required to replace the question symbol with one of several alternatives. Each of the four questions put to her contained two symbols and an object. Premack presents them in truncated English, with schematic drawings for the objects:

1. "Banana? "

2. "Yellow? "

3. "Apple? "

4. "Red? "

Premack rephrases the first question as "What is the relation between banana and the object banana?" and the second as "What is the relationship between yellow and the object banana?" He continues: "Her alternatives were 'name of' and 'color of' plus four or five irrelevant words. She was correct on eight of nine trials." The test was repeated with "chocolate," "brown," and a piece of chocolate substituted for "apple," "red," and the apple, respectively. Says Premack: "She was correct on 19 of 24 trials" (192). There was more to the lesson, but we will stop here.

Since Premack never shows the sentences actually put to Sarah but always gives an English rendering, it is easy to fall into the trap of thinking that any pattern in the original situation is reflected in the translation. When we examine the published data on the language and Sarah's prior exposure to it, however, we find regularities in the association of symbols that are obscured in the English gloss. Given these regularities, it is possible to answer questions such as the four above without any knowledge of the meanings of the "name of" and "color of" symbols.

One peculiar feature of Premack's artificial language is that objects can appear in sentences along with the symbols. Premack brings out this feature by using drawings of an apple and a banana. In Sarah's experience, the "name of" symbol is always followed by an object, never by a symbol. The same is true for "not-name of." There is one exception to this rule. Sarah was given a test with two kinds of instructions: (1) "Sarah insert cracker dish" and (2) "Sarah insert name of cracker dish." The first required her to put a cracker in the dish; the second, to put the plastic word "cracker" in it (167). It is not clear whether this test took place before or after the lesson above.

Another feature of the language is that the symbols for colors are themselves colorless; Premack says that this was done to avoid iconism (45). In every statement of the form "X color of Y" or "X not-color of Y," X is a colorless symbol. Consequently, when a question has the form "? color of Y" and the alternatives are a colored and a colorless symbol, the answer must be the colorless symbol. Furthermore, when a question has the form "X ? Y," where X is a colored symbol, the answer cannot be "color of."

The four questions put to Sarah can be answered simply on the basis of observed associations. The symbol for banana is a pink square, that for apple a blue triangle. "Color of " does not go with the colored symbols, so the answers to questions (1) and (3) must be "name of." As for the other two questions, either answer is logically consistent with the regularities noted above. We do not suppose, however, that Sarah is using logic, only associations. Her previous lesson had drilled her on "color of" but not on "name of," and she was accustomed to using that symbol in connection with "red" and "yellow."

We do not maintain that all of Sarah's accomplishments can be explained entirely in terms of observed associations between symbols. In order to respond appropriately to commands such as "Sarah insert cracker dish," she must have learned to associate the symbols with objects and actions, at least well enough to choose from a small number of alternatives.

Mere association between a piece of plastic and an object does not make the plastic a word for the object. To be a word, the plastic must signify or stand for the object. "The piece of plastic becomes a word when the properties ascribed to it are not those of the plastic but of the object it signifies. In looking at the word, one sees not it, but the object for which it stands" (Premack and Premack 1983, 32).

Premack claims that the plastic symbols became words for Sarah. One of his major items of evidence is this. Sarah was shown an apple and presented with four pairs of alternatives to match with it: a red card versus a green one, a square card versus a round one, a square card with a stem versus one without the stem, and a square card with a stem versus a stemless round one. Sarah "described" the apple as red, round, and stemmed. She was then shown a blue triangle (the symbol for apple) and given the same alternatives. She made the same choices she had previously made for the apple (Premack 1971, 224–25; 1976, 169–71; Premack and Premack 1983, 33). To be sure, the properties ascribed to the symbol "are not those of the plastic but of the object it signifies." But blue and triangular were not presented to Sarah as choices. Since she was not given the option of matching the piece of plastic with its own properties, there is no reason to view her response as anything other than a reversion to previously successful answers (Savage-Rumbaugh, Rumbaugh, and Boysen 1978, 551).

As additional evidence that his chimpanzee subject thinks of the objects when she sees the plastic symbols, Premack reports that Sarah was taught the word "brown" through the sentence "brown color of chocolate" given to her when no chocolate was present. This was the only case in which Sarah learned a word exclusively by means of other words (Premack 1986, 81). When we read the original description of the experiment, we find that there was much more to it than simply showing Sarah a definition.

First Sarah was presented with the question "? color of chocolate" and given "brown" as the only alternative. Next she was asked "? color of grape" with green as the only choice. The words "green" and "grape" were already known to her, as were "color of" and "chocolate." She was then asked "? not-color of grape" and "? not-color of chocolate," with "brown" and "green" respectively as the only choice. All four questions were repeated, this time with the two alternatives "brown" and "green." The next step was a transfer test. She was presented with the symbols "? color of" followed first by a brown card, then by a green card. Again the symbols "brown" and "green" were the alternatives. Finally, she was tested in the grammatical context of instructions. She was given the command "Sarah take brown" and presented with four wooden disks, only one of which was brown (we are not told the colors of the others). This was followed by "Sarah insert brown (in) red dish," where, in addition to the dish, she had to choose between a green and a red dish. She performed these tasks successfully (Premack 1976, 202-3).

On Premack's interpretation, Sarah passed the transfer test with the brown card by drawing upon her mental representation of chocolate. There is a simpler interpretation. She has to choose between two symbols, one of which she had successfully matched with its color (green) in previous sessions. Since the color she was presented with was not that which she has learned to associate with the symbol "green," she chose the other symbol. Having been rewarded for this choice, she used the new association in responding to the sequence "Sarah take brown." The first part of the lesson, the association between "brown" and "chocolate," played no role except to accustom her to working with the new bit of plastic.

What Good Is Language to an Ape?

In Premack's ape language experiments the emphasis was on cognitive function rather than on communication. The plastic symbols were intended to provide Sarah with tools for recognizing relations, forming simple judgments, and reasoning by analogy. Her lessons were structured around topics of human academic concern. Chimpanzees are obviously interested in bananas and notice their color, but the fact that yellow is the color rather than the shape or the name of the fruit is something that only human professors care about. Premack's failure to come up with unequivocal evidence of particular linguistic skills is no indictment of the chimpanzee. Language is a means of communication, albeit a very special one. To conduct a fair test of an animal's ability to learn a language, one must give the animal the means and the opportunity to talk about what an animal would want to talk about.

In the Ameslan projects, as well as in the more limited experiments with Sherman and Austin, the communicative role took precedence over the cognitive. Washoe, Koko, and Nim signed in contexts comparable to those in which children use language. The caretakers taught signs they thought the apes would want to use.

We know what sorts of things human children want to talk about, for we are human and were once young ourselves. Shared history and interests will only take you so far with an ape. Despite concessions to their special needs and interests, the subjects of the ape-signing experiments were required to toe a human line. Not only did they have to communicate by our language; they had to talk about what humans are accustomed to talk about. "Where do gorillas go when they die?" is a human question.

The photographs in Terrace's book *Nim* (1979) show a young chimpanzee resplendent in T-shirt and trousers, washing dishes and doing the laundry at the Delafield Estate, taking instruction in his classroom at Columbia University surrounded by books and toys. Upon completion of the teaching phase of the project, Nim was shipped back to the Institute for Primate Studies in Norman, Oklahoma. Banished from paradise, the simian Adam was stripped of his clothes. No longer was he privileged to use a flush toilet. Gone was the plethora of household objects. When Terrace went to visit Nim a year later, he felt the need to take along "a picture book, a hat, a ball, sunglasses, and various kinds of food and drink" (229) lest the hapless chimp should find himself at a loss for things to sign about.

The vocabularies of the signing apes included some signs that refer to natural activities of the animals—"groom" and "hug," for example. Conspicuous by their absence were any signs having to do with dominance. It is obvious from the reports of Terrace and other investigators that dominance played a big role in the lives of their subjects, just as it does for apes in the wild. Terrace describes how Nim tested new teachers by aggressive displays. Constant vigilance was required even by those who, like himself, had considerable dominance over Nim (1979, 96-98). Yet this aspect of Nim's world was never signed about. Was this because it offended the democratic sensibilities of his caretakers to sign "me boss you"? What a fine opportunity it would have made to test Nim's syntactical ability, to see whether he could distinguish between "Laura boss Nim" and "Nim boss Laura."

Language is clearly advantageous to us humans. Thanks to it we can communicate things we otherwise could not—things that are in our interest to convey to one another. Can the same be said for the subjects of the ape language experiments? Did their training open up significant new vistas for them?

Studies of the natural communicative behavior of chimpanzees, both in the wild and in experimental settings, reveal a rich repertory of natural signals. In experiments conducted by Emil Menzel (1975), one of a group of chimpanzees was shown a hidden object and then returned to the group. A few minutes later all were turned loose. The one shown the object was able to convey the presence, direction, rough location, and desirability or undesirability of the hidden goal. If two chimpanzees were shown different objects, the one with the better goal attracted the larger following. If one was shown two pieces of food and the other four, the latter attracted about twice as many followers. The leader going to a preferred food gained more followers than the one going to a nonpreferred food. The one whose goal was a new toy attracted more followers than the one going to an old toy.

It is often said that language enables us to talk about the past, the future, and the far away, and to make universal judgments. The signing chimps gained none of these benefits. Their language training was confined to the here, now, and concrete, areas in which their own natural communicative talents, if allowed to flourish, would serve them quite well, and in some cases better.

Was it to Sarah's advantage to learn the abstract concepts "color of," "same as," and so on? From one point of view it was: she could earn herself extra bananas or a hug if she did. But like a student taking an examination, she gets the same reward for learning as for giving the appearance of learning. Students sometimes have occasion to put their knowledge to real use after they leave the classroom. Sarah never leaves it. Language for her is a task to be mastered, not a means for broadening her horizons.

With primate language research, the more the data are examined the less impressive they are. It seems that you can lead an ape to words but you can't get it to "speak as we do." To this extent Descartes was right. But the battle for the beast-machine is not declared won by hoisting the banner of human linguistic uniqueness. Human languages are not necessarily the only way to "make one's thoughts understood." With the natural communication systems of animals, the results become more and more impressive as the research goes on. Animal communication turns out to be far more sophisticated than Descartes ever envisaged.

ANIMAL SIGNALS: AFFECTIVE OR SYMBOLIC?

Up through the 1960s the prevailing view on animal communication was that all animal signals are *affective,* in other words, they convey the emotional or motivational state of the signaler and nothing more. This is essentially what Descartes said: animals only express their passions and natural impulses. Although some ethologists were quite willing to ascribe subjective experiences to animals, the affective view of signaling by no means requires this assumption.[2] One could easily follow Descartes further and hold that "emotion" here refers exclusively to states of the central nervous system (CNS).

There is no room in ethology for Descartes's simple-minded anthropocentric view of the appropriateness of an utterance. Animals communicate primarily with other animals, usually of their own species. Whatever relevance their natural signals have must be found in that context. W. John Smith (1965, 1969, 1977), a leading exponent of the affective view, distinguishes between the message and the meaning of a display. The message is encoded in the signal. It "is in some way descriptive of" and "bears a fixed relation to some aspect of the CNS state of the communicator." The meaning is relative to the individual recipient and dependent on that individual's immediate and historical context. The meaning to the recipient is "the response selected by the recipient from all of the responses open to it" (1965, 405–6).

Smith's (1963) research on eastern kingbirds provides an illustration. Kingbirds have a vocal display called the kit-ter. It is given under a variety of circumstances, all involving locomotion or approach towards something, be it a perch, a mate, or another bird. According to Smith, the message

2. See Lorenz and Tinbergen's 1938 joint paper "Taxis and Instinctive Behaviour Pattern in Egg-rolling by the Greylag Goose," in Lorenz 1970–71, 1:316–50, and Lorenz's 1963 lecture "Do Animals Undergo Subjective Experience?" 1970–71, 2:323–36.

encoded in the kit-ter is that the communicator "is experiencing some interference with a tendency to approach" (121). A male newly arrived on a territory frequently gives this call as he moves from place to place in it, alighting on some perches and passing by others. To a migrating female the meaning of the call is that here is an unmated male. To another male in search of a territory it signifies the presence of a rival. When a bird gives the kit-ter display upon approaching its mate, the meaning is appeasement.

Smith's theory has two corollaries. First, the information encoded in the signal is always about the sender, never about the external world. It reflects what Smith (1977, 71) calls the "egocentric perspective." Second, the same message always relates to the the same inner state; a different state requires a different message. Research has cast doubt on both of these claims.

In the 1940s the Austrian zoologist Karl von Frisch decoded the waggle dance of the honeybees. When a bee has discovered a new source of food or other commodity needed by the hive, she returns to the hive and performs a dance while the other bees press close around her. The tempo of the dance indicates the distance or effort needed to get to the food source. The orientation indicates the direction of the food source relative to the position of the sun. The dance is usually performed on a vertical surface in the hive. In this situation straight up stands for the direction of the sun's azimuth. The angle of the waggle run relative to the vertical corresponds to the angle between the food source and the sun. For instance, if the run points sixty degrees left of straight up, the food is sixty degrees to the left of the sun's azimuth. The desirability of the food is conveyed by the liveliness of the dance: the higher the concentration of sugar in the nectar, the more vigorous the movements (von Frisch 1967; J. L. Gould 1975a, b; Lindauer 1985).

In the 1950s Martin Lindauer, a student of von Frisch, discovered that the waggle dance is also used to convey information about possible nesting sites. When the hive becomes overcrowded, scout bees fly out in search of a suitable nesting cavity. They return and dance about the places they have found. They observe the dances of other bees and visit the sites indicated. Some give up their old dance and perform one about the new location. The process of observing dances, visiting, and dancing continues until a consensus is reached. The swarm then flies off to the chosen cavity (Lindauer 1961).

The most obvious interpretation of the data is that the dance is a kind of symbolic representation of the location and desirability of the food source or nesting site. For one committed to the view that all animal signaling is affective, the obvious interpretation will not do. Instead, the information encoded in the dance must be about the internal state of the dancer. This in fact is how Smith (1977) interprets it. The tempo, he insists, is "a measure of the 'intensity' of the forthcoming flight, not of map length" (134). The information given by the orientation of the dance is not about the direction of the food source or potential hive site but "about characteristics of the next flight that the dancing communicator will make" (144). The intensity of the dance "correlates with the value of making that flight—the benefits that will result from it" (152). To restate Smith's position more graphically, the message encoded in the dance is not this: "There is a high concentration of sugar 100 meters away at sixty degrees to the left of the sun." It is rather more like this: "I am going to exert a moderate amount of energy in certain maneuvers and the flight will be worth a great deal to me."

It is hard to see what would count as refuting this interpretation. How could one demonstrate that the message encoded in the dance was really about the external world and not merely about the bee's forthcoming behavior? Part of the rationale for restricting the message to information about the communicator was to allow the same message to have different meanings for different receivers. The trouble with the bee case is that the grounds for distinguishing between the message and the meaning are missing. The dancer is disposed to visit the site; the bees who observe the dance become similarly disposed. The energy needed to fly to the food source is the same for the recruits as it is for the communicator, and the benefits that accrue to them are the same. Thus the meaning of the dance, that flying to a certain location takes a certain effort and has a certain value, is the same as the message conveyed from the so-called egocentric perspective.

Research on vervet monkeys (Seyfarth, Cheney, and Marler 1980a, b; Seyfarth and Cheney 1982) provides a more fruitful area for testing Smith's affective theory of signaling. Like honeybees, vervet monkeys have signals that correlate with certain aspects of the environment and with certain responses on the part of the recipients. Unlike bees, however, monkeys are not all of one mind; they do not share exactly the same history and motivations. So there is at least prima facie ground for distinguishing the message of a signal from its meaning to a recipient.

Vervet monkeys give different types of alarm calls for different types of predators. Each type of call elicits a different behavioral response. One call is given for large mammalian carnivores, especially leopards. Upon hearing this call the monkeys climb into the trees. Another call is used for eagles, primarily martial eagles. The monkeys react by looking up and running into the thick vegetation. A third call, for snakes, leads the monkeys to stand on their hind legs and look around on the ground. This call is used primarily for pythons.

Seyfarth, Cheney, and Marler (1980 a, b) found that when they played recordings of the alarm calls in the absence of any actual predators, the monkeys reacted the same: they climbed the trees at the sound of the leopard alarm, hid in the bushes in response to the eagle alarm, and looked down upon hearing the snake call. Moreover, the pattern of responses remained unchanged when the playbacks were controlled for call length and amplitude. These findings undermine Smith's thesis that the meaning of the signal to the recipient depends upon the context and varies with it. The response selected—climbing a tree, hiding in the bushes, or looking down—depends neither upon the recipient's observation of the predator nor upon sensory input concerning the communicator's level of arousal.

What about the message? Does it encode information about the predator or merely about the caller's motivational state? Let us put the question another way. Which of the following best describes the message: (1) "There's an eagle"; (2) "I see an eagle"; (3) "I see something that makes me want to run into the bushes"; (4) "Run into the bushes"; (5) "I'm going to run into the bushes"? The term "eagle" in (1) and (2) is defined in terms of the characteristics by which an adult monkey recognizes an aerial predator.

The first alternative gives information about the caller's environment. The second is descriptive of an aspect of the caller's CNS state, but it cashes out as symbolic since it conveys the information that a predator is near. The same is true of (3) so long as the escape strategy is shared by the other monkeys. Alternative (4) is an injunction to act in a certain way. It is directly about neither the external world nor the caller's internal state, though indirectly it could be about both. The alternative that most agrees with Smith's theory is (5). The eagle alarm is the natural expression of the caller's intention to escape by hiding in the bushes.

Infant and juvenile vervet monkeys are more likely than adults to give alarm calls to nonpredators. Infants were observed to give the eagle alarm to storks, geese, pigeons, and falling leaves (Seyfarth, Cheney, and Marler 1980a; Seyfarth and Cheney 1980, 1982). These findings raise the following question for an affective theory of signaling: What is the infant monkey's internal state when it gives the alarm call in circumstances that pose no real danger to it? On Smith's theory messages can be incomplete (Smith 1986, 77–78), but there is no such thing as an erroneous message. The message always describes some aspect of the communicator's CNS state, whether that state is appropriate or not. Hence the motivational state of the infant in the presence of the falling leaf must be basically the same as that of an adult upon seeing a martial eagle. This is a testable consequence. Does the infant show signs of fear? Does it try to escape from the leaf?

If not, then the evidence points away from an affective interpretation of the signal.[3]

The strongest evidence against Smith's theory comes from reports of deceptive signaling. The phenomenon has been observed in several species, including the Arctic fox (Rüppell 1986) and chimpanzee (Premack and Woodruff 1979; de Waal 1986). Our favorite example has to do with birds. Charles A. Munn (1986a, b) observed mixed flocks of insect-eating birds in the Amazon basin of Peru. Two species, the bluish-slate antshrike and the white-winged shrike-tanager, act as sentinels for the flocks, giving alarm calls at the sight of hawks. They do not actively forage but dive after arthropods that have been flushed by the other birds. The sentinel birds often give alarm calls when there is no predator but an arthropod has just flushed and is being pursued by a member of the flock. The sentinel sounds the alarm, the other bird hesitates, and the sentinel snatches the prize.

The alarm call is used in insect-chasing situations about as often as it is used in the presence of a predator. The flock members nevertheless exhibit the same startle and escape reactions to the false alarms as to the true ones. In Smith's terms the meaning of the signal to the recipients is the same in both contexts. On Smith's theory, the meaning can vary but the message, which describes some aspect of the signaler's CNS state, is always the same. Here the meaning is the same but the message is surely different. It is highly implausible that the sentinel bird is in the same motivational state when it spots a hawk as when it notices another bird chasing an insect. According to Smith, the information provided by a signal need not be, and indeed never is, complete. "All signalers withhold information," and this withholding can serve to mislead (1986, 77). In order to explain the deception in terms of the withholding of information, however, one must assume that the bird's state when it gives the false alarm has something in common with its state when it gives the true alarm, and that the message is descriptive of this common aspect. The information made available thus is very minimal—so minimal that it cancels out of the analysis. All the theoretical weight falls on the meaning. The difference between the false and the true alarm can be determined only by the context, and in terms of the context the false alarm is seen to be parasitic on the true.

An affective theory of animal communication is one according to which animal signals convey information that is always about the affective state

---

3. Seyfarth, Cheney, and Marler (1980a) do not describe the signaling infant's behavior. They only report that infants are more likely to respond inappropriately to the calls of other monkeys. See also Seyfarth and Cheney 1980, 1986.

of the signaler. Smith's theory, with its distinction between message and meaning, is a refined affective theory. There are two alternatives to the affective approach. One grants that animal signals convey information but denies that the information is always or exclusively about the signaler's CNS state. The other refuses to treat animal signals as information conveyers.[4]

Signals that refer to something other than the animal's affective state are called "semantic" (Seyfarth, Cheney, and Marler 1980a, b) or "symbolic" (Marler 1977a, b, 1985b). We favor the latter term. In the area of animal communication, symbolic signaling may be defined as signaling that conveys information about some feature of the animal's environment to which the signal does not bear a natural resemblance. Construed as symbolic signals, the alarm calls of vervet monkeys give the information that a certain type of predator is near, and the honeybee dance conveys the location and desirability of a food source or nesting site. A symbolic theory of signaling is one according to which some animal signaling is symbolic.

The affective and symbolic views both presuppose that the signal conveys information about something, whether it is the signaler's internal state or a feature of the signaler's environment. It has been proposed that ethology would be better off if this assumption were abandoned. The resulting view of animal signaling constitutes an alternative to both of the aforementioned views. Is it a viable alternative?

THE TOM SAWYER VIEW

Richard Dawkins and John R. Krebs (1978) define communication as a way of manipulating the behavior of other animals. "Communication is said to occur when an animal, the actor, does something which appears to be the result of selection to influence the sense organs of another animal, the reactor, so that the reactor's behavior changes to the advantage of the actor" (283). More informally: "Communication, which we use interchangeably with 'signalling,' could be characterized as a means by which one animal makes use of another animal's muscle power" (283). This view of signaling we call the Tom Sawyer view in honor of Mark Twain's fictional adventurer, whose disquisition on the joys of fence painting was a device to tap his friend's

---

4. The sort of information that is at issue here is not Shannon information, which is defined in terms of the number of available choices, but semantic information, which is information about something. On this all sides agree. See Smith 1963, 117n; Krebs and Dawkins 1984, 395–97.

muscle power rather than a report on his own inner state. It is by no means essential that the reactor should be exploited, as Tom Sawyer's friend was. Dawkins and Krebs explain: "Our definition stipulates that communication results in a net average benefit to the actor, but it says nothing on whether the reactor benefits. The point is irrelevant to the definition" (284). In some cases the reactor also gains an advantage from being manipulated to the benefit of the actor. Courtship displays are an example.

Dawkins and Krebs offer their view as an alternative to what they call "the classical ethological approach" to the evolution of animal signals. According to the classical view, communication is a vehicle for cooperation between individuals. Signals evolve from incidental movements expressive of the signaler's emotions, such as teeth-baring in dogs. The most effective signals are those that are the most unambiguous and informative of the signaler's motivational state. Natural selection favors actors who make their internal states easy to read and reactors who successfully predict their behavior. In contrast to the classical view, Dawkins and Krebs claim that natural selection favors actors who successfully manipulate the behavior of reactors and reactors who resist manipulation if it is to their disadvantage (309).

For Dawkins and Krebs no less than for the affective approach, the problem cases are those in which the signal apparently gives information about the environment. In the case of the bee dance they admit that "the benefit is, in a sense, mutual, but we would still prefer to avoid information terminology and would instead think of the dancing bee as a manipulator, making efficient use of the muscle power of her sisters" (286). As for the alarm calls of songbirds, they state: "It is reasonable here to regard information as flowing from actor to reactor, but it is no less reasonable to eschew the ideas of information and of meaning and to think instead of the caller as 'manipulating' the behavior of its companions" (287).

Charnov and Krebs (1975) argue that the evolution of passerine alarm calls is better explained in terms of manipulation than by altruism. Natural selection favors calling, not because it benefits the flock as a whole, but because it benefits the caller. Calling increases the calling bird's survival chances relative to those of the rest of the flock. Charnov and Krebs explain how the caller might manipulate the flock to its own advantage:

> Having seen the hawk, the bird has two pieces of information: that there is a hawk, and the position of the hawk. If the caller passes on only part of this information to its flock mates, it will be able to use them to enhance its own safety. The noncallers are simply told that there is a hawk, and head for cover without respect to the predator's direction of approach. The caller

can now protect itself by "seeking cover" (Hamilton 1971) on the far side or in the middle of the flock, or benefit from the "confusion effect" (Eibl-Eibesfeldt 1970). Undoubtedly other types of manipulation are possible, but these seem the most obvious. (110)

It is far from obvious that the effects of calling put the caller in a better position than the rest of the flock or in a better position than it would be in by not calling. Having seen the hawk, the bird has two options: call or keep silent. If the strategy is to take advantage of the "confusion effect" by making it difficult for the hawk to concentrate on any one bird, calling will leave the caller better off. It is not clear, however, that the caller is better off relative to the other birds. If the strategy is to seek cover in the middle of the flock, it seems that the bird would fare better by not giving its confederates even the minimal information that a hawk is present. On Hamilton's (1971) models of predation, each individual tries to decrease its "domain of danger," which is the area containing all points nearer to it than to any other animal. A single individual can definitely improve its position by moving nearer to its neighbors while all the others remain stationary. If the others are moving as well, then it may not be able to decrease its domain of danger relative to theirs. Since all the birds will try to decrease their domains upon hearing the alarm, the calling bird is worse off relative to the others than it would be if it had not set the flock in motion by its call.

The alarm calls of vervet monkeys are even less amenable to a Tom Sawyer analysis. The fact that there are different alarm calls for different classes of predators is clearly advantageous to the receivers. The best way to escape from an eagle is a bad move in the presence of a leopard, and vice versa. The specificity of the call prevents potentially disastrous responses. One is hard pressed, however, to see how the caller gains any benefit from eliciting an appropriate response from its fellows as opposed to a random response or no response at all.

In the passage quoted above, the bird's manipulation is described in terms of giving and withholding information. Manipulative signaling and informative communication are by no means mutually exclusive. One can easily encompass the other (cf. Smith 1986). The crucial issue is not whether animal signals *can* be described using semantic information terminology, but whether it is necessary to invoke such terms. Is it possible to avoid informational concepts altogether and still give an adequate account of what the animals are doing?

Dawkins and Krebs (1978; Krebs and Dawkins 1984) maintain that it is. For them the paradigm cases of animal communication are agonistic and courtship encounters, in which sender and receiver direct their attention primarily toward each other. Signaling or response mistakes can in such instances usually be attributed to one party's failure to "read" the other's behavior correctly. The need for informational analysis is more likely to surface in cases of another sort, namely, those in which the sender's attention is on something besides the receiver and in which the receiver's response does not involve monitoring the behavior of the sender.

Vervet monkeys begin to utter alarm calls when they are a few months old. Young monkeys at first call to a wide variety of objects within a general class—flying objects in the case of the eagle call, long, thin objects on the ground for the snake call—and gradually learn to narrow it down to a particular subclass. Even the youngest monkeys succeed in eliciting responses appropriate to a given call. Nearby monkeys will look up upon hearing the eagle alarm, whatever the age of the caller and irrespective of whether the call was elicited by a predator or a nonpredator (Seyfarth, Cheney, and Marler 1980b; Seyfarth and Cheney 1986). The immature monkey's lack of mastery does not, then, consist in the inability to get its hearers to react in a certain way. The young monkey does not need to learn how to give its calls convincingly enough to fool some of the troop some of the time; that much it can do already. It needs to learn what to call about, in other words, the symbolic component. The fact that adult monkeys do or do not take up the call can serve as feedback for learning the correct association between call type and predator species (Seyfarth and Cheney 1982, 1986).

The Tom Sawyer view has the side effect of seriously curtailing the cognitive approach to animal communication. In the early 1980s an experiment was conducted in which honeybees were trained to a feeding station on a boat in the middle of a lake. After observing the dance, the recruits flew to the edge of the lake and proceeded to search along the shore. When the station was moved close to the far shore and the scouts were trained to the new site, the recruits flew across the lake to the feeding station. One interpretation of this result suggested by the researchers is that the recruits compare the directions in the dance to their cognitive map of the locale and "see" (Gould, Dyer, and Towne 1985, 150) or "make some sort of judgment" (J. L. Gould 1986, 861) that the former spot was unsuitable. This interpretation depends upon the assumption that the dance is taken to be about the location of the food source. As such it would have to be disallowed by Dawkins and Krebs. Yet their own conceptual tools seem inadequate to the task of making sense of the data. The failure of the recruits to carry through on their "amplification" of the movements of the dance cannot be due to initial or subsequent "mind-reading" of the dancer, since the dance was performed just like any other and the subsequent behavior of the dancer was not observed by them.

ANIMAL LANGUAGE: UNPACKING THE METAPHOR

Two questions can be asked about the communication systems of animals: (1) Are they languages? (2) Are they comparable to human language? Chomsky observes that in order to determine whether a given communication system counts as a language, one must first answer the question of what language is, and this is a conceptual problem, not a scientific one (1980, 430). By contrast, in order to determine whether a communication system is comparable to human language, one needs some knowledge of both, but there is no need to settle the conceptual problem of what language is.

Representative approaches to the first question are found in *Rationality* by the philosopher Jonathan Bennett (1964) and *The Mind of an Ape* by the psychologists David and Ann James Premack (1983). Bennett argues that bee dances are not language because they are "not literally symbolic," and they are not symbolic because the bees do not have reasons for their behavior (1964, 15). According to the Premacks, the bees do not have language unless they can judge the agreement or disagreement between their dances and the real situation. It is not enough for a bee to do a dance that accurately represents the distance, direction, and desirability of the food source. The bee must also be able, if shown a replica of her dance, to determine whether or not it accurately represents this information (Premack and Premack 1983, 116–17).

The second question seems at first glance to be singularly uninteresting. Animal communication obviously differs from human language in many nontrivial respects. Philosophers are especially fond of pointing this out in regard to man's best friend. Anthony Kenny remarks that there is no way a dog can express the difference between the two thoughts "My master is at the door" and "I think that my master is at the door" (Kenny et al. 1973, 48). Donald Davidson (1975, 16) complains that we have no means to determine whether Fido, who supposedly knows that his master is home, also knows that Mr. Smith (who is his master) or that the president of the bank (who is the same person) is home. Bennett (1964, 88–89) points to the absence of canine communication to the effect that in general bones stay put until retrieved by the burier. John Heil's examples are "Bones are good" and "There is a bone in the butcher shop a mile up the road" (1982, 406). The absence of such expressions proves that the canine signaling system is different from human language in certain important respects. Yet the existence of dissimilarities, even essential dissimilarities, does not mean that there is no common ground for comparison.

There is a widespread conception that the only kind of analogy worth bothering about is a perfect analogy or isomorphism. Two systems are *isomorphic* with each other if and only if for every element in one there is a corresponding element in the other (one-to-one correspondence), and for every relation between elements in one there is a relation between the corresponding elements in the other. Obviously, no communication system of any nonhuman species is isomorphic with human language. None even comes close. An imperfect analogy can still serve a purpose, however. Contrary to popular opinion, there is nothing wrong with comparing apples and oranges. Indeed it is often very worthwhile to make such a comparison.

Is it ever worthwhile to compare animal signaling systems to human language? According to Chomsky (1980, 440), to expect that ape communication will shed light on human language or vice versa is like expecting the study of broad jumping to shed light on bird flight or vice versa. The former analogy is likely to be as useless as the latter. Chomsky is referring to the language systems taught to apes, but his remarks apply equally to the study of natural communication systems. It would be absurd, suggests Chomsky, to define "flying" as "an act in which some creature rises into the air and lands some distance away, with the goal of reaching some remote point" and then to propose that biologists start with the simpler case of human "flight" before taking up the complex mechanisms of bird flight (430).

What is absurd here is the insistence that the difference between human jumping and bird flight is only one of degree. So long as it is recognized that jumping is not the same as flying, it may indeed be useful to examine the physics of jumping to shed light on certain problems in the study of flight.

A comparison between two processes or systems may prove illuminating for one set of problems even though it is unhelpful for another set. Chomsky, concerned as he is with the intricacies of human grammatical structure, sees no point in consulting apes. That is fair enough. But his argument from flying should not dissuade other scientists with different interests from pursuing the analogies he disdains.

Ethologists such as Colin Beer (1976), Peter Marler (1977b), and Charles Snowdon (1982) advocate the use of linguistic and psycholinguistic analogies in the study of animal communication. Beer wryly observes that such talk is sure to raise suspicion in some quarters, for "the serious will agree that anyone who thinks animals can talk is lost in a Disneyland of whimsies" (1976, 416). The Disneyland accusation is unfounded. The ethologists in question are not claiming that animal communication is a type of language. They are merely saying that it is analogous to human language in certain respects that are useful to look at. One takes an analogy as far as it will go, then one leaves it behind. The point of introducing the linguistic analogy is that it can take us further than the traditional conception of animal signaling as a simple, fixed, stereotyped activity (Snowdon 1982, 212; Marler 1985a, 338).

The term "syntax" is used in ethology to refer to any system of rules that allows one to predict sequences of signals (Snowdon 1982, 231). Many animals, especially primates and birds, have complex displays consisting of different elements, some of which are also used alone or in other combinations. In most cases the elements seem to function like phonemes or syllables of human language in that they are not meaning-bearing units (Marler 1977b). There are cases, however, in which the components function more like words or morphemes, so that the meaning of the whole is the sum of the meanings of the parts. One of Snowdon's examples from his research on cotton-top tamarins is a sequence consisting of "a type E (alarm) chirp and a low arousal alerting call. This combination was always given after initial type E (alarm) chirps had aroused the animals. When this combination phrase occurred, the animals remained stationary and scanned the environment with reduced arousal. A short time later they began to move about, giving only the low-arousal alerting call" (Snowdon 1982, 231).

Another example of morphemelike signaling is provided by Beer's research on laughing gulls. The birds have a courtship display that consists of the upright posture followed by facing away or turning the head away from the recipient. The upright by itself conveys hostility in agonistic contexts. The facing away posture "appears to negate the message of hostility" (Beer 1976, 415). When a male laughing gull is with its mate in the presence of a third bird, often the male will attack the outsider while facing away to its partner. In this situation the facing-away display "appears to have the function of indicating to the partner that the manifest hostility is directed elsewhere" (431).

Research on the ontogeny of primate signals suggests parallels with the development of human speech. Snowdon (1982) reports that infant cotton-top tamarins go through a period of fragmented vocalization analogous to the babbling of human infants. Seyfarth and Cheney (1982) compare the over-generalized alarm calls of infant vervet monkeys to human infants' use of "dada" to refer to any male adult. In both cases the utterance is nonrandom, and referential specificity increases as the infant gets older.

Biological investigations such as the ones just mentioned operate from an evolutionary viewpoint. According to the theory of evolution, all complex biological systems have resulted from historical development through various stages. Human speech is no exception. Writes Philip Lieberman (1975, 83): "Human language can be no more disjoint from the communications systems of other living animals than human respiration or human locomotion. The apparent uniqueness of human language, like the apparent uniqueness of fully bipedal locomotion, merely reflects the fact that the intermediate forms are extinct." Darwin and his followers teach us to expect far-reaching similarities in structure and function between species, both in the same line of descent and across parallel lines of development. Birds evolved flight, but so did insects and bats. The evolutionary perspective licenses the search for analogous features of flight, but one cannot say exactly what will be discovered. Insect flight proves to be far more difficult to understand than that of birds, or aircraft for that matter. And jumping, pace Chomsky, plays a role in theories of the origin of bird flight (Ostrom 1979).

8

Three Fables of Animal Mindlessness

Animals show more skill than humans do in some actions, but none at all in many others. This proves, said Descartes, that animals do not act through reason. The conclusion persists to this day. The action test has taken the following form: To determine whether an animal is acting mindlessly or consciously, alter the conditions so that the behavior is no longer appropriate. If the animal does not change its behavior or adapt it to the new circumstances, then it is acting mindlessly. Earlier we criticized Descartes for holding too narrow a conception of acting through reason. A similar charge can be brought against the users of the updated version.

Certain examples figure prominently in the modern discussions of animal mindlessness. The examples have become so laden with philosophical interpretation that they have acquired the status of fables. Our treatment is structured around three of these fables: the stupid wasp, the illogical bees, and the irrational robin.

Wittgenstein (1953, 155) remarks that a main cause of philosophical disease is "a one-sided diet: one nourishes one's thinking with only one kind of example." When it comes to thinking about animals, Wittgenstein's aphorism is off the mark. Here the nutritional deficiency is due not to a lack of variety in the diet but to malabsorption. One fails to look at one's examples hard enough.

THE STUPID WASP

Douglas R. Hofstadter (1982) proposes the term "sphexishness" to denote the kind of mindless behavior typified by the wasp *Sphex*. The term is defined ostensively. After giving a description of the wasp's behavior, Hofstadter writes: "Something about the wasp's action seems supremely unconscious, a quality totally opposite to what we human beings think *we* are all about, particularly when we talk about our own consciousness. I propose to call the *Sphex* wasp's quality 'sphexishness' and its opposite 'antisphexishness.' I then propose that consciousness is simply the possession of antisphexishness to the highest possible degree" (22). Daniel Dennett borrows the term "sphexishness" from Hofstadter. He too defines it ostensively, first describing the wasp's behavior and then saying that "this unnerving property, so vividly manifested by the wasp" is called "sphexishness" (1984, 11).

In our view the notion of sphexishness is so ill defined as to be useless. The wasp example is far more complex than the authors let on.

The yellow-winged Sphex (*Sphex flavipennis*), a hunting wasp, lays her eggs in a nest provisioned with a cricket for food. The wasp stings the cricket in a way that paralyzes but does not kill it. She brings the prey to the mouth of the burrow. Leaving it there, she goes into the burrow for a few seconds. Then she reappears, drags the cricket inside, lays her eggs on it, and closes the cell. The French entomologist Jean Henri Fabre (1915) found that if he moved the cricket a few inches away while it was left unattended, the wasp would fetch it back and enter the burrow again without it. Forty times he moved the cricket. Each time the wasp went through the sequence of dragging it to the threshold, entering the cavity for a few seconds, and re-emerging. Fabre found the same "inflexible obstinacy" in other wasps of the same colony, but upon trying the experiment with a different group he got different results. After he had moved the cricket a few times, the wasp seized it and brought it directly into the hole.

What Fabre calls "the ignorance of instinct" manifested itself on other occasions as well. Once Fabre took a wasp in the process of closing her burrow. Setting her aside, he removed the prey, with the eggs upon it, from the hole. Returned to her place, the wasp went inside for a few moments. She obviously could have seen that there was nothing in there, yet she came out and resumed her work as if nothing were amiss. Asserts Fabre: "I conclude therefore as I began: instinct knows everything, in the undeviating paths marked out for it; it knows nothing, outside those paths. The sublime inspirations of science and the astounding inconsistencies of stupidity are both its portion, according as the insect acts under normal or accidental conditions" (211).

Humans have a behavior that is superficially similar to the above case. It is called locking the barn after the horse has been stolen. Humans who do this may be stupid, but their stupidity is not the sort that Fabre had in mind. Humans at least know what they are doing, whereas the wasp does not know what it is doing.

The story of the persistent wasp has been retold a number of times, always with the same curious description of the wasp's preliminary entry into the burrow. Sir John Lubbock writes in his book *On the Senses, Instincts, and Intelligence of Animals* (1897, 245): "Thus one solitary wasp, *Sphex flavipennis*, which provisions its nest with small grasshoppers, when it returns to the cell, leaves the victim outside, and goes down for a moment to see that all is right." Lubbock is quoted by L. T. Hobhouse in *Mind in Evolution* (1915, 76). Dean E. Wooldridge writes in *The Machinery of the Brain* (1963, 82): "The wasp's routine is to bring the paralyzed cricket to the burrow, leave it on the threshold, go inside to see that all is well, emerge, and then drag the cricket in." Wooldridge's account is based on Wells, Huxley, and Wells (1931, 2:1161), but he omits the qualification in their phrase "apparently to see that all is well." Wooldridge in turn is quoted by Hofstadter (1982, 22) and by Dennett (1978, 65; 1984, 11). In each case the pregnant phrase "to see that all is well" passes by without comment. None of the authors considers what the grounds are for ascribing such a purpose to a wasp or what constitutes all being well. It is as though the phrase crept in from somewhere else. In fact it comes from Fabre.

Fabre puzzled over the function of the extra step of entering the burrow prior to bringing in the prey. "Could it not be," he speculated, "that, before descending with a cumbrous burden, the Sphex thinks it wise to take a look at the bottom of her dwelling, so as to make sure that all is well and, if necessary, to drive out some brazen parasite who may have slipped in during her entrance?" (1915, 72). Note that Fabre is asking a question, not giving an answer. Moreover, he gives a meaning to the phrase "all is well" by specifying what would count as all *not* being well, namely, the presence of a parasite. The subsequent borrowing of his phrase without any attempt at explication invites a superficial assessment of the wasp's behavior.

The subroutine repeated by the wasp involves three steps: bring the prey to the threshold, enter the burrow without it, and come out again. Of the first step per se there is nothing to complain. Knowing the function of the behavior, one sees the point of the repetitions. Suppose that instead of waiting until the cricket was deposited on the threshold, the experimenter snatched it from the wasp as she was dragging it along. In such circumstances it would not seem stupid for the wasp always to go back for it before proceeding on her journey. Although we might disagree with her about when to give up the task as hopeless, we must admit that logic is on her side to this extent: if the burrow has one entrance and the cricket is to be placed inside, the cricket must first be brought up to the entrance.

The aura of stupidity emanates from the second step. In the course of describing Fabre's experiment, Wooldridge, following Wells, Huxley, and Wells, remarks: "The wasp never thinks of pulling the cricket straight in" (1963, 83). In *Elbow Room* Dennett assesses the wasp's performance and finds it pathetic:

> By the time we arrive at such a sophisticated creature as our *Sphex*, we can assign quite an elaborate catalog of interests to the creature. If it were not so, if we did not have a clear and detailed vision of where her interests lay, her performance in the strange experiment described in chapter one would not seem so pathetic. We measure her performance against her interests and see how poorly she does. Were we to act as her guardian, we could advise much better courses of action to her—if only she could take our advice! She is a very imperfect guardian of her own interests, it seems. (1984, 22-23)

Dennett has nothing against the wasp's preliminary entry in normal circumstances, for a few pages later he states: "*Sphex*, in her normal surroundings (that is, when tricky biologists are not interfering), typically does what reason dictates, for surely reason does proclaim the wisdom of reconnoitering her pathways ('Look before you leap!')" (1984, 25-26).

Why does the reconnoitering step seem wise in the single instance but pathetic in the multiple instances? There is no general law of nature that once things are checked they stay checked. One can easily imagine a case in which it would be wise to repeat forty times or more the process of looking before you leap. You are on the fifteenth floor of a burning building. A safety net is being held out for you below. Forty times the smoke and falling debris drive you back. Each time you approach the ledge you check to make sure that the net is still there, for the firemen could have moved it to rescue someone else in the meantime.

Fabre failed to discover the function of the reconnoitering step (1915, 76). Nevertheless, his initial speculation about parasites shows how conditions inside the burrow could change from moment to moment, making repeated visits useful. Depending on what she is looking for, it may be that the wasp is well advised, like the person in the burning building, to keep on looking until she leaps.

Behavior that is prima facie useful may prove to be counterproductive in certain circumstances. According to Dennett, what makes the wasp's performance in the experiment seem pathetic is that it goes against her interests. It is counterproductive to keep going through the reconnoitering step, since every repetition of it gives the experimenter yet another opportunity to practice his treachery. The wasp cannot proceed with the important business of egglaying until the cricket is safely inside the burrow. The only way she will ever get the prey inside is to drag it straight in, and to do this she must omit the reconnoitering visit. Before we give her any definite advice, however, we should make sure we have set up the decision problem properly.

The problem is to determine which course of action has the higher expected utility or desirability: to reconnoiter each time or to omit this step after it has been performed a few times. If the wasp persists in reconnoitering and the experiment continues indefinitely, the nest will never be provisioned. This outcome is obviously undesirable. If she does not reconnoiter and the experimenter keeps the same protocol, the wasp will be able to provision the nest and to lay her eggs. The value assigned to this outcome must take into account any cost that may accrue from omitting the step. Is there a cost and if so what is it? Answering this question requires putting more flesh on the vague phrase "to see that all is well." Unless we know what counts as something being wrong, we cannot assess the harm to the larvae if they are shut up in such a cavity. Nor can we determine the probability that this something will occur during the interval since the last visit.

One might protest that it makes no difference what the cost is since the wasp has everything to lose by taking the other alternative. At best the choice is between a sure loss and a virtually certain gain; at worst it is between a sure loss and a small chance of gain. This assumes that the experiment will continue indefinitely and that the protocol will remain unaltered.

There are other possible states of the world, however. The experiment could be discontinued. The experimenter could remove the cricket after it has been deposited in the burrow or simply destroy the whole edifice. Under these conditions the outcomes of the wasp's actions would be different from those envisaged above. To figure the expected utilities of the alternative actions, we must take into account the probabilities of the conditions on the assumption that a given alternative is chosen. If the probability that the experiment will be discontinued is sufficiently high, and the cost of an unchecked nest is likewise high, then the expected utility of reconnoitering will be higher than that of omitting the step.

As a matter of fact Fabre did not keep the experiment going indefinitely but gave up after forty trials. And what happened then? Fabre goes off to relax and reflect upon the wondrous stupidity of instinct. Meanwhile the wasp retrieves her prey for the forty-first time, deposits it on the threshold, steps inside for a few seconds, emerges—and triumphantly pulls the cricket into the burrow!

The wasp, of course, does not know that she is in an experiment, let alone that experiments usually end. The decision problem for the rational wasp is different from that of a human advising the wasp. By *rational wasp* we mean a hypothetical construct with a wasp's powers of perception and a human ability to reason. The rational wasp, being ignorant of the conditions known by us to affect the outcome, must go on what she knows. One might be tempted to say that on the basis of prior experience, the rational wasp will judge it to be highly probable that the cricket will move the next time it is abandoned. This view becomes less tempting when we examine the problem more closely.

Wasps, like other animals, go through many kinds of repetitions in their normal activities. Digging, for instance, consists of removing load after load, eating is a matter of taking bite after bite, and so on. All of these sequences terminate. Whatever is going on in the cricket's perambulations is either like the wasp's own repeated actions, or else it is like a uniform physical process, such as an object sliding down a slope every time it is placed there. Or it is a completely mysterious, "supernatural" event. In the first case persistence on the part of the wasp has a good chance of paying off. In the second case it probably will not pay off unless the wasp takes care to place the cricket in a different position or blocks it somehow. In the third case there is no way to determine the probability of recurrence.

According to Hofstadter, what makes human beings antisphexish is their sensitivity to sameness. They notice when they are in a loop or rut, and they are able to break out of it. The wasp fails to manifest this ability (1982, 24). Failure to break out of a loop seems mindless and mechanical only because one thinks the creature's interests would be served by getting out of it. Hofstadter treats loops as though they were all on a par, "tedious" routines to be "nipped in the bud by the same kind of mechanism that enables you to cut off a bore at a party. 'Excuse me, I think I'll go get some more punch' " (27). Loops are not necessarily infinite, and finite loops are not necessarily bad. Sometimes it pays to forgo the punch and stay with the bore, at least for a while. Workers on an assembly line provide an apt illustration.

We have not shown that Fabre's wasp is conscious, let alone rational. We have only called into question the claim that her behavior is rigid when reason calls for flexibility. The problem is to determine what reason calls for. This problem resurfaces in the second fable.

THE ILLOGICAL BEES

At the 1981 Dahlem Workshop on Animal Mind-Human Mind, J. L. Gould proposed the following as a necessary condition for consciousness: "an ability to recognize, in a variety of cases, a logical conflict between a token or sign stimulus and the context which it is supposed to represent" (Seyfarth et al. 1982, 392). His example is "a bee using the odor of oleic acid as a token to indicate a dead bee, whereupon it removes the corpse from the hive" (392; cf. Gould and Gould 1982, 283).

The same behavior is observed in ants and described by Wilson, Durlach, and Roth (1958). When *Pogonomyrmex badius* workers come across the corpse of a sister ant, they carry it away from the nest. In an effort to determine the nature of the releasing stimuli for this behavior, the experimenters treated small squares of paper with an extract derived from worker corpses. These were placed near the nest together with untreated squares. The treated squares were carried off to the refuse pile whereas the untreated squares were not. The extract was then daubed on live workers. They too were carried off. After they were deposited on the refuse pile, they got up and returned to the nest only to be carried off again. The cycle was observed to continue for one to two hours. Some corpses were leached by being soaked in acetone. They were not transported, but when subsequently daubed with corpse extract, they were carried off the same as normal corpses. It was determined that oleic acid was the chief chemical stimulus for the behavior.

Transporting their sisters again and again only to have them return to the nest, the ants call to mind Fabre's wasp with her wandering cricket. Unlike the wasp case, where the appearance of mindlessness stems from the repetition of the behavior, the ants and the bees seem to act mindlessly from their first encounter with an oleic-acid-treated worker. The mere act of transporting the live worker is taken to be in violation of Gould's necessary condition of consciousness: "By the operational definition described above, we can provide a logical mismatch—a live bee with a drop of oleic acid on it—and observe that other bees nevertheless (and with considerable difficulty) throw the bee with acid on it out of the hive. Clearly the bees cannot be said by this definition to be in any meaningful sense conscious of their actions" (Seyfarth et al. 1982, 392).

The issue here is not whether it is meaningful to ascribe consciousness to insects at all. It is simply whether their behavior in this instance violates the alleged necessary condition of consciousness. The first order of business is to pinpoint the logical conflict. According to Seyfarth et al., "a live bee with a drop of oleic acid on it" constitutes a logical mismatch. More precision is needed. There is no logical contradiction between the statements "This bee has oleic acid on it" and "This bee is alive." It is quite possible for both to be true, as indeed they are in the experiment. The logical contradiction arises from simultaneously holding the following two statements: "All bees with oleic acid on them are dead" and "All bees that move are alive." Since the bee has oleic acid on it, it follows from the first statement that it is dead; but since it moves, it follows from the second that it is alive.

The next order of business is to determine whether it is justified to accuse the bees of failing to recognize the logical conflict. Let us pose the problem for a rational bee. This hypothetical creature, we shall say, believes that oleic acid is a sure sign of death. Here is a sister who reeks of oleic acid, yet she prances about as though nothing were wrong with her. What is a rational bee to do? Should she conclude that oleic acid is not a sure sign of death after all, or that this is a walking corpse?

However distasteful it may be to us, the latter alternative is as much a resolution of the logical mismatch as the former. True, modern medical science and common sense agree that corpses cannot walk. Yet we can easily imagine the sort of case that would incline us to reconsider this opinion. The horror literature is full of chain-dragging skeletons, headless horsemen, and the like. In reading these stories we may think that the characters give up scientific laws too easily, but not that they are guilty of logical contradiction.

The situation for the rational bee is analogous to that of a human society in which the absence of breathing is taken as a sure sign of death. When there are conflicting indicators, a decision must be made about which is to be believed. Suppose there is no breathing but the heart still beats. If the people pronounce the patient dead and proceed with the burial, we can hardly accuse them of failing to perceive a logical mismatch, let alone of not being conscious of their act of burial. Why then are we so quick to make such a judgment against the bees? Is it because they show no puzzlement at the antics of their "dead" sister? Puzzlement is a product of uncertainty. If confidence in one sign is high enough to override all others, then puzzlement will not be in evidence.

Gould's criterion conceals a double standard. For humans, on the one hand, allowances are made for ignorance, for credulity, for lack of logical skill. No one would ever dream of denying people consciousness on the grounds that they persist in beliefs in the face of overwhelming evidence to the contrary. Animals, on the other hand, are expected to be perfect little scientists. In order to earn the epithet "conscious" they must be proficient in logic, ever ready to change their beliefs in the face of available evidence, careful to take all considerations into account. When people fail to live up to this ideal, we say they are all too human. When animals fail, they are said to be machine-like.

The image of bees as little scientists is evoked by Dennett in his 1983 article "Intentional Systems in Cognitive Ethology: The 'Panglossian Paradigm' Defended." According to Dennett (1971, 1978), there is room in science for the intentional stance. To adopt the intentional stance toward a thing is to think of it as something with beliefs, desires, and so on. One can do this with animals, plants (violets like to grow near streams), and computers. The role of the intentional stance is to generate predictions that would otherwise be hard to come by and to pose questions that are difficult to put in any other terms. One does not claim that the creature actually has intentional states, only that it simplifies matters to think of it as though it did. Dennett gives the following intentional story of the bees to show how gaps and defects in the intentional profile of an animal can point to "shortcuts and stopgaps" in the biological design:

> Suppose, for example, that we adopt the intentional stance toward bees, and note with wonder that they seem to *know* that dead bees are a hygiene problem in a hive; when a bee dies its sisters *recognize* that it has died, and, *believing* that dead bees are a health hazard, and *wanting,* rationally enough, to avoid health hazards, they *decide* they must remove the dead bee immediately. Thereupon they do just that. Now if that fancy an intentional story were confirmed, the bee system designer would be faced with an enormously difficult job. Happily for the designer (if sadly for bee romantics), it turns out that a much lower order explanation suffices: dead bees secrete oleic acid; the smell of oleic acid turns on the "remove it" subroutine in the other bees; put a dab of oleic acid on a live, healthy bee, and it will be dragged, kicking and screaming, out of the hive. (1983, 350)

There seems to be a "shortcut" only because the story makes the bees into diminutive public health officials going about their business in a cool and objective manner. It is possible to take another sort of intentional stance toward the bees. Consider this story. Bees abhor the odor given off by the dead. When a bee dies its sisters *recognize* that it has the odor of death, and *wanting* to be rid of the hateful smell, they *decide* they must remove the dead bee. Thereupon they do just that. Unlike Dennett's story, this one stands up as well after the experiment as before. The behavior of the bees toward their live sister is consistent with and predictable from it.

"In fact there is an eerie resemblance between many of the discoveries of cognitive ethologists working with lower animals and the sorts of prowess mixed with stupidity one encounters in the typical products of AI," writes Dennett (1983, 350). This remark says less about animals than it does about theoretical kinship of the two disciplines. Dennett assesses animal behavior analogously to the output of a computer program. Programs are designed for a certain purpose. The programmer's purpose is attributed to the program. The latter shows prowess insofar as it achieves the programmer's purpose, stupidity insofar as it fails. Likewise Mother Nature is considered the programmer of biological systems, and animals are deemed to act mindlessly when their behavior fails to achieve the function for which nature designed it.

Dennett recognizes that the analogy is flawed: there is no Mother Nature (351). To fill the gap he postulates "free-floating rationales" that do not belong to the animal or to nature or to the human observer. This move puts Dennett in line with the pre-evolutionary theological thinking of biologists such as Fabre rather than with modern theory of evolution. The free-floating rationales correspond to the instincts with which God equipped the animals in lieu of reason. The narrowness and rigidity of behavior, a mark of instinct for Fabre, becomes a sign of the computer subroutine under the new regime.

There are no such free-floating rationales in the detheologized evolutionary process. There are only the traits that the animals actually possess and the scientific descriptions we invent to comprehend the process. From the evolutionary adaptationist point of view, one at first thinks that the behavior pattern of removing dead bees has been selected for. Wilson's experiments prove this initial guess wrong. The behavior that has been selected for is the removal of objects that secrete oleic acid. One can easily see the increase in fitness conferred by this trait.

Since there is no bee designer in nature, nor any mock designer (free-floating rationales), Dennett is not entitled to separate the intentional system from the design in the way he does. An appropriate intentional system must exactly match the design. One achieves the fit not by postulating shortcuts in the design but by adjusting the intentional profile. If the resulting profile deviates from the ideal of the perfect reasoner, then so be it. This brings us to the third fable.

THE IRRATIONAL ROBIN

David Lack describes the territorial behavior of English robins in his classic *The Life of the Robin* (1946). When one robin ventures into another's territory, it is pursued by the territory holder. If the intruder perches and does not retreat, the owner displays by stretching its red breast out toward the intruder. The owning robin resorts to attack only if its display fails to dislodge the intruder. Lack set up a mounted robin in territories occupied by nesting robins. The birds postured at the stuffed specimen and then attacked it, some feebly and briefly, others quite violently. One belligerent female pommeled it so hard that she knocked its head off. Lack continued the experiment, removing more and more parts until all that was left was a bundle of red feathers. This was enough to release a typical display in half the robins. Lack also tried a stuffed juvenile robin, which looks much like an adult except that the breast is brown speckled rather than red. It was ignored by twelve of fourteen robins. He took an adult specimen and painted the breast brown. It was not attacked by any of them.

Tinbergen (1965) found a similar pattern of behavior in three-spined sticklebacks. The red belly of the male is an eliciting stimulus like the robin's red breast. The fish were presented with models of various shapes, some with red bellies, some without. They attacked the red-bellied models more vigorously than stickleback-shaped models without the red. The shape and size of the red models made no difference. Tinbergen reports that when a red mail van passed by the window where the aquaria were located, "all males dashed towards the window side of their tanks and followed the van from one corner of their tank to the other" (66).

Behavior of this type is undoubtedly the inspiration for Dennett's inclusion of fish and birds in the following passage from *Elbow Room:*

> Another feature lurking in the tale of the wasp is that spooky sense one often gets when observing or learning about insects and other lower animals: all that bustling activity but *there's nobody home!* We are looking at a world that appears to have been cleverly designed but then deserted by its designer. The ants and bees, and even the fish and the birds, are just "going through the motions." *They* don't understand or appreciate what they are up to, and no other comprehending selves are to be found in the neighborhood. (Dennett 1984, 13)

The birds' senses are more than adequate to register the differences between a robin and a bunch of feathers, yet they react to the latter as though they were seeing a real bird. Their behavior in the abnormal case puts a new light on their behavior in the normal case. The red breast, not the robin gestalt, releases the display. Are we therefore to say that the birds are just going through the motions and that there's nobody home?

Several authors have noted that people sometimes react somewhat like

Lack's robins and Tinbergen's sticklebacks. Colin Beer's (1982) examples are recoiling in horror at the sight of blood and being "blind with anger." Krebs and Dawkins (1984) give the example of a man sexually aroused by a picture of a nude woman. In each of these cases what is released is a single emotion: horror, rage, lust. By contrast, the robin and the stickleback act out an extended sequence of behavior that is directed at a specific recipient. Their displays seem pointless because there is no sentient audience for them.

Beer asks whether we are "ever so uncoupled from our normal perceptual proficiency as to be duped into 'miscarriages' of response by the kinds of experiment used by ethologists to probe the perceptual worlds of lower animals" (1982, 259). If natural experiments are allowed to count then the answer is clearly yes. Complex communicative displays characteristic of our species are sometimes provoked by and directed toward inanimate objects. Computer users, stymied by the rigidities of a given program, have been known to vent their frustration by typing profanities or insults as though the recipient of the message were human. If asked whether they thought the computer was really affected by such an outburst, they probably would admit that it was not. They are fully aware of the silliness of insulting a machine; in Dennett's words they "understand or appreciate what they are up to." But they do it anyway because it makes them feel better.

Occasionally people become so captivated by a machine that it becomes a moot issue whether or not they understand or appreciate what they are doing. Weizenbaum (1976, 6) writes in reference to the psychiatric version of the ELIZA program: "I was startled to see how quickly and how very deeply people conversing with DOCTOR became emotionally involved with the computer and how unequivocally they anthropomorphized it. Once my secretary, who had watched me work on the program for many months and therefore surely knew it to be merely a computer program, started conversing with it. After only a few interchanges with it, she asked me to leave the room."

The more lifelike the output, the more we are inclined to excuse emotional involvement on the part of the user. What makes the robin's behavior seem so inexcusable is that the tuft of red feathers is obviously different from a live robin. This is not a fair way to set up the analogy, however. In the case of the person's reaction to the computer, one is judging the similarity of the behaviors, whereas in the robin case it is the similarity of the objects. A computer console has even less in common with the human figure than a cluster of feathers has with a bird. The person is seduced not by the appearance of the object but by its message. Why not likewise for the robin? The bundle of feathers is set upright so that the red is prominent, just as it is on a posturing adult robin. The owner of the territory is reacting to the stimulus not as object but as display. In the language of intentionality our point is this: the bird believes, not that the object is a displaying robin, but merely that a display is taking place in its territory.

Some might contend that it is silly to attack a meaning-bearing object. Maybe so, but people do it all the time. Annoying letters are angrily torn up and thrown into the waste basket. "No Hunting" signs are shot at. Burning crosses on lawns are approached with horror, and not because of the fire hazard. It would never occur to the residents to think that this is only a symbol and that so long as the Ku Klux Klansmen themselves are not standing on the lawn there is nothing to worry about.

Some might object that posturing displays, unlike the objects mentioned above, cannot exist where the displayer is not. If the robin believes that posturing can occur without a posturer then it is being downright irrational. Maybe so, but irrational belief systems are still belief systems and can have laws of their own. Herein lies another bone of contention.

Dennett maintains that "the use of intentional idioms carries a presupposition or assumption of *rationality* in the creature or system to which the intentional states are attributed" (1983, 345). When irrationality is encountered, the intentional stance must give way. The following passage from his 1971 article "Intentional Systems" is especially revealing:

> The presumption of rationality is so strongly entrenched in our inference habits that when our predictions prove false we at first cast about for adjustments in the information-possession conditions (he must not have heard, he must not know English, he must not have seen x, been aware that y, etc.) or goal weightings before questioning the rationality of the system as a whole. In extreme cases personalities may prove to be so unpredictable from the Intentional stance that we abandon it, and if we have accumulated a lot of evidence in the meanwhile about the nature of response patterns in the individual, we may find that a species of design stance can be effectively adopted. This is the fundamentally different attitude we occasionally adopt toward the insane. To watch an asylum attendant manipulate an obsessively countersuggestive patient, for instance, is to watch something radically unlike normal interpersonal relations. (Dennett 1971, 93-94; 1978, 9-10)

To adopt the intentional stance is to explain or predict the individual's behavior in terms of beliefs, desires, and so on. Hence to abandon the intentional stance is to avoid any reference to beliefs and desires in predicting the individual's behavior. Successful handling of the mentally ill surely does not call for so callous an attitude. The patient's beliefs may be bizarre, the logic tortured, but there is method in the madness, as the saying goes. Attempts at computer simulation of paranoid processes have proceeded on the assumption that the paranoid holds a network of delusional beliefs and routinely searches linguistic expressions for indications of malevolent intent (Colby, Weber, and Hilf 1971; Colby 1975). Like the chess-playing computer, the paranoid computer invites the intentional stance. You can handle the "patient" better if you figure out what remarks are likely to make the computer think you are out to get it.

In taking the intentional stance toward animals, there is no need to restrict oneself to belief systems that would be considered acceptable for a normal, civilized adult human being. The minimum condition is that one should be able to understand the perspective that one attributes to the animal, at least well enough to gain the sorts of benefits one expects from the intentional stance. Some linguistic philosophers adopt overly restrictive criteria for understanding belief systems. Their attitude borders on xenophobia. You *can* understand what you *do* understand. Or, you can understand belief systems different from your own, but only slightly different.[1] Our approach is more pragmatic. You don't know what you can or cannot understand until you try.

To illustrate the intentional stance from an alien perspective, we ask the reader to suspend disbelief while we construct an intentional profile of birds. By "suspend disbelief" we mean that the reader should ignore the question of whether birds actually have the intentional states we ascribe to them. As Dennett states and we have already noted, to treat a creature as an intentional system is not to assume that it really has intentional states, but only that its behavior can be predicted by ascribing them to it. Our intentional profile is constructed with an eye toward the sorts of behaviors described in the early papers of Konrad Lorenz.

The European cuckoo is a brood parasite: it lays its eggs in the nests of other birds. The young cuckoo, bigger and stronger than its foster siblings, pushes them out of the nest. Lorenz describes the reaction of warblers to the sight of their own displaced young: "Very young warblers which had been carried to the edge of the nest by a young cuckoo were given absolutely no attention by the adult warming the cuckoo, although the beak of the adult projected over the edge of the nest only centimeters away from the undercooled offspring" (1970-71, 1:178). From a purely intellectualistic intentional stance, the adult warbler is either stupid or callous, or both.

---

1. See, for instance, Stich 1979, especially the argument that we cannot specify the content of a dog's beliefs.

Any creature with a modicum of sense would surely realize that those are its own babies fallen from the nest, and any parent with an ounce of parental feeling would make some effort to retrieve them.

This assessment is based on a belief system according to which one's own infants are objects of continuing parental concern. One's own infants are defined historically as those that hatched from one's own eggs, or at least from eggs in one's own nest. It is possible to construct an alternative belief system in which the object of parental concern is not the infant per se but the infant in a certain situation: the gaping baby is in need of food, the baby in the nest is in need of warming or cooling, and so on. The baby birds outside the nest are judged not to need temperature regulation precisely because they are outside the nest. Since they are not in need of warming or cooling, there is no reason to bring them back in!

This example suggests that if you want to design a computer program to simulate the behavior of birds, you should assume that you are dealing with an alien way of looking at the world—one in which individuals are defined and responded to in terms of specific situations and roles. This aspect of the avian world view is even more evident in the examples that follow.

Jackdaws give a rattling call when they see an animal carrying a live or dead corvid or some other black, dangling object. A single crow pinion feather carried by a fellow jackdaw is enough to elicit rattling. Lorenz inadvertently brought an attack upon himself by carrying his wet black bathing trunks across the lawn. Yet when he held out a black pigeon to the jackdaws, instead of rattling and attacking him, they attacked the pigeon. Once a jackdaw caught its toe in the wire mesh of the cage and tore off its claw. Though it shrieked in pain and distress, there was no rattling response from its fellows. "None of the jackdaws paid the slightest attention to the plight of their companion, but a rattling chorus immediately commenced as I rushed up and grasped the bird in my hand in order to free it!" (Lorenz (1970-71, 1:7).

A similar selectivity of concern is exhibited by male golden pheasants toward their young. Like other birds of the order Galliformes, the male golden pheasant leaves to the female the work of caring for the progeny, although he does aid in their defense. Lorenz reports: "I was greatly surprised by a *Chrysolophus* cock which angrily flew at my face when I caught one of his half-grown chicks, although he had otherwise paid no attention to them and had trampled on them in the crudest fashion whilst courting the hen" (1:179).

The most obvious intentional profile of the birds is the one that suits them least: the birds care about the welfare of their confederates or their young, recognize that one of their kind is in trouble, and desire to help.

That they act out of general concern is belied by the jackdaws' disregard for the plight of the injured bird and by the male pheasant's carelessness towards his chicks. One possible alternative is that they act not out of desire to rescue the victim, but because they wish to discourage future predation by depriving the predator of the leisurely enjoyment of its spoils. The problem with this account is that it fails to explain why the jackdaws attacked one of their own members (Lorenz 1970-71, 1:8).

Both of these alternatives proceed from the assumption that the birds have a "rational" end in view and have figured out a "rational" means of achieving it. A more fruitful approach takes its cue from a remark Lorenz attributes to his teacher Oskar Heinroth. When accused of making animals into machines, Heinroth would jokingly reply: "On the contrary, animals are emotional people with very little ability to reason" (Lorenz 1970-71, 2:334; cf. 1:251). In adopting the intentional stance towards animals, one does well to heed this man whom Lorenz considered to be one of the few real experts on animal behavior (1:xv).[2] Keep your intentional story light on the intellectualizing and heavy on the emotion. It will last longer that way.

Keeping it light on the intellectualizing means not being a stickler for the belief-and-desire format. Dennett admits that there are other intentional idioms besides believing and desiring, yet he tends to rely exclusively on these two. The following passage is typical: "One predicts behavior in such a case by ascribing to the system *the possession of certain information* and by supposing it to be *directed by certain goals,* and then by working out the most reasonable or appropriate action on the basis of these ascriptions and suppositions. It is a small step to calling the information possessed the computer's *beliefs,* its goals and subgoals its *desires*" (Dennett 1971, 90; 1978, 6).

For the sorts of cases usually discussed by philosophers, the belief-and-desire format works well enough that there is no need to look for other ways of constructing one's intentional profile. George sees an old man walking down the street. He believes that the man is an influential person who can put him in contact with potential clients. Desiring to generate more business for himself, he goes up to the old man and shakes his hand. Or, George believes that the man is his landlord and that he will ask for the overdue rent. Wishing to avoid being pressed for payment, George ducks into an alley. Or, believing the man is carrying diamonds and wishing to acquire wealth in a hurry, George attacks the man and robs him of his stones.

---

2. For discussion of Heinroth and others who agreed with the spirit of his maxim, see Durant 1981.

Other cases do not easily fit into the belief-and-desire mold. George sees an old man approach. Something about the man's manner makes George uneasy, so he crosses over to the other side of the street. Let us have George admit that he does not think the old man really is crazy or dangerous. George does not believe that the man will actually do anything to him. At most he believes that the man looks sinister. This belief does not play a role in the analysis comparable to the belief that the man is his landlord and will ask for money. George crosses over because the man seems sinister to him, not because he *believes* that the man seems sinister. The basis for action in the landlord case is a belief about the man, whereas in the case of the sinister-looking man it is a feeling toward the man. George may act on the basis of this feeling even though he realizes that it is silly. Call him irrational if you want, but his action is as amenable to treatment in intentional terms as if it were based upon belief.

The most workable intentional story of the jackdaws is one constructed along the lines of George and the sinister-looking man. The story should be told in such a way that things in the world take on emotional significance for the birds. The jackdaws watch the man as he walks through the garden. He is a familiar figure to them, but now there is something in his manner that makes them uneasy. Their gaze falls on the thing he holds in his hands. Carrying the limp black object, he seems sinister. So they give the rattling call and attack.

There is some question whether a straightforward information-and-goals approach such as Dennett describes is adequate even for computers (Dreyfus and Dreyfus 1986). On this issue we have nothing to say, for our concern, as always, is with animals. However, in the latter context a remark of Marvin Minsky, quoted by Dreyfus and Dreyfus, appears all the more apt. Cognitive psychologists believe that their proposition-centered devices such as semantic networks are simpler and more basic than dispositional notions such as feelings and understandings. "But what if feelings and viewpoints are the simpler things? If such dispositions are the elements of which the others are composed, then we must deal with them directly" (Minsky 1980, 118).

9

Making Room for Consciousness

Copernicus's *Revolutions of the Heavenly Spheres* was published in 1543 with an unsigned preface by Andreas Osiander, a Lutheran clergyman. It said that the theory ought not to be taken literally, but merely as a convenient method for astronomical calculation. Adopting the intentional stance is a bit like doing Copernican astronomy à la Osiander: one is not supposed to ask whether the hypothesis is true.

Is it possible to go beyond the intentional stance and treat animal consciousness as a natural phenomenon open to scientific investigation? Donald R. Griffin is one scientist who believes that it is. His two books *The Question of Animal Awareness* (1981) and *Animal Thinking* (1984) have attracted much attention, both favorable and unfavorable. Three refrains run through the critical reviews. The first is that the key terms have not been adequately explicated. The following is from a review of the first edition of *The Question of Animal Awareness:*

> He bandies about mentalistic terms without regard to sense or relevance. The 'rough-and-ready *un*sophisticated definitions' on which he prides himself are no definitions at all but empty verbiage: '*Awareness* is the whole set of interrelated mental images of the flow of events. . . . An *intention* involves mental images of future events in which the intruder pictures himself as a participant . . . The presence of mental images, and their use by an animal to regulate its behavior, provide a pragmatic, working definition of *consciousness.*' A pragmatic working definition? It doesn't work for me. (Humphrey 1977, 522)

Another reviewer comments: "There is no attempt subsequently to sharpen or clarify these working definitions or to articulate them systematically with current developments in the study of animal and human cognition" (Mason 1976, 930).

The second objection is that the hypothesis of animal consciousness is untestable. Latto (1986) remarks that it is not possible to investigate animal consciousness directly and that indirect approaches fail to yield any definitive answers. "Conscious awareness in other animals is a closed world about which we can do no more than speculate" (309). John Krebs (1977) writes: "The test of the value of any scientific hypothesis is whether or not it generates new experiments, and it seems to me that the awareness hypothesis fails this test." If it generates no predictions, then nothing can count against it. This puts it in the realm of pseudoscience.

The third objection is that the hypothesis is superfluous. "It should be perfectly possible to give a full and satisfactory account of animal thinking and cognition in terms of representations without referring to either consciousness or awareness," insists Latto (1986, 313). "The problem of animal mind has not been as completely neglected as he believes," declares Mason (1976, 930), who goes on to criticize "Griffin's failure to appreciate the methods and accomplishments of previous investigations of animal cognition" (931).

These three objections reflect a general philosophical unease which goes beyond the details of Griffin's thesis. In this chapter we examine the unease about attributing subjective experiences to animals. Our position is that the reasons usually given for excluding consciousness from the domain of scientific inquiry—that it is ill-defined, untestable, and superfluous—are themselves open to attack.

EXPLICATION

The history of science shows that there are two ways for concepts to be obsolete. One is illustrated by phlogiston and ether. The later scientists did not criticize their predecessors for having wrongly conceived phlogiston or ether; they claimed there were no such things. The new theories had no counterparts for the old concepts. The other type of obsolescence is exemplified by the scholastic concept of motion. The proponents of the new mechanics rejected the concept of motion as a kind of change or passage from potentiality to actuality. They redefined the concept and thereby introduced a new way of distinguishing between what is moving and what is at rest. Yet the terms "motion" and "rest" continued to be applied to the same range of phenomena as before. At least some clear cases of motion under the old theory remain clear cases under the new theory.

Patricia Churchland (1983) suggests that the traditional concept of consciousness may well be on the way to obsolescence. Is this alleged obsolescence like that of phlogiston and ether (her examples) or like that of motion? That is, are we on the way toward denying that conscious states exist, or toward redefining the concept of consciousness? Moreover, what exactly is this traditional concept of consciousness that science is in the process of rendering obsolete?

Descartes is considered to be the primary exponent of the traditional concept of consciousness. The usual interpretation of Descartes is that one is conscious of all one's mental states in the sense that one is introspectively aware of them. According to Churchland, this concept is undermined by evidence of unconscious mental states and the unreliability of introspection.

If our account in chapter 1 is right, then Descartes did not hold the view that philosophers are wont to attribute to him. The usual interpretation conflates the immediate awareness that is the ingredient of every mental act with introspective awareness of the act. More is at stake here than just interpreting Descartes. Much of the current dissatisfaction with the concept of consciousness stems from the belief that the only viable definition of consciousness is in terms of introspective availability. This opinion needs to be reexamined. Descartes, as we interpret him, is useful in this regard. One can learn from Descartes without committing oneself to the whole Cartesian theory of mind.

Against the "venerable dogma that one's mental life is self-intimating and introspectively available," Churchland argues that "a great deal of intelligent and sentient activity, perhaps the lion's share, goes on without benefit of self-conscious awareness" (1983, 80–81). One item of evidence is unconscious cognitive processing. She cites an example from the 1977 review article by Richard Nisbett and Timothy Wilson:

> Thus Nisbett and Wilson (1977) have shown that when subjects are set the task of evaluating candidates for a job by examining the candidates' files, if they are told they will subsequently meet a particular candidate, this typically results in a more favorable judgment of that candidate than if they are not so told. For the evaluators, this effect on their judgment of expecting to meet the candidate was utterly dumbfounding, for they supposed their evaluations to be based entirely on other considerations. (81)

Is the traditional view really threatened by this data? The subjects were aware of being told which candidates would be interviewed. They were also aware of their own evaluations. What they were not aware of was the causal relation between the two. Who ever maintained that people are always or even usually aware of the causal connections among their various mental states? Certainly not Descartes or any other philosopher in the Cartesian tradition. Indeed, Malebranche went so far as to maintain that we cannot be directly aware of such connections since they do not exist; God causes every mental state. Malebranche's approach, bizarre as it seems, illustrates that the assignment of causes and effects, as well as the nature of the relation between them, depends on what causal theory you subscribe to. This is the very point Nisbett and Wilson are trying to make: subjects are no better than observers at determining the factors that influence their performance, since their reports are based upon a priori causal theories, not upon introspection (Nisbett and Wilson 1977, 249–50). Far from offering a wholesale indictment of introspection, Nisbett and Wilson grant that one has direct access to mental content: "The individual knows a host of personal historical facts; he knows the focus of his attention at any given point in time; he knows what his current sensations are and has what almost all psychologists and philosophers would assert to be 'knowledge' at least quantitatively superior to that of observers concerning his emotions, evaluations, and plans" (255).

Churchland has other items in her arsenal of evidence against the so-called traditional conception of consciousness. Instead of going through all of them, we have selected two that relate to incorrigibility and evidence, the two problematic theses commonly thought to be entailed by the Cartesian theory of mind. The incorrigibility thesis, it will be remembered, is that if I believe I am in a certain state then I am in that state. The evidence thesis is that if I am in a certain state, I know I am in it. The clinical syndrome of blindness denial serves as evidence against the first, subliminal perception against the second. Blindness denial is described by Churchland as follows:

> Certain patients who suffer a sudden onset of blindness due to lesions or trauma to the visual cortex, do not recognize that they have lost their vision and can no longer see. The clinical pattern here is that these patients cannot see, but they are unaware that they are blind, tend to deny their visual deficit, and persist in behaving as though they can see. Often they invent excuses to explain why they bump into the furniture (e.g. "I lost my glasses," "there is too much stuff in here") and they may confabulate when asked to describe what they see (e.g. when the doctor holds up two fingers and asks the patient how many

she sees, she may reply with assurance that she sees four, or she may describe the curtains in the room as red when they are really white, and so on). (Churchland 1983, 82)

The syndrome of blindness denial as described by Critchley (1979) includes a number of different reactions. Some patients refuse to admit that they are blind; others admit it but act as though it is unimportant. Some believe they still have the capacity to see even though it is not being exercised in this instance. Others believe they are exercising the capacity when in fact they are not. The last situation is the important one for Churchland's purposes. She comments: "In some sense, incredible as it may seem, these patients do not know that they do not see. . . . Philosophers may be so dismayed and shocked by the idea, that they may insist the syndrome is wrongly described" (83).

Why would philosophers be dismayed? Presumably because they think it is impossible to be mistaken about one's own mental states. It cannot be the case that the patient believes she sees but in fact does not see. If she believes she sees then she sees.[1] Why do philosophers hold this? Presumably because the incorrigibility thesis is part and parcel of the traditional concept of consciousness. Earlier we showed that it is perfectly consistent with the Cartesian theory of mind to admit that people sometimes misidentify their acts of thinking. Descartes's own example was mistaking conceiving for imagining. There is no reason why the blindness-denial syndrome cannot be treated along similar lines: the patient confuses seeing with imagining that she sees.

In subliminal perception the subject's behavior is affected by a stimulus that is below the threshold for awareness. "The stimulus is subthreshold for awareness in a verbally competent subject if he cannot report the occurrence of the stimulus and denies that he perceived it" (Churchland 1983, 93n). One perceives but does not know that one perceives. Subliminal perception counts against the Cartesian theory of mind only if that theory

---

1. Churchland's description of the situation makes it sound as though the evidence thesis is at stake: "it does seem astonishing that one could fail to know that one has no vision at all" (1983, 83). This is also true of her account in *Neurophilosophy* (1986), where she reports that "several philosophers" have insisted to her that "so long as one is conscious, and so long as one can make judgments at all, *then* if one is not having visual experiences, one will be aware that one is not having visual experiences, and vice versa. In a word, you cannot fail to know whether you are blind" (229). This is not the usual interpretation of the evidence thesis, nor is it a corollary of it. One can be aware of every state one is in without being aware of every state one is not in.

entails the evidence thesis. We argued earlier that it does not. According to Descartes, one can have a mental episode without reflecting on it while it is occurring, and one can forget one's mental episodes immediately after they happen. Cartesian philosophy is in basic agreement with the following statement by Nisbett and Wilson (1977, 240): "We cannot perceive without perceiving, but we can perceive without remembering." Far from posing a threat to Cartesianism, the phenomenon of subliminal perception readily admits of Cartesian explanation. As with the thoughts of fetuses and sleeping adults, the perceptions do not produce the sorts of brain traces that are required for memory and verbal report.

Churchland's error is to equate the "transparency" and "self-intimating" nature of mental life with introspective availability. The terms properly refer to nonreflective, immediate consciousness. Before we follow Churchland in consigning the "venerable dogma that one's mental life is self-intimating . . . to the museum of quaint and antiquated myths" (80), we should consider whether the Cartesian distinction between two types of consciousness is a viable one.

David Rosenthal (1986) advocates a distinction between reflective and nonreflective awareness, but his way of drawing it is different from that which we have ascribed to Descartes.

Cartesian mentality is defined in terms of consciousness; all mental states are conscious states. Not so for Rosenthal. Conscious states are a subclass of mental states. They differ from unconscious mental states in that they are accompanied by higher-order thoughts, whereas the latter are not. A mental state is conscious, says Rosenthal, if and only if one has "a roughly contemporaneous thought that one is in that mental state" (335). For Descartes, to think that one is in a mental state is to be introspectively aware of that state. Not for Rosenthal. Introspective or reflective awareness requires a *conscious* thought that one is in a mental state; that is, the thought that one is in a mental state must itself be the object of a higher-order thought. "Introspective awareness of a particular mental state is having a thought that one is in that mental state, and also a thought that one has that thought. Having a conscious mental state without introspectively focusing on it is having the second-order thought without the third-order thought" (337).

The advantage of this account, according to Rosenthal, is that it puts us "in a position to advance a useful, informative explanation of what makes conscious states conscious. Since a mental state is conscious if it is accompanied by a suitable higher-order thought, we can explain a mental state's being conscious by hypothesizing that the mental state itself causes that higher-order thought to occur" (336). The disadvantage of the Cartesian approach is that by defining mentality in terms of consciousness, it rules out the possibility of explaining consciousness in terms of mentality. "It is plain that we cannot explain or analyze consciousness at all unless we can do so in terms of some sort of mental phenomenon" (340). Hence the Cartesian view "prevents us from explaining consciousness in any useful way" (341).

The phrase "to explain consciousness" has two meanings: to give a causal explanation of the phenomenon, and to provide an explication or analysis of the concept. When Rosenthal proposes "a useful, informative explanation" in terms of the mental state causing the higher-order thought, he is using "explanation" in the first sense. When he criticizes the Cartesian view for not "explaining consciousness in any useful way," he is using the term in the second sense. His objection to Cartesian consciousness is not that it is causally unexplainable, but that the concept is unanalyzable.

Rosenthal acknowledges that there is an alternative to his own analysis: "Conscious mental states are conscious . . . because they are about themselves. And this self-reference is intrinsic; it does not result from some connection those states have with other mental states" (345). This is essentially the position taken by Franz Brentano in his *Psychology from an Empirical Standpoint* (1973, 128): "We can say that the sound is the *primary object* of the *act* of hearing, and that the act of hearing itself is the *secondary object*. . . . The act of hearing appears to be directed toward sound in the most proper sense of the term, and because of this it seems to apprehend itself incidentally and as something additional." Rosenthal admits that it is possible to pursue this line of reasoning within a Cartesian framework. He fails to see that Descartes actually held a version of this view. The Cartesian distinction between C1 (consciousness as a mental act) and C2 (consciousness as the ingredient of an act) is analogous to Brentano's distinction between introspection or inner observation, which requires a separate act, and inner perception, which does not. Unlike Brentano, Descartes believed that introspection was possible: one mental act can have another as its primary object. The cognitive role that Brentano assigns to inner perception is thus fulfilled in Descartes's system by C1.

Rosenthal's main objection to consciousness as intrinsic to the act is that "there is no nonarbitrary way to distinguish this view from an account in terms of higher-order thoughts" (345). We take issue with this statement. There is an important theoretical difference that bears on the question of animal consciousness.

Rosenthal's account is heavily committed to the philosophical thesis that awareness is propositional. Both immediate and introspective awareness

consist in having a thought that something is the case. In immediate awareness one has the thought that one is in a certain state; in introspection,
one has the thought that one has this thought. He does not specify the
mode of thought other than to say that it "is not mediated by any inference
or perceptual input" (335–36). It seems to be either a judgment or a nonsensory
perception, perhaps both.

However one construes it, a fair degree of mental sophistication is
obviously involved even for the second-order thought that one is in a mental
state. Are infants and animals capable of forming such a thought? They
must be if they have conscious mental states. Rosenthal's response is that
infants and animals have sufficient mental ability to think such thoughts:
"But one need not have much ability to think to be able to have a thought
that one is in a particular sensation. Infants and nonhuman animals can
discriminate among external objects, and master regularities pertaining to
them. So most of these beings can presumably form thoughts about such
objects, albeit primitive thoughts that are very likely not conscious. No more
is needed to have thoughts about one's more salient sensory experiences"
(350). This answer will not do. It is not enough to be able to discriminate
among external objects and form thoughts about them. As Rosenthal has
set up the situation, one must be able to form a thought about *oneself*,
namely, the thought that one is in a certain mental state.

The alternative account places no such cognitive burden on infants and
animals. Consciousness as the ingredient of a mental act is nonpropositional,
being directed toward the mental episode itself rather than toward the fact
that one is having it. Since it involves neither judgment nor intellectual
apprehension, it need not be associated exclusively with higher cerebral
processes.

The issue here is the explication of consciousness, not of mentality.
The following two questions can and should be separated: (1) Is the Cartesian
view of consciousness, with its distinction between C1 and C2, workable?
(2) Was Descartes right that all mental states are conscious states? An
affirmative answer to either question by no means entails a like answer
to the other. In particular, one can accept and use the Cartesian distinction
between immediate and reflective consciousness without committing oneself
to the Cartesian thesis that the subject has immediate consciousness of all
its mental states.

In Cartesian C2 consciousness, being conscious of mental state x is
both necessary and sufficient for the existence of x. One can accept this
as a characterization of immediate consciousness without holding that all
mental states can be filled in for x. The result is a division of mental states

into those of which the subject is immediately conscious and those of which it is not. The latter can occur without the subject's being aware of them whereas the former cannot. The subject can introspect either kind through the introduction of a further thought.

How can there be introspection of an unconscious mental state? The question brings out an ambiguity in the term "introspect." It has both a wide and a narrow meaning. The wide meaning is thinking about what is or was going on in one's own mind. The narrow meaning is reflecting upon mental phenomena of which one is or was conscious at the time of their occurrence. You can think about the cognitive process by which you solved a given problem even though you were unaware of the process at the time. This is introspection in the first sense but not in the second. One of the problems confronting cognitive psychologists is to determine which sense of introspection is involved in subjects' verbal reports of their own cognitive processes. Are they reporting on how it seemed to them at the time, or are they theorizing on how they must have done it? (cf. Nisbett and Wilson 1977; Ericsson and Simon 1980).

TESTABILITY

According to conventional wisdom, conscious experiences, especially those of nonverbal individuals, are not amenable to scientific study because statements about them cannot be observationally verified or falsified. The argument has roots in the logical positivist criterion of factual meaningfulness (Hempel 1965) and Popper's (1959) criterion of demarcation. It has two forms corresponding to two notions of falsifiability. The first form we call the *privacy* argument, the second the *predictability* argument.

The privacy argument can be summarized thus: Consciousness is private to the individual who has it. Science is by nature a public enterprise. Therefore consciousness is not open to scientific investigation. The following passage by a neurologist shows the privacy argument in action:

> As a clinical neurologist I have been trained not to deal with the concept of consciousness. I can deal with responsiveness, for that I can test with a stimulus, grading the response or noting the nonresponse. What is going on in that patient's brain between the stimulus and the response is his own province. Presumably, what is going on is consciousness or awareness of the stimulus and response— but it is still the private domain of that individual. Therefore, I will deal with responsiveness and hope that "consciousness" fades into a well-deserved obscurity. (Joynt 1981, 109)

How my pain feels to me, what it is like for me to see green, what it seems me I am doing when I solve a problem—such experiences are my private domain. I can tell you about them and you can use my reports as behavioral data, but you should not consider them to be part of the corpus of scientific assertions. Others have, at least in principle, the means to determine my behavior and my neurological states, but only I have access to my subjective experiences. The same is true of animals, supposing they have subjective experiences. Because consciousness is private, any statement about it, whether made by the individual who has it or by an observer, is irrefutable and hence not a scientific statement at all but something else instead: pseudoscience, metaphysics, fairy tale, or nonsense.

The privacy argument assumes that the only kind of access that counts is direct access. The privacy of consciousness renders any hypothesis about it unverifiable or falsifiable by direct observation, where "observation" means "intersubjective experience." One cannot enter another individual's mind for a firsthand look at what it is like for that individual. In this respect hypotheses about the conscious experiences of others are like hypotheses about what happened in the distant past: they, too, cannot be established as true or false by directly observing the events they describe.

The privacy argument is analogous to an argument often given by creationists: Neither creation nor evolution is a scientific theory because neither is falsifiable, and neither is falsifiable since we cannot go back and observe origins. Like the creationist argument, the privacy argument works from too narrow a conception of what counts as falsifiable. A hypothesis itself need not refer to publicly observable events so long as it has publicly observable consequences (Radner and Radner 1982). This principle is accepted in virtually every scientific field. Why not then apply it to hypotheses about consciousness, including animal consciousness?

The predictability argument applies the criterion of indirect falsifiability to consciousness hypotheses and finds them wanting. The argument goes like this. Consider the hypothesis that individuals of a certain class have subjective experiences. This is a testable hypothesis if and only if some observable state of affairs follows from it but not from its denial. No such empirical prediction follows from it. Thus there is no prediction the falsity of which would constitute evidence against it. Therefore the hypothesis does not deserve the label "scientific."

The key step in the argument is the premise that every empirical consequence of the consciousness hypothesis is also a consequence of its denial. Two strategies are commonly used to support this premise. One is the "show me" challenge. Where is the prediction that can serve as the basis for a crucial experiment to decide the issue? The other strategy, favored in arguments against human consciousness, is to propose an imaginary situation in which no empirical consequences follow from the hypothesis that an individual is in a certain conscious state. The fact that one can successfully complete such a thought experiment is supposed to show that consciousness hypotheses cannot be tested empirically. We shall examine the latter strategy first. Two venerable thought experiments, the inverted spectrum and the zombie, will serve as illustrations.

Suppose that Ralph's experience of seeing red is exactly like Mabel's experience of seeing green and vice versa. Both individuals have learned the appropriate circumstances for applying the color names, so they both call the same things "red." When they drive up to a traffic light, both of them correctly stop on "red" and proceed on "green," but the stoplight looks to Mabel as the go light looks to Ralph. No empirical test will show that their subjective experiences are different, for they always give identical responses in all color identification problems. How do we know that we are not in the same situation as Ralph and Mabel, that what looks green to you looks red to me and vice versa? No empirical test can settle the issue. Therefore the question is scientifically meaningless. Therefore—here comes the crucial step—consciousness is not amenable to scientific study.[2]

The nice thing about imaginary setups is that they can be left fuzzy wherever it is convenient to the argument and adjusted willy-nilly whenever challenged. The inverted spectrum puzzle focuses on the individuals' behavior and blithely ignores their physiology. If one ventures the reasonable suggestion that some sort of neurological wire-crossing must have occurred (e.g., Putnam 1981, 80), the story can easily be amended. Oh yes, I forgot to tell you that their brain states are identical. Thus neurological as well as behavioral tests are useless.

The zombie is the end of the line for this train of thought experiment. Suppose that instead of seeing green where the rest of us see red, Ralph sees nothing at all. To be more precise, he behaves appropriately in response to color stimuli—he stops at red lights, calls them "red," and so on—but he has no subjective experience of seeing anything. Nagel (1974) describes conscious or subjective experience in terms of its being "like something" for the individual. Following this description we must confess that it is not like anything for Ralph to see red.

There is more to the story. Ralph does not simply lack the experience of seeing red; he has no conscious experience whatsoever. Yet in spite of

---

2. For an abbreviated version of this argument see Kosslyn 1983, xiv–xv.

it he behaves exactly as we do. Question him about how he feels or how things seem to him, and he will answer just like anyone else. If you think that consciousness is a phenomenon to be investigated scientifically, then you must believe that there is some meaningful difference between zombies and ordinary conscious folks. But there is no difference that makes a difference. Writes Dennett toward the close of his zombie exercise: "I have been playing along with this zombie idea—for tactical reasons that should now be obvious—but in fact I think (in case you have not already guessed) that the concept is just incoherent" (1982, 178).

A child hearing the story of Ralph the zombie would want to know how he got to be that way. Is there something wrong with Ralph's brain? Is he a robot? Under a magic spell? The purveyors of the thought experiment would have us believe the answer doesn't matter. The story treats consciousness independently of any causal connections it might have with particular physiological processes. For this very reason the argument fails to make its point.

To see why this is so, let us set aside the consciousness question for a moment and turn to another thought experiment: the perfect forgery.

Suppose a group of clever craftsmen creates a forgery of Holbein's portrait of Sir Brian Tuke. Somehow they manage to smuggle it into the National Gallery of Art in Washington, D.C., and hang it beside the original. Then they swallow cyanide capsules and fall dead on the floor, where they are found the next morning along with the two paintings. So skillfully executed is their masterpiece that all the experts and all the tests in the world fail to detect the least difference between the two paintings. There is no way to figure out which is the original and which is the forgery.

Does our little flight of fancy have any consequences for the art world as it actually exists? In particular, does it establish that the concept of a forgery is incoherent or that there is no meaningful difference between a forgery and an original? Of course not. Proposing an imaginary situation of this sort does nothing to undermine the efficacy of the tests in the real world. Many forgeries are in fact detected and originals authenticated, subject of course to revision in light of future evidence. The thought experiment provides no grounds for systematically doubting such judgments. All it does is to bring out the meanings of the concepts. Even though the two paintings are indistinguishable with respect to their observable properties, one of them is still the original *Sir Brian Tuke* and the other a forgery. The original is the one painted by Hans Holbein the Younger. Aestheticians are welcome to argue whether the perfect forgery is art, but they would be misguided indeed if they used the story as an excuse to abandon factual discussions of original works of art and how they differ from forgeries. Originals and forgeries fit into different causal networks. They have different histories. Those histories are discoverable in principle if not always in fact.

In order to rectify the story so the forgery is undetectable in principle, we must have the forgers duplicate the causal network of the original. Then we can no longer call it "forgery." The reason, however, is not that the concept of forgery has been demonstrated to be incoherent, but only that it no longer makes sense in this particular imaginary case.

Something similar is going on with the zombie and the inverted spectrum. One describes the behavior of the individuals and leaves aside any questions about their physical makeup. The tacit assumption is that consciousness is by nature causally independent of any particular brain processes. Who subscribes to this assumption? Certainly not those of us who favor a materialist approach to consciousness. Dualists insist that conscious states are something over and above physical states; but even the most flagrant dualist need not assume that there is no causal connection between the two kinds of states.[3] The thought experiments make us realize that, as with other direct unobservables, the way to get at consciousness is to consider it as an element in a causal network. To maintain the illusion of the perfect zombie, the child's question has to be confronted. The zombie's neurophysiology as well as its behavior exactly matches our own but the causal laws are suspended—in other words, magic is involved. Zombiehood is undetectable, not because consciousness is unobservable in principle, but because the story has cut off the means to observe it. The fact that one can imagine a perfect zombie no more shows the untestability of consciousness than the fact that one can paint oneself into a corner shows the impossibility of painting a whole floor.

The remaining strategy for undermining testability is the "show me" challenge. Take the hypothesis that bats have conscious experiences, or as Nagel (1974) says, there is "something that it is like to be a bat." If this is a testable hypothesis, what predictions follow from it that do not also follow from hypotheses in which consciousness plays no role? Griffin (1981, 1984) offers a large body of evidence in support of animal awareness. At no point is the opposition forced to say, "Yes, that can only be explained by bringing in the subjective experiences of the animal."

We believe that the quest for a smoking gun is misguided. Testable consequences do not always cash out as incontrovertible evidence. This is

---

3. The impossibility of causal interaction between the mental and the physical is not a corollary of dualism per se, although it does follow from dualism plus a certain causal theory (R. A. Watson 1966; Radner 1985).

especially true when the hypothesis itself is in need of, but lacks, a higher-order explanation. Once again we shall avail ourselves of an analogy before we elaborate with regard to consciousness.

Biologists distinguish between what they call the fact and the theory of evolution. The fact of evolution is that all species are descended from a common ancestor. Darwin's term for it was "descent with modification." The theory of evolution deals with the mechanisms by which the changes occur. Debates concerning Darwinian natural selection, Wright's sampling drift, Eldredge and Gould's punctuated equilibrium, and Kimura's neutral mutations all pertain to evolutionary theory. Stephen Jay Gould draws a strict line between fact and theory: "And facts and theories are different things, not rungs in a hierarchy of increasing certainty. Facts are the world's data. Theories are structures of ideas that explain and interpret facts" (1983, 254). The line is not so simply drawn. A fact in one context may be a theory in another, depending on whether it is being explained or doing the explaining. The "fact" of evolution, descent with modification, is itself an idea that explains a body of data that includes the fossil record and the hierarchical arrangement of similarities among living organisms. It in turn is explained in terms of the mechanisms described in the theory of evolution. Niles Eldredge, in contrast to Gould, downplays the distinction between fact and theory: "Philosophers of science have argued long and hard over the differences between facts, hypotheses, and theories. But the real point is this: they are all essentially the same. All of them are ideas" (1982, 29).

Both Gould and Eldredge are addressing the creationist charge that evolution is "just a theory." Their point is that a theory is not a poor cousin of a fact, that uncertainty is not the defining feature of a theory. We are not interested here in creationist misunderstandings. Our analogy has to do with the triumvirate of fossil record, fact of evolution, and theory of evolution.

That all organisms are descended from a common ancestor is not something that can be directly observed. But if it did happen, then there should be traces of it—objects or events that are available for direct examination now. The fossil record provides a strong body of evidence for descent with modification. Yet there was a time when eminent scientists could look at the fossil record, as much of it as was then available to them, and deny the transmutation of species. Charles Lyell, the great geologist and friend of Darwin, believed that species were immutable. Some species went extinct when they could no longer adapt to local circumstances. Other species were created or "called into being." In this way the number of species remained constant. Darwin was converted to transformationism before he formulated his theory of natural selection (Kohn 1980). Until he had a mechanism to explain it, however, its status as fact was far from secure. The evidence that led to his conversion, such as the two ostrich species he found in South America, posed difficulties for the immutability view, but not fatal ones.

The hypothesis of animal consciousness is in roughly the same position as the fact of evolution before the formulation of a theory of evolution. It is supported by behavioral evidence and physiological analogies. An explanatory mechanism for consciousness still eludes us. Since the clearest case of a conscious being, namely oneself, has a brain, and since the brain obviously has something to do with consciousness, it is safe to assert that the explanation of consciousness must ultimately be in terms of the functioning of the brain and must wait until significant advances have been made in neurophysiology. Because there is at present no viable physiological theory of consciousness, the "fact" of animal consciousness is far from secure. The evidence offered in support of it is not likely to attain smoking-gun status. Nevertheless, predictions can be made from it. What kind of predictions? Much the same sort as follow from the fact of evolution, to wit, if you keep looking for data, you will find more of the same.

Simpler forms of life appear earlier in the fossil record than do the more complex. One prediction of descent with modification is that this pattern will be upheld as more evidence comes in. If the pattern turns out to be significantly violated, this would count against the fact of evolution. Likewise, prediction from the "fact" of animal consciousness has to do not with any specific behavior, but with the filling in of a pattern. The pattern involves similarities—both structural and functional—between animal and human brains, as well as similarities of animal behaviors to those that in humans are indicative of subjective experiences. If similarities are systematically absent in a given species, this would count against the ascription of consciousness to that species.

SUPERFLUITY

A hypothesis may be testable yet superfluous. Testability has to do with the relation between hypothesis and evidence. Superfluity is a relation of the hypothesis to some alternative hypothesis. A hypothesis is testable provided it generates predictions that are in principle capable of refuting it. It is superfluous if another available hypothesis can do everything it can do and do it better.

Is the hypothesis of animal consciousness superfluous? If it is, what alternative makes it so? The usual answer is that cognitive psychology provides models of mental processes that make no appeal to consciousness. One can study the mental states and processes of animals, and use this information to explain various behaviors, without raising any questions about the animals' subjective experiences. Tightly knit as it seems, the answer contains a loose thread. Let us try pulling it and see what happens.

Scientific concepts can function either on the level of facts or phenomena to be explained, or on the level of theories that do the explaining. A given concept can play one role in one context and the other in another. Darwinian descent with modification, for instance, explains the fossil record and is in turn explained by natural selection, and so on. When animal consciousness is dismissed as superfluous, we must ask whether the dismissal refers to consciousness as a phenomenon to be explained or as an explanatory device. The most plausible answer is that consciousness is superfluous in the latter role. Anything that can be explained by it can be explained equally well without it.

When cognitive psychologists study human mental performances such as problem solving, they typically ask the subjects for verbal reports on what they are thinking. The verbal reports are data that require explanation in terms of cognitive mechanisms (Ericsson and Simon 1980). The psychologists have the option of formulating their explanation such that consciousness does not play an explanatory role. They may find later on that this was the wrong choice, just as the "energeticists" in the late nineteenth century attempted to formulate all their explanations of physical processes without acknowledging atoms and ultimately failed. Should it turn out that consciousness is a causal factor in the process of generating introspective reports, then cognitive psychology would not have rendered superfluous the hypothesis that humans have conscious experiences.

What has just been said about human introspective reporting holds equally for the performances of any organism: if consciousness is a causal factor in any cognitive process, then the hypothesis that the individual has conscious experiences of a given kind is not superfluous. To illustrate how this cashes out in cognitive ethology, we shall ask some new questions about an old topic: vocal mimicry in birds.

Avian vocal mimicry, or interspecific vocal imitation by birds, is usually studied with a view to the evolutionary function of the behavior (e.g., Howard 1973; Rechten 1978). The evolutionary debate revolves around two questions. First, are the imitations a means of "cheating" or merely of increasing repertoire size? Second, are they directed toward the singer's own species, the model species, or a third species?[4] Relatively little attention has been paid to the mimicking process itself, to what the bird is doing when it mimics. It has been suggested that loquacious birds are apt to mimic by chance, and that shared environmental factors or a shared history can give rise to resemblances in vocalization (Baylis 1982). A research program can be set up to determine the extent to which good mimics such as mockingbirds derive their vocalizations from previously heard songs of other species. Once this has been established, one can go on to ask about the cognitive processes involved.

At the risk of being branded hopeless sentimentalists, we wish to suggest that from a strictly cognitive point of view, avian vocal imitation can be treated on a par with human representational art. The avian imitator represents (literally re-presents) a part of its environment. Some of the same sorts of questions that are asked about artistic representation can be asked about vocal imitation by good mimics. These questions include the following: What features of the auditory environment interest the imitator? What role, if any, is played by the phenomenology of perceiving? Does it make any difference to the final product what it was like for a mockingbird to hear a whip-poor-will?

The statement that consciousness is a causal factor in a certain type of cognitive process means that the existence and nature of the individual's subjective experience affect the unfolding of the process. The claim that consciousness plays no explanatory role in animal cognitive psychology, then, amounts to this: even if an animal has subjective experiences, they in no way influence the animal's cognitive states or processes. In no problem-solving situation does it make any difference how things seem to the animal or, indeed, whether they seem at all. It is by no means a corollary of cognitive theory that this should be the case. If it is being put forward as the best position on animal cognition, it should be argued for.

In dismissing consciousness as superfluous, one sets limits on one's explanatory apparatus. It is important to realize that the limits are set by

---

4. Biological mimicry as defined by Wickler (1968) involves three roles: (1) the mimic, which resembles another species and gains an advantage thereby; (2) the model, which it resembles; and (3) the signal receiver, which mistakes the mimic for the model. A familiar instance of visual mimicry is that certain nonpoisonous butterflies are avoided by predators because they look like poisonous species. In this example the mimic, the model, and the signal receiver are all different species. A signal receiver can also belong either to the mimic's species or to the model's. This characterization, though useful in regard to visual mimicry, is inadequate when applied to avian vocal mimicry, especially insofar as it rules out functional accounts in which no one mistakes the mimic for the model (Baylis 1982).

choice, self-imposed, not dictated by any fundamental principles of scientific methodology. There is room for consciousness if one is willing to make room for it.

10

Relevance to Ethics

We have tried in this book to clear away some of the metaphysical and methodological stumbling blocks to the study of animal consciousness. If animal consciousness is indeed open to empirical investigation, then the results of such an inquiry will obviously have some bearing on the morality of our treatment of animals. This moral relevance is the subject of the present chapter. Our aim is not to advance one ethical theory over another but only to show how information gained from the study of animal consciousness can be put to use in ethics.

By themselves data about animal consciousness have no ethical consequences. To argue directly from "Calves suffer from extreme confinement" to "Calves ought not to be so confined" is to go from what is to what ought to be. Inferences of this type are generally dismissed as fallacious. It has recently been argued that some moves from is to ought are not fallacies, that ethical norms can be derived from facts about human evolution (Richards 1986a, b). Whether this argument succeeds or not, our original point still stands: no ethical consequences follow directly from data about animal consciousness. Even if it is possible to derive ethical norms from facts about human nature, it is not possible to derive injunctions about how to treat animals directly from facts about animal nature. In order to arrive at the conclusion "Calves ought not to be confined," one needs the premise that, special considerations aside, one ought not to inflict suffering on a being capable of suffering. This premise must be grounded in an ethical theory.

It might be objected that although the fact that certain animals have conscious experiences has no direct moral consequences, the fact that certain animals lack them does have a direct moral consequence, namely, that it is morally permissible to mistreat those animals. The term "mistreat" has the same meaning here as when applied to an automobile or a sewing machine: to mistreat a thing is to handle it in such a way as to contribute to its malfunction or breakdown. This argument fails for the same reason as the previous one about not inflicting suffering. An additional premise is needed to get to the desired conclusion. In this case, the premise is that it is morally permissible to mistreat a being lacking conscious experiences. This premise, too, must be grounded in an ethical theory. Something is morally permitted only if it is not morally prohibited. What are the limits of moral prohibition? There are ways of setting the limits so that it becomes wrong to mistreat inanimate objects—not because wrong has been done to the object, but because in mistreating it one does wrong to persons. If moral prohibitions can cover acts done to inanimate objects, they can also extend to treatments of nonconscious organisms.

Most people agree that it is wrong to perform certain types of actions with regard to animals, for example, to inflict gratuitous suffering on them. Why is it wrong to do such things? The question can only be answered in the context of an ethical theory. Different theories give different answers.

"Act so that you treat humanity, whether in your own person or in that of another, always as an end and never as a means only." So reads one formulation of Kant's famous categorical imperative (Kant 1969, 54). The justification for restricting it to humanity is that only rational beings are ends in themselves, and humans are the only rational beings we know of. The Cartesians sought to keep animals out of the kingdom of heaven. Kant's concern is to keep them out of the kingdom of ends. According to Kant, animals are not ends in themselves. They have value merely as means and as such they are "things." Since we have duties only to beings that are ends in themselves, we have no duty *to* animals. We do, however, have a duty *with regard to* them. This indirect duty is based on a direct duty to humanity. Kant explains in the *Lectures on Ethics* (1963, 240): "If a man shoots his dog because the animal is no longer capable of service, he does not fail in his duty to the dog, for the dog cannot judge, but his act is inhuman and damages in himself that humanity which it is his duty to show towards mankind. If he is not to stifle his human feelings, he must practice kindness towards animals, for he who is cruel to animals becomes hard also in his dealings with men."

Kant is hardly being "indulgent to men" in their dealings with animals, as Descartes was. Kant's idea of what counts as maltreatment is, if anything, even stricter than the usual one; the passage above bears witness. Many people find the Kantian position on animals disturbing. Their disquiet stems not from the kind of treatment it enjoins, but from the reason for the injunction: that cruelty to animals tends to make one callous towards human suffering and kindness to animals fosters kindly feelings towards people. The British moral philosopher Henry Sidgwick (1966, 241) called it "a hard-hearted paradox" insofar as it gives no weight to the animal's suffering per se (cf. Hoff 1983).

One strategy for getting around the paradox is to give animals moral status in their own right. This can be done either by attributing reason (the morally relevant brand) to them, or else by denying the Kantian premise that only rational beings are ends in themselves. Few people are willing to take the first alternative, although Richard A. Watson (1979) suggests that some animals, including chimpanzees, dolphins, dogs, and pigs, sometimes intend to act with reference to moral principles and at other times lapse into a state of amorality like Camus's stranger. Defenders of the second alternative argue that animals, at least the higher forms, have moral status simply in virtue of having interests. In the oft-quoted words of the nineteenth-century philosopher Jeremy Bentham, "The question is not, Can they *reason?* nor, Can they *talk?* but, Can they *suffer?*" (1962, 1:143).

At this point there is a further divergence of views. Of those who link inherent value with interests, some defend rightness or wrongness in terms of consequences, whereas others hold that moral worth does not stem from consequences. Theories of the first kind, in which consequences determine moral worth, are called *teleological;* theories of the second kind, *deontological.* Teleological theories include the class of theories known as *utilitarianism.* There are two main types of utilitarian theory: act and rule utilitarianism. Act utilitarians consider the consequences of individual actions, whereas rule utilitarians look to the consequences of rules or general policies.

Bentham was an act utilitarian. According to his principle of utility, an action is good if it tends to increase the balance of happiness or pleasure in the total number of individuals affected by the action, and bad if it tends to increase the balance of unhappiness or pain. Higher pleasures are given no more weight in the calculation than lower pleasures. "Prejudice apart, the game of push-pin is of equal value with the arts and sciences of music and poetry. If the game of push-pin furnish more pleasure, it is more valuable than either" (2:253). Here Bentham compares two sets of activities that are at least in part intellectual. A pig can enjoy push-pin no more than poetry. Nevertheless, the spirit of Bentham's aphorism supports animal interests. When intensity, duration, and so on, are taken into account, simple porcine pleasures can outweigh either push-pin or poetry.

John Stuart Mill, himself a utilitarian, objected to this sort of disregard for the quality of pleasure. "It is better to be a human being dissatisfied than a pig satisfied; better to be Socrates dissatisfied than a fool satisfied. And if the fool, or the pig, is of a different opinion, it is because they only know their own side of the question. The other party to the comparison knows both sides" (Mill 1969, 212). We shall return to this passage shortly.

The way to grant animals moral standing in a utilitarian theory is to include their interests among the consequences to be taken into account. The way to bring animals into the moral realm in a deontological theory is to include them among the beings who have moral rights. Peter Singer (1975, 1978) is a utilitarian. He denies that his case for animal liberation is based upon extending rights to animals. "The only right I ever attribute to animals is the 'right' to equal consideration of interests, and anything that is expressed by talking of such a right could equally well be expressed by the assertion that animals' interests ought to be given equal consideration with the like interests of humans" (1978, 122). Tom Regan (1982, 1983) is a deontologist. His argument for giving moral status to animals can be summarized as follows: Animals have interests. Whatever has interests has inherent value. Whatever has inherent value has rights. Therefore animals have rights. The concepts of right and duty are correlative: a being having rights is a being to whom duties are owed. Since one must know one's duty in order to do it, and only rational beings can know their duty, animals have no duties. We have duties to them, but they have none to us or to one another. They are moral patients but not moral agents.

On the question of whether animal interests are better defended by utilitarian or by deontological principles, we have nothing to say. The answer to this question would require a detailed assessment of the relative merits of the two kinds of ethical theory, a task far beyond the scope of the present work. Our concern here is not with the validity of this or that moral theory, but only with the relevance of data on animal consciouness to moral judgments having to do with animals.

Once animals are let into the moral domain, moral agents are obligated to take their interests into account in actions affecting them. In order to take animal interests into account, one must know what they are. An adequate moral theory will provide principles for deciding whose interests take precedence when there is a conflict between the interests of one individual or group and those of another. This is true whether the conflict is between the interests of two humans, an animal and a human, or two animals. In matters involving the weighting of interests, both animal rightists and utili-tarians tend to confine their discussions to the most general categories:

nonsentient versus sentient beings, animals versus humans. Questions involving comparison betweeen species of higher animals are either sidestepped altogether or else given cursory treatment. The attitude seems to be, How can we compare their interests when we have no access to their conscious experiences? By undermining this sort of skepticism, we open the door for a more extended analysis of ethical choice involving animals.

We shall use two examples to show what happens when inadequate consideration is given to the unique interests of different species. One concerns Mill's satisfied pig. The other has to do with animal rights and the predator question.

A PIG SATISFIED

For utilitarians as well as for the defenders of animal rights, whenever one set of interests is allowed to trump another, and a choice has to be made on the basis of the quality of the individuals' lives, humans always win out over nonhumans. Mill's remark about the satisfied pig illustrates this attitude in a utilitarian context. The interesting thing about this passage is Mill's insistence that whereas the pig and the fool know only their own sides of the question, the other party to the comparison knows both sides. That is to say, the wise man knows what it is to be a fool satisfied, and the person knows what it is to be a pig satisfied. Some would respond to Mill that no human being could possibly have such knowledge about pigs. This is not our position, for we have argued that animal consciousness is knowable, albeit indirectly and incompletely. Our quarrel with Mill has to do with *how* the person knows the quality of the pig's satisfaction.

We presume that Mill is not thinking of cases such as Konrad Lorenz knowing what it is like for a jackdaw to be satisfied; since this sort of knowledge comes only with long years of experience, and few people have studied pigs or the ethological literature pertaining to them. For Mill, the knowledge of pig satisfaction is gained, not by observing pigs, but by observing oneself. Mill takes the person-pig relation to be analogous to that between a wise man and a fool. Take wisdom away from a wise man and you have a fool. Analogously, take away a person's ability to reason and you have just another animal—like a pig. The wise man deems the fool's satisfaction inferior, because he is himself capable of it and also, by virtue of his wisdom, capable of a superior satisfaction. Likewise, the person deems the animal's satisfaction inferior, because he is capable of the same sort of satisfaction, plus a higher satisfaction by virtue of his intellectual faculties.

There is great potential for mischief in letting the matter be resolved in this way. The wise man values his wisdom more than he values whatever he shares with fools. But he is apt to underrate foolishness if he bases his assessment of it purely on his own case. A wise man gains less satisfaction from playing the fool than fools enjoy from their tomfoolery. In extrapolating from his own case, the wise man should consider that the fulfillment of foolish desires may give higher satisfaction when those desires are unified and integrated into a fool's way of life.

The question of unity or structure becomes all the more pressing when human satisfactions are compared to those of pigs. Deprive a person of his or her specifically human faculties and you get a deficient human being. Deprive a pig of those same faculties and you have a perfectly normal, well-functioning pig. Human beings have certain desires more or less in common with pigs. They also have other desires unique to their species. Pigs, too, have other desires of their own. Humans judge in their own case that their uniquely human desires admit of a higher quality of satisfaction than their piggish desires. But the quality of satisfaction afforded by piggish desires is not necessarily the same for people and pigs. Because these desires are integrated differently in a pig, their fulfillment may give satisfaction of a higher order than fulfillment of the corresponding desires in a human being. For this reason, the person is well advised to look to the pig before claiming to know both sides of the comparison.

Undoubtedly, the student of animal behavior will come to the same conclusion as Mill's introspective wise man: it is indeed better to be a person dissatisfied than a pig satisfied. Why then bother to examine the pig at all? Mill sticks to the easy case of people versus pigs. How are we to settle the matter when the parties to the comparison are both animals? Is it better to be a pig dissatisfied than a mouse satisfied? This may seem to be a frivolous question, but it is not at all frivolous if you are both an experimenter on animals and a utilitarian who allows animals into the moral sphere. Then the choice of animals for experimentation becomes, in part, a moral choice, and its settlement by utilitarian principles requires a judgment about relative capacities for satisfaction. To make an informed judgment in this regard, the experimenter needs to know about the life styles of the experimental candidates.

THE PREDATOR QUESTION

The predator-prey situation has been used alternatively to illustrate both nature's disregard for the plight of her creatures ("nature red in tooth and claw") and nature's beneficence ("the balance of nature"). As a purely natural process, predation is not subject to moral commendation or condemnation. It is neither right nor wrong. Yet once animals are admitted into the moral domain, a moral question about predation arises. Predation represents a case of conflicting interests, at least on the individual level. It is in the fox's interest to catch the rabbit and in the rabbit's interest to escape. Assuming that both animals are beings with moral status, the question of whether or not to intervene becomes a moral question for human moral agents observing the process. Tom Regan discusses the predator question in the context of his theory of animal rights. Principles that Regan uses in human versus human and human versus animal situations, when applied to this case of animal versus animal, yield a conclusion that is contrary to the one Regan himself offers. We believe that Regan's failure to come to terms with the implications of his theory stems from a reluctance to get into the position of having to make detailed comparisons of animal satisfactions.

"With regard to wild animals, the general policy recommended by the rights view is: *let them be!*" declares Tom Regan in *The Case for Animal Rights* (1983, 361). If animals have a right to be treated in ways that respect their inherent value, then do we not have a prima facie duty to protect prey from predators? In answering this question Regan points out, quite correctly, that the relationship between animal predator and prey is not one of correlative rights and duties. *"Only moral agents can have duties,* and this is because only these individuals have the cognitive and other abilities necessary for being held morally accountable for what they do or fail to do. Wolves are not moral agents" (285). Hence the wolf has no duty to respect the sheep's inherent value, and the sheep has no right to have its inherent value respected by the wolf. So far so good. Regan concludes: "In claiming that we have a prima facie duty to assist those animals *whose rights are violated,* therefore, we are not claiming that we have a duty to assist the sheep against the attack of the wolf, since the wolf neither can nor does violate anyone's rights" (285). The italicized words impose an undue limitation on the moral assessment of the situation. We want to know whether our duty to respect the inherent value of the prey animal implies that we ought to defend it against the predator, given that both have the status of moral patients.

Before we tackle this question directly, permit us to pose a series of problems for the delectation of casuists.

1. You are out hiking in the wilderness. You discover an old man trapped under a fallen tree. Do you have a duty to help him?

2. You find a wood duck trapped in the ice along the edge of a shallow pond. Do you have a duty to try to free it?

3. You are hiking in the wilderness. A rabid fox steps out from behind a tree and is about to bite you. Is it wrong to harm the fox to save yourself?

4. You notice a rabid fox going after a healthy fox. Is it wrong to harm the rabid animal to save the healthy one?

5. A small child is firing a gun at two other children. Ought you to save the two children even if you must harm the gunholder?

6. A leopard is about to pounce on two children. Ought you to save the children even if you must harm the leopard?

The first two problems involve victims of natural processes. In neither case can it be said that the individual's rights are violated in the mishap. Regan says: "Nature *could* violate our rights only if . . . nature has direct duties to us to do or forbear doing certain acts that are our due. But nature has no duties; only moral agents do. . . . Nature no more violates our rights than it respects them" (1983, 272; cf. R. A. Watson 1981). According to an old and disputed proverb, if a tree falls in the forest where there is no one to hear, there is no sound. If a man is standing under the tree when it falls, no wrong is done to him. Just as the introduction of a perceiver changes the situation with respect to sound, so, too, the presence of a moral agent changes the moral character of the situation. At the very least, the observer of a natural misfortune has a duty of benevolence. Of such duties it is generally true that the agent has discretion in how the duty is to be carried out; no particular individual or group can claim the right to be the beneficiary of one's charity. In problem 1, however, the old man arguably has a claim to your assistance since (a) there is no one else to turn to, (b) no allocation of resources is involved, and (c) the risk and the cost to the helper are negligible. If someone refused to help under these circumstances, one would have to question that person's commitment to the duty of benevolence.

Problem 2 is similar to problem 1 in all morally relevant respects, assuming of course that wood ducks have moral status as subjects-of-a-life. For some reason, Regan is reluctant to classify birds as moral patients; his confidence extends only to "normal mammalian animals aged one or more" (81). In any event, the particular species and type of natural misfortune are not important: it is the form of the problem that matters. The example given by Peter Singer (1975, 251–52) will do just as well: "For instance, if a landslide blocks the exit to a valley, so that the valley begins to flood and animals are trapped by rising waters, human beings can and should put their knowledge to work in enabling the trapped animals to escape."

Problems 3 and 5 are examples of what Regan calls "innocent threats." In order to rescue the victim, one must take action against an individual with moral standing. In this respect the problems are different from problems 1 and 2. One does not have to worry about damage inflicted on the tree or the ice in the course of freeing the trapped victim, but the interests of the gun-wielding child and the rabid fox do figure in the moral equation. As moral patients they have no duties and thus do nothing right or wrong. Is it wrong to harm a moral innocent when it poses a threat to another individual? Regan's answer is that assuming the threatened individual is innocent of any morally relevant wrong and given that all nonviolent options have been explored, it is not wrong to harm a moral patient who poses an innocent threat. This holds whether the moral patient is a gun-wielding child (293) or a rabid animal (296).

Regan only considers innocent threats to human beings: a child firing a gun "at us," a rabid dog that "attacks us." Once animals are granted moral status, however, there is no reason why a situation like that described in problem 4 should be treated otherwise than as a case of one moral patient posing an innocent threat to another moral patient. If animals can be innocent threats to us, they can also be innocent threats to one another. Since the healthy fox is innocent of any morally relevant wrongdoing, it cannot be wrong to defend it by harming the rabid fox, given that all nonviolent options have been exhausted.

Problems 3 and 4 raise the question of whether it is wrong to harm an innocent threat when the victim is also innocent. To say that something is not morally wrong is to say that it is prima facie morally permissible to do it. Problem 5 raises the question of one's moral obligation in a situation of innocent threat. Ought one to put the victims' interest ahead of the innocent threats? Our answer to the question about the wrongness of harming an innocent threat does not imply an affirmative answer to the question about obligation, for one is not obligated to do all that one is permitted to do. Nor does it rule out a negative answer, for there may be cases in which it would be wrong to save the victims at the expense of the innocent threat. It would be wrong, not because the innocent threat is innocent, but because some other principle is violated. In order to determine one's moral obligation in a situation of innocent threat, one must take into account both the nature and the number of individuals involved.

Regan offers two principles for choosing between the rights of the few and the rights of the many: the miniride principle and the worse-off principle. He primarily has in mind cases such as choosing whom to take on a lifeboat, where the choice is between two sets of victims of a natural disaster. However, the principles work equally well for innocent threat situations, where one has the choice either to do nothing and let the victims come to harm or else to do harm to the innocent threat. The miniride principle is the following: "Special considerations aside, when we must choose between overriding the rights of many who are innocent or the rights of few who are innocent, and when each affected individual will be harmed in a prima facie comparable way, then we ought to choose to override the rights of the few in preference to overriding the rights of the many" (305). Suppose that A is a child who poses an innocent threat to children B and C, and that the only way to save the lives of B and C is to kill A. As individuals with inherent value, A, B, and C all have "a basic prima facie right not to be harmed" (287). Since all of them are human children and the harm to each is death, the harms are prima facie comparable. To refrain from interfering out of respect for A's rights would be to override the rights of B and C in favor of A. But this violates the miniride principle. Consequently one ought to harm A rather than let A do what will harm B and C.

Problem 6 differs from problem 5 in that the innocent threat is nonhuman. Although it is just a healthy animal going about its normal carnivorous business, the leopard is definitely a *threat* to the children, and it must be an *innocent* threat because it is a moral patient. To simplify matters, let us ignore the question of how the children got so close to the animal in the first place. For purposes of argument let us say that no moral agent is in any way to blame for the children's predicament and that they were just unlucky to meet up with the beast.

Death is not a comparable harm for a leopard and a human child since, according to Regan, humans have more opportunities for satisfaction than animals and thus more to lose by dying. Consequently the miniride principle does not apply to problem 6. Regan's principle for choosing between unequal harms is the worse-off principle: "Special considerations aside, when we must decide to override the rights of the many or the rights of the few who are innocent, and when the harm faced by the few would make them worse-off than any of the many would be if any other option were chosen, then we ought to override the rights of the many" (308). When the choice is between a greater harm to one individual and a lesser harm to many, one ought to choose the latter. What counts is the magnitude of harm done to each individual, not the aggregate amount of harm done to the group. If a child is firing a gun at ten cats, and the choice is between killing the child or letting the child kill the cats, then by the worse-off principle one ought to let the cats die. Even if all of them are killed, the harm to each of them is less than the harm that would be inflicted on the child. In the reverse situation, where the innocent threat is a cat and the victims are children, one should save the many at the expense of the few, since death is a greater harm to each individual victim than it is to the innocent threat.

So far everything accords pretty well with our intuitions. Now we come to the really interesting problem:

7. A coyote is about to pounce on two prairie dogs. Ought you to save the prairie dogs even if you must harm the coyote?

The insights of the previous six problems come together in this one. The prairie dogs are about to die as the result of a natural process. When a moral agent observes an innocent victim in distress and is able to help, at no cost and negligible risk, benevolence enjoins the agent to assist the victim. Although the coyote is as morally innocent as the victims, it is not wrong to harm the coyote, since it is morally permissible to harm an innocent threat in order to save innocent victims. Whether one is obliged to put the prairie dogs' interests ahead of the coyote's depends on whether the harm one would do to the coyote is greater than that which would come to the rodents. Let us say that the harm to each is death. Assuming that the opportunities for satisfaction are roughtly equal for coyotes and prairie dogs, death is as great a harm to one species as to the other. Thus by the miniride principle one ought to save the prairie dogs.

Our problem stacks the deck against the coyote by positing two prey animals. In a one-on-one situation where the harms are comparable, there is no obligation to put the prey's interests ahead of the predator's. Most familiar predation situations involve one predator against one prey at a time, or several predators against one prey. In such situations the rights view accords with the common intuition that one ought not to interfere. Note, however, that even with these ratios, the justification for noninterference depends on the assumption that death is a comparable harm for predator and prey. Is this assumption based on evidence or ignorance? Where there are choices to be made about the lives of moral patients, it behooves the moral agent to gather enough data to make an informed decision. The lives of some prey may afford more opportunities for satisfaction than the lives of some predators, in which case killing the predator is preferable to letting the prey be killed.

Does the animal rights view imply that we should try to eliminate all predators out of consideration for their innocent victims? The following is from a review of *The Case for Animal Rights:*

> Since some animals can and do pose innocent threats to other (rights holding) animals, as a matter of strict justice, we ought to deal with such threats no differently than we would if they were threats to (rights holding) humans. If we ought to protect humans' rights not to be preyed on by both human and animal predators, then we ought to protect animals' rights not to be preyed upon by both human and animal predators. In short, then, Regan's theory of animal rights implies a policy of humane predator extermination, since predators, however innocently, violate the rights of their victims. (Callicott 1985, 371)

The animal rights view does not imply that predation by animals is on a par with the human practice of hunting. Hunters are moral agents whereas animal predators are not. Human predators can "violate the rights of their victims"; animal predators cannot. It makes no sense to speak of either animal or human rights being violated in animal predation unless there is a moral agent who is in a position to help the victim. In such cases the victim has the right to have its interests taken into account— not by the predator but by the third-party moral agent.

The human right not be to be preyed on by human predators is a right against prospective predators as well as against society. Do humans have a similar right not to be preyed on by animal predators? If they do, it is a right not against the predator, but only against society. Does society have a duty to protect humans from animal predators? It does if the animals are in zoos or have otherwise been purposely brought into human company. What about predators in the wild? If a dangerous animal wanders into a human settlement, a decision has to be made on what to do with it. The human inhabitants have the right to have their interests taken into account, as does the animal. It is the same if humans wander into the animal's territory and find themselves in danger. Does this mean that we should go out and systematically eliminate all dangerous animals lest they wander into our territory or we into theirs? Of course not. Society does not have a duty to make the wilderness safe for humanity. Or for prey. The animal rights theory no more implies a policy of humane predator extermination than the human rights theory does.

The animal rights theory does imply that there is a need to rethink the practice of hand rearing predators and reintroducing them back into the wild. The predators, of course, still do no wrong. The question is whether the human caretaker is morally justified in putting the predator's interests ahead of the prey's. If a person raises an owl and feeds it mice, the mice are preyed upon by the person, against whom they have a claim not to be harmed. When the owl is grown and the person sets it free, the mice it preys upon have no claim against it, but they do, on the animal rights view, arguably have a claim against the person who set this evil in their midst.

THE BALANCE OF NATURE

Some will object that the above analysis overlooks the beneficial side of predation. Coyotes and prairie dogs live together in ecological balance. One coyote can devour many prairie dogs in its lifetime, yet the proportion of prairie dogs to coyotes remains the same. Fiddle with the ratio and you court disaster. Start killing coyotes, and soon there will be vast hordes of prairie dogs digging holes everywhere. Cows and horses will step into the holes and break their legs. The prairie dogs themselves will suffer from overcrowding. Coyotes are nature's way of keeping prairie dogs in check. Three cheers for coyotes! As for the reintroduction of predatory species in various regions, the people who undertake these projects do good, not harm, since they are reestablishing the natural balance. They are merely putting back into the environment what human "development" took away.

These sentiments may stem from a dissatisfaction either with animal rights in general, or with our treatment of it in particular. We shall reply first from within the framework of animal rights, then from outside it.

As a deontological theory, the animal rights theory denies that moral worth can be determined by consequences alone. Individuals having inherent value have rights. Actions that violate their rights are prima facie wrong. Sometimes it is justifiable to override the rights of some individuals, when this is the only way to respect the rights of others. But one cannot justify ignoring any individual's rights simply on the grounds that doing so will increase that individual's satisfaction or the satisfaction of everyone else. If the killing of coyotes is justifiable by either the miniride or the worse-off principle, then the mere fact that this action is likely to cause trouble in the long run does not constitute a sufficient reason to refrain from doing it. Similarly, the fact that the rehabilitation of owls increases the satisfaction of the owls, keeps down the population of mice, and gives pleasure to people, must give way to considerations based on rights in determining the moral worth of the practice.

It makes no difference whether the predatory species is on the verge of extinction or not. As Regan notes, the animal rights view does not recognize the rights of species, nor does it allow that members of endangered species ipso facto have more right not to be harmed. "If, in a prevention situation, we had to choose between saving the last two members of an endangered species or saving another individual who belonged to a species that was plentiful but whose death would be a greater prima facie harm to that individual than the harm that death would be to the two, then the rights view requires that we save that individual" (Regan 1983, 359).

Within the framework of the rights view, bad consequences do not turn a right action into a wrong one, and good consequences do not make wrong into right. It is often held that a legitimate test of moral principles is how well they agree with our considered moral beliefs, that is, with moral beliefs we hold after having reflected clearly, impartially, and with as much relevant information as we can muster. Regan accepts this test (133–35). Does not the animal rights view lead to a conclusion that clashes with the considered belief that it is best not to interfere with the balance of nature?

Our answer is a resounding "Yes, but. . . ." There are three buts. First, this belief is not a moral belief. Second, it is not as "considered" as one might think. Third, when the policy of noninterference in nature conflicts with a moral belief, the considered moral opinion is that the moral belief ought to determine one's action. We shall consider each of these points in turn.

The belief that it is best not to interfere with the natural balance is a belief about the rationality of a certain course of action in light of its possible or probable outcomes. The content of the belief can be rendered along the following lines. If you try to increase x, you will probably end up by decreasing x. If you try to eliminate situation y, you might bring about situation z, which is far worse on your scale of utilities. Such a principle can be offered in support of a moral judgment, but it is not itself a moral judgment.

Suppose someone says that we ought to undertake the systematic extermination of wolves in order to increase the sum total of pleasure in the deer population. There are two strategies for combatting this proposal; each can be pursued independently of the other. One strategy is to argue that it is wrong to achieve increased pleasure for deer at their predators' expense. This is a moral argument. The other is to argue that the proposed extermination will not increase the sum total of deer pleasure but instead will have the opposite effect of increasing their suffering. There will be more deer—they will overgraze, ruin the vegetation, and eventually they will all starve. This is an argument from the harmful effects of interfering in nature, and it is an empirical argument. The inefficacy of the proposed action is a reason why the action ought not to be done, but it is not a moral reason.

The issue is not whether it is morally good to increase deep pleasure, or morally permissible to achieve this result by killing wolves, but merely whether this particular means will have the desired result.

We turn now to the second but. The belief that it is best not to disturb the natural balance is not as "considered" as one might think. "The balance of nature" is a slippery term. You can apply or withhold it as you wish. Consider the aforesaid dire consequences of killing coyotes: hordes of prairie dogs digging holes everywhere, horses and cows stepping into the holes and breaking their legs. (Here our imaginary opponent is not just imaginary, for this objection was actually made to us by a fellow philosopher.) The prairie dogs are running amuck, but from whose point of view? The farmer's. From a more global perspective, one could say that prairie dogs are nature's way of keeping the population of horses and cows in check.

What counts as being in accordance with the balance of nature? If "balance of nature" is taken to mean that the population ratios remain roughly the same among species in a given locality, then much of what goes in nature is not "in balance." Habitats change. Open fields become thickets. Thickets become forests. There is no biological law that says that one species shall not take over and ruin things for other species. Oak and beech trees regularly ruin things for bull thistles and wild strawberries and the animals that like them. Moreover, vast fluctuations in population size are cyclical among some species. There is no biological law prohibiting a species from becoming so numerous that it ruins things for its own members. Boom and bust are part of nature's way, as is the extinction of species.

What counts as disturbing the natural balance, and what counts as restoring it? The answer is apt to be influenced by the respondent's own interests. Take the introduction of predatory birds into urban habitats. Is this disturbance or restoration? Some participants in these projects attempt to justify the practice by saying that it is an effort to restore the natural balance, at least in part. Yet the habitat into which the birds are introduced is quite different from when they originally lived there. There is a new set of inhabitants—house sparrows, starlings, and pigeons—whose food sources and perils are quite different from those of the falcon's original prey. Does the present habitat really need this additional predator to keep the prey population within the carrying capacity of the land? Are the human participants in the falcon projects worried that the bird population in our cities will become so numerous that the food supply will run out and there will be a pigeon and starling population crash?

Killing predators to save prey goes against the belief that it is best not to interfere in nature. But when the policy of noninterference comes into conflict with a moral principle, then the considered moral opinion is that the moral principle takes precedence. This is the third but. We humans deem it best not to disturb the balance of nature, but only when nature is doing her balancing act on some other species. The natural constraints on human population growth—disease, famine, even infertility—are considered problems in urgent need of solution. This special treatment of the human case cannot be justified in terms of a difference in the efficacy of interference. Humans have made a great effort to improve the lot of human beings, both individually and collectively. If we took the same pains on behalf of any other single species, there is every reason to think that we would be equally successful.

Suppose that tomorrow it is decided that the welfare of whitetail deer, both individually and collectively, is the highest goal of mankind, and that their interests take precedence over those of all other species, including man. When whitetail deer are sick or injured, they are taken care of. Cures are sought for their most crippling diseases. Every effort is made to increase their life expectancy, and it is considered especially tragic when a young one dies. As the deer population increases, farmland is given over to their use. Towns and suburbs are razed; trees and shrubs are planted in their place. New varieties of plants are developed that are resistant to overgrazing. Famine relief efforts are organized to aid the victims of drought. Under such a setup, the deer will surely prosper, just as humanity has prospered. If the deer population continues to grow, at some point there will be too many deer for the earth to support; but the same is true for humans. Incurable optimists will insist that eventually technology will develop to the stage when we can send the deer out into space to colonize other planets.

Why single out whitetail deer as opposed to some other species? Why favor any nonhuman species at the expense of humans? These are at bottom moral questions. The point of the parable is that in decisions to interfere or refrain from interfering in nature on behalf of an individual or group, the key factor is not whether interference, if pursued far enough, will work; it is whether or not there are moral grounds for undertaking it. The policy of noninterference can be overridden by moral considerations.

Obviously, we are not suggesting that any single species of animal should be exalted like the whitetail deer in our story. Nor do we advocate extending to animals the same extraordinary measures now taken in the name of human welfare. Maybe the human species shouldn't be exalted quite as much as it is. Garrett Hardin (1974) and others have argued that famine relief efforts and so on, when unaccompanied by efforts to curb population growth, eventually lead to greater misery for everyone. All we are suggesting is that there may, in particular cases, be moral reasons for rescuing animals from natural calamities, including predation by other species, just as there are acknowledged moral reasons for doing so in the case of humans.

Once we grant animals moral status, we must be prepared to take them seriously. Taking animals seriously means considering them as individuals in their own right. It means recognizing them as beings with interests and capacities for satisfaction, some of which are species-specific. In order to appreciate the full range of animal experience, we must be prepared to step beyond the simple dichotomy of human versus nonhuman. Other animals deserve the same careful scrutiny that we have hitherto lavished on our own species.

References

AT—Descartes 1964-76.
C—Descartes 1976
CSM—Descartes 1984-85
HR—Descartes 1955
K—Descartes 1970
OC—Malebranche 1958-67
S—Malebranche 1980

Adam, C., and Tannery, P., eds. 1964–76. *Oeuvres de Descartes,* by R. Descartes. 12 vols. Paris: J. Vrin. Cited in the text as AT.

Adams, D. K. 1928. "The Inference of Mind." *Psychological Review* 35: 235–52.

Aelian. 1958–59. *On the Characteristics of Animals.* Trans. A. F. Scholfield. 3 vols. Cambridge, Mass.: Harvard University Press.

André, Y. M. 1970. *La vie du R. P. Malebranche.* Paris, 1886. Genève: Slatkine Reprints.

Aquinas, Saint Thomas. 1945. *Basic Writings of Saint Thomas Aquinas.* Trans. A. C. Pegis. 2 vols. New York: Random House.

Arnauld, A. 1775–83. *Oeuvres de Messire Antoine Arnauld.* 43 vols. Paris: Sigismond d'Arnay.

Baerends, C. P., and Kruijt, J. P. 1973. "Stimulus Selection." In *Constraints on Learning,* ed. R. A. Hinde and J. Stevenson-Hinde, 23–49. New York: Academic Press.

Barber, T. X. 1993. *The Human Nature of Birds.* New York: St. Martin's Press.

Bateson, P. P. G., and Klopfer, P. H., eds. 1991. *Perspectives in Ethology.* Vol. 9: *Human Understanding and Animal Awareness.* New York: Plenum Press.

Bayle, P. 1965. *Historical and Critical Dictionary (Selections).* Trans. R. H. Popkin. Indianapolis: Bobbs-Merrill.

227

Baylis, J. R. 1982. "Avian Vocal Mimicry: Its Function and Evolution." In *Acoustic Communication in Birds,* ed. D. E. Kroodsma and E. H. Miller, 2: 51–83. New York: Academic Press.

Beer, C. G. 1961. "Incubation and Nest Building Behavior of Black-headed Gulls. I: Incubation Behavior in the Incubation Period." *Behavior* 18: 62–106.

————. 1976. "Some Complexities in the Communication Behavior of Gulls." *Annals of the New York Academy of Sciences* 280: 413–32.

————. 1982. "Study of Vertebrate Communication—Its Cognitive Implications." In *Animal Mind-Human Mind,* ed. D. R. Griffin, 251–67. Berlin: Springer-Verlag.

————. 1992. "Conceptual Issues in Cognitive Ethology." *Advances in the Study of Behavior* 21: 69–109.

Bekoff, M. 1992. "Scientific Ideology, Animal Consciousness, and Animal Protection: A Principled Plea for Unabashed Common Sense." *New Ideas in Psychology* 10: 79–94.

Bekoff, M., and Jamieson, D., eds. 1990. *Interpretation and Explanation in the Study of Animal Behavior.* Vol. 1: *Interpretation, Intentionality, and Communication.* Boulder, Colo.: Westview Press.

Bennett, J. 1964. *Rationality.* London: Routledge & Kegan Paul.

Bonner, J. T. 1980. *The Evolution of Culture in Animals.* Princeton: Princeton University Press.

Bowler, P. J. 1983. *The Eclipse of Darwinism.* Baltimore: Johns Hopkins University Press.

Brentano, F. 1973. *Psychology from an Empirical Standpoint.* Trans. A. C. Rancurello, D. B. Terrell, and L. A. McAlister. London: Routledge & Kegan Paul.

Browne, J. 1983. *The Secular Ark: Studies in the History of Biogeography.* New Haven: Yale University Press.

Bunge, M. 1980. *The Mind-Body Problem: A Psychobiological Approach.* Oxford: Pergamon Press.

Burkhardt, R. W., Jr. 1977. *The Spirit of System: Lamarck and Evolutionary Biology.* Cambridge, Mass.: Harvard University Press.

————. 1983. "The Development of an Evolutionary Ethology." In *Evolution from Molecules to Men,* ed. D. S. Bendall, 429–44. Cambridge: Cambridge University Press.

————. 1985. "Darwin on Animal Behavior and Evolution."In *The Darwinian Heritage,* ed. D. Kohn, 327–65. Princeton: Princeton University Press.

Callicott, J. B. 1985. Review of *The Case for Animal Rights,* by T. Regan. *Environmental Ethics* 7: 365–72.

Carruthers, P. 1989. "Brute Experience." *Journal of Philosophy* 86: 258–69.

Changeux, J.-P. 1985. *Neuronal Man.* Trans. L. Garey. New York: Random House.

Charnov, E. L., and Krebs, J. R. 1975. "The Evolution of Alarm Calls: Altruism or Manipulation?" *American Naturalist* 109: 107–12.

Cheney, D. L., and Seyfarth, R. M. 1990. *How Monkeys See the World.* Chicago: University of Chicago Press.

Cheney, D. L., and Seyfarth, R. M. 1992. "Précis of How Monkeys See the World." *Behavioral and Brain Sciences* 15: 135–82.

Chomsky, N. 1966. *Cartesian Linguistics.* New York: Harper & Row.

———. 1980. "Human Language and Other Semiotic Systems." In *Speaking of Apes: A Critical Anthology of Two-Way Communication with Man,* ed. T. A. Sebeok and J. Umiker-Sebeok, 429–40. New York: Plenum Press.

Churchland, P. S. 1983. "Consciousness: The Transmutation of a Concept." *Pacific Philosophical Quarterly* 64: 80–95.

———. 1986. *Neurophilosophy.* Cambridge, Mass.: MIT Press.

Clifford, W. K. 1879. *Lectures and Essays.* Ed. L. Stephen and F. Pollock. 2 vols. London: Macmillan.

Cohen, D. H., and Karten, H. J. 1974. "The Structural Organization of Avian Brain: An Overview." In *Birds: Brain and Behavior,* ed. I. J. Goodman and M. W. Schein, 29–73. New York: Academic Press.

Colby, K. M. 1975. *Artificial Paranoia: A Computer Simulation of Paranoid Processes.* New York: Pergamon Press.

Colby, K. M.; Watt, J. B.; and Gilbert, J. P. 1966. "A Computer Method of Psychotherapy: Preliminary Communication." *Journal of Nervous and Mental Diseases* 142: 148–52.

Colby, K. M.; Weber, S.; and Hilf, F D. 1971. "Artificial *Paranoia.*"*Artificial Intelligence* 2: 1–25.

Coren, S. 1994. *The Intelligence of Dogs: Canine Consciousness and Capabilities.* New York: Free Press.

Costa, M. J. 1983. "What Cartesian Ideas Are Not." *Journal of the History of Philosophy* 21: 537–50.

Cottingham, J. 1978. " 'A Brute to the Brutes?' Descartes' Treatment of Animals." *Philosophy* 53: 551–59.

Cottingham, J., trans. 1976. *Descartes' Conversation with Burman.* Oxford: Clarendon Press. Cited in the text as C.

Cottingham, J.; Stoothoff, R.; and Murdoch, D., trans. 1984–85. *The Philosophical Writings of Descartes.* 2 vols. Cambridge: Cambridge University Press. Cited in the text as CSM.

Critchley, M. 1979. *The Divine Banquet of the Brain.* New York: Raven.

Curley, E. M. 1978. *Descartes against the Skeptics.* Cambridge, Mass.: Harvard University Press.

Cyrano de Bergerac, S. de. 1965. *Other Worlds: The Comical History of the States and Empires of the Moon and the Sun.* Trans. G. Strachan. London: Oxford University Press.

Daniel, G. 1692. *A Voyage to the World of Cartesius.* Trans. T. Taylor. London: Thomas Bennet.

Darwin, C. 1859. *On the Origin of Species by Means of Natural Selection, or the Preservation of Favoured Races in the Struggle for Life.* London: John Murray.

Darwin, C. 1871. *The Descent of Man, and Selection in Relation to Sex.* 2 vols. London: John Murray.

———. 1874. *The Descent of Man, and Selection in Relation to Sex.* 2d ed. New York: A. L. Burt.

———. [1872] 1965. *The Expression of Emotion in Man and Animals.* Chicago: University of Chicago Press.

Davidson, D. 1975. "Thought and Talk." In *Mind and Language,* ed. S. Guttenplan, 7–23. Oxford: Clarendon Press.

Dawkins, R., and Krebs, J. R. 1978. "Animal Signals: Information or Manipulation?" In *Behavioural Ecology: An Evolutionary Approach,* ed. J. R. Krebs and N. B. Davies, 282–309. Sunderland, Mass.: Sinauer.

DeGrazia, D. 1994. "Wittgenstein and the Mental Life of Animals." *History of Philosophy Quarterly* 11: 121–37.

Dennett, D. C. 1971. "Intentional Systems." *Journal of Philosophy* 68: 87–106.

———. 1978. *Brainstorms: Philosophical Essays on Mind and Psychology.* Montgomery, Vt.: Bradford Books.

———. 1982. "How to Study Human Consciousness Empirically or Nothing Comes to Mind." *Synthese* 53: 159–80.

———. 1983. "Intentional Systems in Cognitive Ethology: The 'Panglossian Paradigm' Defended." *The Behavioral and Brain Sciences* 6: 343–55.

———. 1984. *Elbow Room.* Montgomery, Vt.: Bradford Books.

———. 1988. "Précis of *The Intentional Stance.*" *Behavioral and Brain Sciences* 11: 495–546,

———. 1989. "Cognitive Ethology: Hunting for Bargains or a Wild Goose Chase?" In *Goals, No-Goals and Own Goals,* ed. A. Montefiore and D. Noble, 101–16. London: Unwin Hyman.

———. 1991. *Consciousness Explained.* Boston: Little, Brown.

Descartes, R. 1955. *The Philosophical Works of Descartes.* Trans. E. S. Haldane and G. R. T. Ross. 2 vols. New York: Dover. Cited in the text as HR.

———. 1964–76. *Oeuvres de Descartes.* Ed. C. Adam and P. Tannery. 12 vols. Paris: J. Vrin. Cited in the text as AT.

———. 1970. *Philosophical Letters.* Trans. A. Kenny. Oxford: Clarendon Press. Cited in the text as K.

———. 1976. *Descartes' Conversation with Burman.* Trans. J. Cottingham. Oxford: Clarendon Press. Cited in the text as C.

———. 1983. *Principles of Philosophy.* Trans. V. R. Miller and R. P. Miller. Dordrecht: D. Reidel.

———. 1984–85. *The Philosophical Writings of Descartes.* Trans. J. Cottingham, R. Stoothoff, and D. Murdoch. 2 vols. Cambridge: Cambridge University Press. Cited in the text as CSM.

Desmond, A. 1982. *Archetypes and Ancestors: Palaeontology in Victorian London, 1850–1875.* Chicago: University of Chicago Press.

de Waal, F. 1986. "Deception in the Natural Communication of Chimpanzees." In *Deception: Perspectives on Human and Nonhuman Deceit,* ed. R. W. Mitchell and N. S. Thompson, 221–44. Albany: SUNY Press.

Dewsbury, D. A. 1984. *Comparative Psychology in the Twentieth Century.* Strouds-
burg, Pa.: Hutchinson Ross.

Dilly, A. 1676. *De l'ame des bêtes.* Lyon: Anisson & Poysuel.

Dreyfus, H. L., and Dreyfus, S. E. 1986. *Mind over Machine.* New York: Free Press.

Durant, J. R. 1981. "Innate Character in Animals and Man: A Perspective on the Origins of Ethology." In *Biology, Medicine and Society, 1840–1940,* ed. C. Webster,
157–92. Cambridge: Cambridge University Press.

―――. 1985. "The Ascent of Nature in Darwin's *Descent of Man.*" In *The Darwinian Heritage,* ed. D. Kohn, 283–305. Princeton: Princeton University Press.

Eldredge, N. 1982. *The Monkey Business: A Scientist Looks at Creationism.* New
York: Washington Square Press.

Endler, J. A. 1986. *Natural Selection in the Wild.* Princeton: Princeton University
Press.

Ericsson, K. A., and Simon, H. A. 1980. "Verbal Reports as Data." *Psychological
Review* 87: 215–51.

Evans, C. S.; Evans, L.; and Marler, P. 1993. "On the Meaning of Alarm Calls: Functional Reference in an Avian Vocal System." *Animal Behaviour* 46: 23–38.

Fabre, J. H. 1915. *The Hunting Wasps.* Trans. A. T. de Mattos. New York: Dodd, Mead.

Fisher, J., and Hinde, R. A. 1949. "The Opening of Milk Bottles by Birds." *British
Birds* 42: 347–57.

Fontaine, N. 1738. *Mémoires pour servir à l'histoire de Port-Royal.* 2 vols. Cologne:
Compagnie.

Fouts, R. S. 1974. "Language: Origins, Definitions and Chimpanzees." *Journal of
Human Evolution* 3: 475–82.

Fuller, B. A. G. 1949. "The Messes Animals Make in Metaphysics." *Journal of Philosophy* 46: 829–38.

Gaita, R. 1992. "Animal Thoughts." *Philosophical Investigations* 15: 227–44.

Gardner, B. T., and Gardner, R. A. 1971. "Two-Way Communication with an Infant
Chimpanzee." In *Behavior of Nonhuman Primates,* ed. A. M. Schrier and F. Stollnitz, 4: 117–84. New York: Academic Press.

Gardner, M. 1981. *Science: Good, Bad and Bogus.* Amherst, N.Y.: Prometheus Books.

Gardner, R. A., and Gardner, B. T. 1969. "Teaching Sign Language to a Chimpanzee."
Science 165: 664–72.

Ghiselin, M. 1969. *The Triumph of the Darwinian Method.* Berkeley: University of
California Press.

Gill, T. V., and Rumbaugh, D. M. 1974. "Mastery of Naming Skills by a Chimpanzee.
Journal of Human Evolution 3: 483–92.

Glickman, S. E. 1985. "Some Thoughts on the Evolution of Comparative Psychology."
In *A Century of Psychology as a Science,* ed. S. Koch and D. E. Leary, 738–82.
New York: McGraw.

Gottlieb, G. 1979. "Comparative Psychology and Ethology." In *The First Century of Experimental Psychology,* ed. E. Hearst, 147–73. Hillsdale, N.J.: Lawrence Erlbaum.

———. 1985. "Anagenesis: Theoretical Basis for the Ecological Void in Comparative Psychology." In *Issues in the Ecological Study of Learning,* ed. T. D. Johnston and A. T. Pietrewicz, 59–72. Hillsdale, N.J.: Lawrence Erlbaum.

Gould, J. L. 1975a. "Communication of Distance Information by Honey Bees." *Journal of Comparative Physiology* 104: 161–73.

———. 1975b. "Honey Bee Recruitment: The Dance-Language Controversy." *Science* 189: 685–93.

———. 1986. "The Locale Map of Honey Bees: Do Insects Have Cognitive Maps?" *Science* 232: 861–63.

Gould, J. L.; Dyer, F. C.; and Towne, W. F. 1985. "Recent Progress in the Study of the Dance Language." In *Experimental Behavioral Ecology and Sociology,* ed. B. Hölldobler and M. Lindauer, 141–61. Sunderland, Mass.: Sinauer.

Gould, J. L., and Gould, C. G. 1982. "The Insect Mind: Physics or Metaphysics?" In *Animal Mind—Human Mind,* ed. D. R. Griffin, 269–97. Berlin: Springer-Verlag.

Gould, S. J. 1983. *Hen's Teeth and Horse's Toes.* New York: W. W. Norton.

Gray, P. H. 1968. "Prerequisite to an Analysis of Behaviorism: The Conscious Automaton Theory from Spalding to William James." *Journal of the History of the Behavioral Sciences* 4: 365–76.

Griffin, D. R. 1981. *The Question of Animal Awareness.* 2d ed. Los Altos, Calif.: William Kaufmann.

———. 1984. *Animal Thinking.* Cambridge, Mass.: Harvard University Press.

———. 1992. *Animal Minds.* Chicago: University of Chicago Press.

Griffin, D. R., ed. 1982. *Animal Mind—Human Mind.* Berlin: Springer-Verlag.

Gruyer, P. 1922. *Saint-Germain.* Paris: Henri Laurens.

Gunderson, K. 1964. "Descartes, La Mettrie, Language, and Machines." *Philosophy* 39: 193–222.

Gyger, M., and Marler, P. 1988. "Food Calling in the Domestic Fowl, *Gallus gallus*: The Role of External Referents and Deception." *Animal Behaviour* 36: 358–65.

Gyger, M.; Marler, P.; and Pickert, R. 1987. "Semantics of an Avian Alarm Call System: The Male Domestic Fowl, *Gallus domesticus*." *Behaviour* 102: 15–40.

Hailman, J. P. 1985. "Historical Notes on the Biology of Learning." In *Issues in the Ecological Study of Learning,* ed. T. D. Johnston and A. T. Pietrewicz, 27–57. Hillsdale, N.J.: Lawrence Erlbaum.

Hailman, J. P., and Ficken, M. S. 1986. "Combinatorial Animal Communication with Computable Syntax: Chick-a-dee Calling Qualifies as 'Language' by Structural Linguistics." *Animal Behavior* 34: 1899–1901.

Haldane, E. S., and Ross, G. R. T., trans. 1955. *The Philosophical Works of Descartes.* 2 vols. New York: Dover. Cited in text as HR.

Hamilton, W. D. 1971. "Geometry for the Selfish Herd." *Journal of Theoretical Biology* 31: 295–311.

Hanna, P. 1990. "Must Thinking Bats be Conscious?" *Philosophical Investigations* 13: 350–56.

Hardin, C. L. 1988. *Color for Philosophers: Unweaving the Rainbow.* Indianapolis: Hackett.

Hardin, G. 1974. "Living on a Lifeboat." *BioScience* 24: 561–68.

Harrison, P. 1989. "Theodicy and Animal Pain." *Philosophy* 64: 79–92.

———. 1991. "Do Animals Feel Pain?" *Philosophy* 66: 25–40.

———. 1992. "Descartes on Animals." *Philosophical Quarterly* 42: 219–27.

———. 1993. "Animal Souls, Metempsychosis, and Theodicy in Seventeenth-Century English Thought." *Journal of the History of Philosophy* 31: 519–44.

Hartshorne, C. 1973. *Born to Sing.* Bloomington: Indiana University Press.

Hautecoeur, L. 1959. *Les jardins des dieux et des hommes.* Paris: Hachette.

Hayes, K. J., and Hayes, C. 1951. "The Intellectual Development of a Home-Raised Chimpanzee." *Proceedings of the American Philosophical Society* 95: 105–109.

Hearst, E., ed. 1979. *The First Century of Experimental Psychology.* Hillsdale, N.J.: Lawrence Erlbaum.

Heil, J. 1982. "Speechless Brutes." *Philosophy and Phenomenological Research* 42: 400–406.

Hempel, C. G. 1965. *Aspects of Scientific Explanation and Other Essays in the Philosophy of Science.* New York: Free Press.

Heppenheimer, T. A. 1985. "Man Makes Man." In *Robotics,* ed. M. Minsky, 29–69. Garden City, N.Y.: Anchor Press/Doubleday.

Herrnstein, R. J. 1980. "Fish as a Natural Category for People and Pigeons." In *The Psychology of Learning and Motivation,* ed. G. H. Bower, 14: 59–95. New York: Academic Press.

Hobhouse, L. T. 1915. *Mind in Evolution.* 2d ed. London: Macmillan.

Hodos, W., and Campbell, C. B. G. 1969. "Scala Naturae: Why There Is No Theory in Comparative Psychology." *Psychological Review* 76: 337–50.

Hoff, C. 1983. "Kant's Invidious Humanism." Environmental Ethics 5: 63–70.

Hofstadter, D. R. 1982. "Can Inspiration be Mechanized?" *Scientific American* 247(3): 18–34.

Hofstadter, D. R., and Dennett, D. C., eds. 1981. *The Mind's I.* New York: Basic Books.

Hölldobler, B., and Lindauer, M., eds. 1985. *Experimental Behavioral Ecology and Sociology.* Sunderland, Mass.: Sinauer.

Hölldobler, B., and Wilson, E. O. 1983. "The Evolution of Communal Nest-Weaving in Ants." *American Scientist* 71: 490–99.

House, I. 1991. "Harrison on Animal Pain." *Philosophy* 66: 376–79.

Howard, R. D. 1973. "The Influence of Sexual Selection and Interspecific Competition on Mockingbird Song (*Mimus polyglottos*)." *Evolution* 28: 428–38.

Hull, D. L. 1973. *Darwin and His Critics.* Cambridge, Mass.: Harvard University Press.

Humphrey, N. K. 1977. Review of *The Question of Animal Awareness,* by D. R. Griffin. *Animal Behavior* 25: 521–22.

Huxley, T. H. 1863. *Evidences as to Man's Place in Nature.* London: Williams & Norgate.
————. 1896. *Collected Essays.* 9 vols. New York: D. Appleton.

James, W. 1890. *The Principles of Psychology.* 2 vols. New York: Henry Holt.
Jamieson, D., and Bekoff, M. 1992. "Carruthers on Nonconscious Experience." *Analysis* 52: 23–28.
Jenkins, H. M. 1979. "Animal Learning and Behavior Theory." In *The First Century of Experimental Psychology,* ed. E. Hearst, 177–228. Hilisdale, N.J.: Lawrence Erlbaum.
Jerison, H. J. 1973. *Evolution of the Brain and Intelligence.* New York: Academic Press.
Johnston, T. D., and Pietrewicz, A. T., eds. 1985. *Issues in the Ecological Study of Learning.* Hillsdale, N.J.: Lawrence Erlbaum.
Jolley, N. 1995. "Sensation, Intentionality, and Animal Consciousness: Malebranche's Theory of Mind." *Ratio* 8: 128–42.
Joynt, R. J. 1981. "Are Two Heads Better Than One?" *The Behavioral and Brain Sciences* 4: 108–109.

Kant, I. 1963. *Lectures on Ethics.* Trans. L. Infield. New York: Harper & Row.
————. 1969. *Foundations of the Metaphysics of Morals.* Trans. L. W. Beck. Indianapolis: Bobbs-Merrill.
Kawai, M. 1965. "Newly-acquired Pre-Cultural Behavior of the Natural Troop of Japanese Monkeys on Koshima Islet." *Primates* 6: 1–30.
Kenny, A. 1968. *Descartes: A Study of His Philosophy.* New York: Random House.
Kenny, A., trans. 1970. *Philosophical Letters,* by R. Descartes. Oxford: Clarendon Press. Cited in the text as K.
Kenny, A. J. P.; Longuet-Higgins, H. C.; Lucas, J. R.; and Waddington, C. H. 1973. *The Development of Mind.* Edinburgh: Edinburgh University Press.
Kingsley, C. 1869. *The Water Babies: A Fairy Tale for a Land Baby.* New ed. London: Macmillan.
Kluender, K. R.; Diehl, R. L.; and Killeen, P. R. 1987. "Japanese Quail Can Learn Phonetic Categories." *Science* 237: 1195–97.
Kohn, D. 1980. "Theories to Work By: Rejected Theories, Reproduction, and Darwin's Path to Natural Selection." *Studies in History of Biology* 4: 67–170.
Kohn, D., ed. 1985. *The Darwinian Heritage.* Princeton: Princeton University Press.
Kosslyn, S. M. 1983. *Ghosts in the Mind's Machine.* New York: W. W. Norton.
Kottler, M. J. 1974. "Alfred Russel Wallace, the Origin of Man, and Spiritualism." *Isis* 65: 145–92.
Krebs, J. R. 1977. Review of *The Quesion of Animal Awareness,* by D. R. Griffin. *Nature* 266: 792.
Krebs, J. R., and Davies, N. B. 1981. *An Introduction to Behavioural Ecology.* Sunderland, Mass.: Sinauer.

Krebs, J. R., and Dawkins, R. 1984. "Animal Signals: Mind-Reading and Manipulation." In *Behavioural Ecology: An Evolutionary Approach,* ed. J. R. Krebs and N. B. Davies, 2d ed., 380–402. Sunderland, Mass.: Sinauer.

Krebs, J. R.; Erichsen, J. T.; Webber, M. I..; and Charnov, E. L. 1977. "Optimal Prey Selection in the Great Tit, *Parus major.*" *Animal Behavior* 25: 30–38.

Lack, D. 1946. *The Life of the Robin.* 2d ed. London: H. F. & G. Witherby.

La Mettrie, J. O. de. 1961. *Man a Machine.* Trans. G. C. Bussey. LaSalle, Ill.: Open Court.

La Motte, A. H. de. 1754. *Oeuvres de Monsieur Houdar de la Motte.* 11 vols. Paris: Prault.

Laporte, J. 1950. *Le rationalisme de Descartes.* Paris: Presses Universitaires de France.

Latto, R. 1986. "The Question of Animal Consciousness." *Psychological Record* 36: 309–14.

Le Conte, J. 1896. "From Animal to Man." *The Monist* 6: 356–81.

Lieberman, P. 1975. "The Evolution of Speech and Language." In *The Role of Speech in Language,* ed. J. F. Kavanagh and J. E. Cutting, 83–106. Cambridge, Mass.: MIT Press.

Lindauer, M. 1961. *Communication among Social Bees.* Cambridge, Mass.: Harvard University Press.

———. 1985. "The Dance Language of Honeybees: The History of a Discovery." In *Experimental Behavioral Ecology and Sociology,* ed. B. Hölldobler and M. Lindauer, 129–40. Sunderland, Mass.: Sinauer.

Locke, J. 1959. *An Essay Concerning Human Understanding.* Ed. A. C. Fraser. 2 vols. New York: Dover.

Lorenz, K. 1970–71. *Studies in Animal and Human Behavior.* Trans. R. Martin. 2 vols. Cambridge, Mass.: Harvard University Press.

———. 1991. *Here Am I—Where Are You? The Behavior of the Greylag Goose.* Trans. R.D. Martin. New York: Harcourt Brace Jovanovich.

———. 1996. *The Natural Science of the Human Species: An Introduction to Comparative Behavioral Research. The "Russian Manuscript" (1944–1948).* Ed. A. von Cranach; trans. R.D. Martin. Cambridge, Mass.: MIT Press.

Lubbock, J. 1897. *On the Senses, Instincts, and Intelligence of Animals.* New York: D. Appleton.

Lubinski, D., and Thompson, T. 1993. "Species and Individual Differences in Communication Based on Private States." *Behavioral and Brain Sciences* 16: 627–80.

Lumsden, C. J., and Wilson. E. O. 1983. *Promethean Fire: Reflections on the Origin of Mind.* Cambridge, Mass.: Harvard University Press.

Macedonia, J. M. 1990. "What is Communicated in the Antipredator Calls of Lemurs: Evidence from Playback Experiments with Ringtailed and Ruffed Lemurs." *Ethology* 86: 177–90.

Macedonia, J. M., and Evans, C. S. 1993. "Variation among Mammalian Alarm Call Systems and the Problem of Meaning in Animal Signals." *Ethology* 93: 177–97.

McRae, R. 1972. "Descartes' Definition of Thought." In *Cartesian Studies,* ed. R. J. Butler, 55–70. Oxford: Basil Blackwell.

Malcolm, N. 1973. "Thoughtless Brutes." *Proceedings and Addresses of the American Philosophical Association* 46: 5–20.

Malebranche, N. 1958–67. *Oeuvres complétes de Malebranche.* 20 vols. Paris: J. Vrin. Cited in the text as OC.

———. 1980. *The Search after Truth.* Trans. T. M. Lennon and P. J. Olscamp. Columbus: Ohio State University Press. Cited in the text as S.

Marler, P. 1977a. "Primate Vocalizations: Affective or Symbolic?" In *Progress in Ape Research,* ed. G. H. Bourne, 85–96. New York: Academic Press.

———. 1977b. "The Structure of Animal Communication Sounds." In *Recognition of Complex Acoustic Signals,* ed. T. H. Bullock, 17–35. Berlin: Abakon.

———. 1985a. "Hark Ye to the Birds: Autobiographical Marginalia." In *Leaders in the Study of Animal Behavior,* ed. D. A. Dewsbury, 315–45. Lewisburg: Bucknell University Press.

———. 1985b. "Representational Vocal Signals of Primates." In *Experimental Behavioral Ecology and Sociology,* ed. B. Hölldobler and M. Lindauer, 211–21. Sunderland, Mass.: Sinauer.

Marler, P.; Evans, C. S.; and Hauser, M. D. 1992. "Animal Signals: Motivational, Referential, or Both?" In *Nonverbal Vocal Communication: Comparative and Developmental Approaches,* ed. H. Papousek, U. Jürgens, and M. Papousek, 66–86. Cambridge: Cambridge University Press.

Marx, J. L. 1980. "Ape-Language Controversy Flares Up." *Science* 207: 1330–33.

Mason, W. A. 1976. Review of *The Question of Animal Awareness,* by D. R. Griffin. *Science* 194: 930–31.

Mayr, E. 1960. "The Emergence of Evolutionary Novelties." In *Evolution after Darwin,* ed. S. Tax, 1: 349–80. Chicago: University of Chicago Press.

Menzel, E. 1975. "Natural Language of Young Chimpanzees." *New Scientist* 65: 127–30.

Miles, M. 1994. "Leibniz on Apperception and Animal Souls." *Dialogue* 33: 701–24.

Mill, J. S. 1969. *Essays on Ethics, Religion, and Society.* Vol. 10 of *Collected Works.* Toronto: University of Toronto Press.

Miller, V. R., and Miller, R. P., trans. 1983. *Principles of Philosophy,* by R. Descartes. Dordrecht: D. Reidel.

Minsky, M. 1980. "K-lines: A Theory of Memory." *Cognitive Science* 4: 117–33.

Mitchell, R. W., and Thompson, N. S., eds. 1986. *Deception: Perspectives on Human and Nonhuman Deceit.* Albany: SUNY Press.

Mivart, St. G. J. 1871. "Darwin's Descent of Man." *Quarterly Review* 131: 47–90.

Møller, A. P. 1988. "False Alarm Calls as a Means of Resource Usurpation in the Great Tit *Parus Major.*" *Ethology* 79: 25–30.

Montaigne, M. de. 1957. "Apology for Raymond Sebond." In *The Complete Works of Montaigne,* trans. D. M. Frame, 318–457. Stanford: Stanford University Press.

Morgan, C. L. 1894a. *An Introduction to Comparative Psychology.* London: Walter Scott.

———. 1894b. "Three Aspects of Monism." *The Monist* 4: 321–32.

Morton, D. B.; Burghardt, G. M.; and Smith, J. A. 1990. "Critical Anthropomorphism, Animal Suffering, and the Ecological Context." *Hastings Center Report* 20 (Special Supplement, May-June): 13–19.

Mounce, H. O. 1992. "On Nagel and Consciousness." *Philosophical Investigations* 15: 178–84.

Munn, C. A. 1986a. "Birds that 'Cry Wolf,' " *Nature* 319: 143–45.

———. 1986b. "The Deceptive Use of Alarm Calls by Sentinel Species in Mixed-Species Flocks Of Neotropical Birds." in *Deception: Perspectives on Human and Nonhuman Deceit,* ed. R. W. Mitchell and N. S. Thompson, 169–75. Albany: SUNY Press.

Nagel, T. 1974. "What Is It Like to Be a Bat?" *Philosophical Review* 83: 435–51. Reprinted in *The Mind's I,* ed. D. R. Hofstadter and D. C. Dennett, 391–403. New York: Basic Books, 1981.

Naragon, S. 1990. "Kant on Descartes and the Brutes." *Kantstudien* 81: 1–23.

Nisbett, R. E., and Wilson, T. D. 1977. "Telling More Than We Can Know: Verbal Reports on Mental Processes." *Psychological Review* 84: 231–59.

O'Donnell, J. M. 1985. *The Origins of Behaviorism: American Psyhology, 1870–1920.* New York: New York University Press.

Olton, D. S., and Samuelson, R. J. 1976. "Remembrances of Places Past: Spatial Memory in Rats." *Journal of Experimental Psychology* 2: 97–116.

Oppenheim, J. 1985. *The Other World: Spiritualism and Psychical Research in England, 1850–1914.* Cambridge: Cambridge University Press.

Ostrom, J. H. 1979. "Bird Flight: How Did It Begin?" *American Scientist* 67: 46–56.

Pardies, I. G. 1672. *Discours de la connoissance des bastes.* Paris: Sebastien Mabre-Cramoisy.

Patterson, F. 1978. "Conversations with a Gorilla." *National Geographic* 154: 438–65.

———. 1981. "Ape Language." *Science* 211: 86–87.

Patterson, F., and Linden, E. 1981. *The Education of Koko.* New York: Holt, Rinehart and Winston.

Pereira, M. E., and Macedonia, J. M. 1991. "Ringtailed Lemur Anti-predator Calls Denote Predator Class, Not Response Urgency." *Animal Behaviour* 41: 543–44.

Plutarch. 1957. "The Cleverness of Animals." In *Plutarch's Moralia,* trans. H. Cherniss and W. C. Helmbold, vol. 12. Cambridge, Mass.: Harvard University Press.

Popper, K. R. 1959 *The Logic of Scientific Discovery.* New York: Basic Books.

Prasteau, J. 1968. *Les automates.* Paris: Grund.

Premack, D. 1971. "On the Assessment of Language Competence in the Chimpanzee."
In *Behavior of Nonhuman Primates,* ed. A. M. Schrier and F. Stollnitz, 4:
185–228. New York: Academic Press.

———. 1976. *Intelligence in Ape and Man.* Hillsdale, N.J.: Lawrence Erlbaum.

———. 1978. "On the Abstractness of Human Concepts: Why It Would Be Difficult to
Talk to a Pigeon." In *Cognitive Processes in Animal Behavior,* ed. S. H. Hulse, H.
Fowler, and W. K. Honig, 423–51. Hillsdale, N.J.: Lawrence Erlbaum.

———. 1986. *Gavagai! or the Future History of the Ape Language Controversy.*
Cambridge, Mass.: MIT Press.

Premack, D., and Premack, A. J. 1983. *The Mind of an Ape.* New York: W. W. Norton.

Premack, D., and Woodruff, G. 1978. "Does the Chimpanzee Have a Theory of
Mind?" *The Behavioral and Brain Sciences* 1: 515–26.

Putnam, H. 1981. *Reason, Truth and History.* Cambridge: Cambridge University
Press.

Radner, D. 1971. "Descartes' Notion of the Union of Mind and Body." *Journal of the
History of Philosophy* 9: 159–70.

———. 1977. "Berkeley and Cartesianism." In *New Essays on Rationalism and
Empiricism,* ed. C. E. Jarrett, J. King-Farlow, and F. J. Pelletier, 165–76. *Cana-
dian Journal of Philosophy,* supplementary volume 4.

———. 1978. *Malebranche.* Assen: Van Gorcum.

———. 1985. "Is There a Problem of Cartesian Interaction?" *Journal of the History
of Philosophy* 23: 35–49.

———. 1988. "Thought and Consciousness in Descartes." *Journal of the History of
Philosophy* 26: 439–52.

———. 1993. "Directed Action and Animal Communication." *Ratio* 6: 135–54.

———. 1994. "Heterophenomenology: Learning about the Birds and the Bees." *Journal of Philosohy* 91: 389–403.

Radner, D., and Radner, M. 1982. *Science and Unreason.* Belmont, Calif.: Wadsworth.

———. 1995. "Cognition, Natural Selection, and the Intentional Stance." *Interna-
tional Studies in the Philosophy of Science* 9: 109–19.

Rechten, C. 1978. "Interspecific Mimicry in Birdsong: Does the Beau Geste Hypothesis Apply?" *Animal Behavior* 26: 305–306.

Regan, T. 1982. *All That Dwell Therein.* Berkeley: University of California Press.

———. 1983. *The Case for Animal Rights.* Berkeley: University of California Press.

Régis, P. S. 1692. *Reponse aux reflexions critiques de M. du Hamel de la philosophie
de Mr. Régis.* Paris: Jean Cusson.

———. [1691], 1970. *Cours entier de philosophie ou système general selon les
principes de M. Descartes, contenant la logique, la métaphysique, la physique et
la morale.* 3 vols. New York: Johnson Reprint.

Richards, R. J. 1986a. "A Defense of Evolutionary Ethics." *Biology and Philosophy* 1:
265–93.

———. 1986b. "Justification through Biological Faith: A Rejoinder." *Biology and
Philosophy* 1: 337–54.

Richards, R. J. 1987. *Darwin and the Emergence of Evolutionary Theories of Mind and Behavior.* Chicago: University of Chicago Press.

Ristau, C.A., ed. 1991. *Cognitive Ethology: The Minds of Other Animals.* Hillsdale, N.J.: Lawrence Erlbaum Associates.

Rollin, B. E. 1989. *The Unheeded Cry: Animal Consciousness, Animal Pain and Science.* Oxford: Oxford University Press.

Romanes, G. J. 1882. "The Fallacy of Materialism." *The Nineteenth Century* 12: 871–88.

———. 1897. *Essays by George John Romanes.* Ed. C. L. Morgan. London: Longmans, Green.

Rosenfield, L. C. 1968. *From Beast-Machine to Man-Machine: Animal Soul in French Letters from Descartes to La Mettrie.* 2d ed. New York: Octagon Books.

Rosenthal, D. M. 1986. "Two Concepts of Consciousness." *Philosophical Studies* 49: 329–59.

Rumbaugh, D. M., ed. 1977. *Language Learning by a Chimpanzee: The Lana Project.* New York: Academic Press.

Rumbaugh, D. M., and Gill, T. V. 1976a. "Language and the Acquisition of Language-type Skills by a Chimpanzee (*Pan*)." *Annals of the New York Academy of Sciences* 270: 90–123.

———. 1976b. "Mastery of Language-type Skills by the Chimpanzee (*Pan*)." *Annals of the New York Academy of Sciences* 280: 562–78.

Rumbaugh, D. M.; Gill, T. V.; and von Glasersfeld, E. C. 1973. "Reading and Sentence Completion by a Chimpanzee (*Pan*)." *Science* 182: 731–33.

Rüppell, V. G. 1986. "A 'Lie' as a Directed Message of the Arctic Fox (*Alopex lagopus* L.)." Trans. B. A. Sabel and C. A. Munn. In *Deception: Perspectives on Human and Nonhuman Deceit,* ed. R. W. Mitchell and N. S. Thompson, 177–81. Albany: SUNY Press.

Ryle, G. 1949. *The Concept of Mind.* New York: Barnes & Noble.

Sainte-Beuve, C. A. 1908. *Port-Royal.* 7th ed. 10 vols. Paris: Libraire Hachette.

Savage-Rumbaugh, E. S.; Rumbaugh, D. M.; and Boysen, S. 1978. "Linguistically Mediated Tool Use and Exchange by Chimpanzees (*Pan troglodytes*)." *The Behavioral and Brain Sciences* 1: 539–54.

———. 1980. "Do Apes Use Language?" *American Scientist* 68: 49–61.

Savage-Rumbaugh, S. 1994. *Kanzi.* New York: John Wiley.

Schneirla, T. C. 1972. *Selected Writings of T. C. Schneirla.* Ed. L. R. Aronson, E. Tobach, J. S. Rosenblatt, and D. S. Lehrman. San Francisco: W. H. Freeman.

Schrier, A. M., and Stollnitz, F., eds. 1971. *Behavior of Nonhuman Primates,* vol. 4. New York: Academic Press.

Sebeok, T. A. 1980. "Looking in the Destination for What Should Have Been Sought in the Source." In *Speaking of Apes: A Critical Anthology of Two-Way Communication with Man,* ed. T. A. Sebeok and J. Umiker-Sebeok, 407–27. New York: Plenum Press.

Sebeok, T. A., and Umiker-Sebeok, J. 1981–82. "Clever Hans and Smart Simians: The Self-Fulfilling Prophecy and Kindred Methodological Pitfalls." *Anthropos* 76: 89–165; 77: 574–78.

———. eds. 1980. *Speaking of Apes: A Critical Anthology of Two-Way Communication with Man.* New York: Plenum Press.

Seligman, M. E. P., and Hager, J. L., eds. 1972. *Biological Boundaries of Learning.* New York: Appleton-Century-Crofts.

Seyfarth, R. M.; Beer, C. G.; Dennett, D. C.; Gould, J. L.; Lindauer, M.; Marler, P. R.; Ristau, C. A.; Savage-Rumbaugh, E. S.; Solomon, R. C.; and Terrace, H. S. 1982. "Communication as Evidence of Thinking: State of the Art Report." In *Animal Mind-Human Mind,* ed. D. R. Griffin, 391–406. Berlin: Springer-Verlag.

Seyfarth, R. M., and Cheney, D. L. 1980. "The Ontogeny of Vervet Monkey Alarm Calling Behavior: A Preliminary Report." *Zeitschrift für Tierpsychologie* 54: 37–56.

———. 1982. "How Monkeys See the World: A Review of Recent Research on East African Vervet Monkeys." In *Primate Communication,* ed. C. T. Snowdon, C. H. Brown, and M. R. Peterson, 239–52. Cambridge: Cambridge University Press.

———. 1986. "Vocal Development in Vervet Monkeys." *Animal Behavior* 34: 1640–58.

Seyfarth, R. M.; Cheney, D. L.; and Marler, P. 1980a. "Monkey Responses to Three Different Alarm Calls: Evidence of Predator Classification and Semantic Communication." *Science* 210: 801–803.

———. 1980b. "Vervet Monkey Alarm Calls: Semantic Communication in a Free-Ranging Primate." *Animal Behavior* 28: 1070–94.

Sidgwick, H. 1966. *The Methods of Ethics.* 7th ed. New York: Dover Publications.

Singer, P. 1975. *Animal Liberation: A New Ethics for Our Treatment of Animals.* New York: New York Review.

———. 1978. "The Fable of the Fox and the Unliberated Animals." *Ethics* 88: 119–25.

Slobodchikoff, C. N.; Kiriazis, J.; Fischer, C.; and Creef, E. 1991. "Semantic Information Distinguishing Individual Predators in the Alarm Calls of Gunnison's Prairie Dogs." *Animal Behaviour* 42: 713–19.

Smith, W. J. 1963. "Vocal Communication of Information in Birds." *American Naturalist* 97: 117–25.

Smith, W. J. 1965. "Message, Meaning, and Context in Ethology." *American Naturalist* 99: 405–409.

———. 1969. "Messages of Vertebrate Communication." *Science* 165: 145–50.

———. 1977. *The Behavior of Communicating: An Ethological Approach.* Cambridge, Mass.: Harvard University Press.

———. 1986. "An 'Informational' Perspective on Manipulation." In *Deception: Perspectives on Human and Nonhuman Deceit,* ed. R. W. Mitchell and N. S. Thompson, 71–86. Albany: SUNY Press.

Snowdon, C. T. 1982. "Linguistic and Psycholinguistic Approaches to Primate Communication." In *Primate Communication,* ed. C. T. Snowdon, C. H. Brown, and M. R. Peterson, 212–38. Cambridge: Cambridge University Press.

Snowdon, C. T.; Brown, C. H.; and Peterson, M. R., eds. 1982. *Primate Communication.* Cambridge: Cambridge University Press.

Sober, E. 1985. *The Nature of Selection.* Cambridge, Mass.: MIT Press.

Sorabji, R. 1993. *Animal Minds and Human Morals: The Origins of the Western Debate.* Ithaca: Cornell University Press.

Squadrito, K. 1991. "Thoughtful Brutes: The Ascription of Mental Predicates to Animals in Locke's *Essay.*" *Dialogos* 26: 63–73.

Stich, S. P. 1979. "Do Animals Have Beliefs?" *Australasian Journal of Philosophy* 57: 15–28.

Terrace, H. S. 1979. *Nim.* New York: Alfred A. Knopf.

———. 1983. "Apes Who 'Talk': Language or Projection of Language by Their Teachers?" In *Language in Primates: Perspectives and Implications,* ed. J. de Luce and H. T. Wilder, 19–42. New York: Springer-Verlag.

———. 1984. "Animal Cognition." In *Animal Cognition,* ed. H. L. Roitblat, T. G. Bever, and H. S. Terrace, 7–28. Hillsdale, N.J.: Lawrence Erlbaum.

Terrace, H. S.; Petitto, L. A.; Sanders, R. J.; and Bever, T. G. 1979. "Can an Ape Create a Sentence?" *Science* 206: 891–902.

Thompson, E.; Palacios, A.; and Varela, F. J. 1992. "Ways of Coloring: Comparative Color Vision as a Case Study for Cognitive Science." *Behavioral and Brain Sciences* 15: 1–74.

Thorpe, W. H. 1974. *Animal Nature and Human Nature.* Garden City, N.Y.: Doubleday.

Tinbergen, N. 1953. *The Herring Gull's World.* London: Collins.

———. 1965. *Social Behaviour in Animals.* London: Chapman and Hall.

Tolman, E. C. 1948. "Cognitive Maps in Rats and Men." *Psychological Review* 55: 189–208.

Trublet, N. C. J. 1761. *Memoires pour servir à l'histoire de la vie et des ouvrages de M. de Fontenelle.* Amsterdam: Marc-Michel Rey.

Turing, A. M. 1950. "Computing Machinery and Intelligence." *Mind* 59: 433–60. Reprinted in *The Mind's I,* ed. D. R. Hofstadter and D. C. Dennett, 53–67. New York: Basic Books, 1981.

Turner, F. M. 1974. *Between Science and Religion: The Reaction to Scientific Naturalism in Late Victorian England.* New Haven: Yale University Press.

Tyndall, J. 1889. *Fragments of Science: A Series of Detached Essays, Addresses, and Reviews.* 7th ed. 2 vols. London: Longmans, Green.

Umiker-Sebeok, J., and Sebeok, T. A. 1980. "Questioning Apes." In *Speaking of Apes: A Critical Anthology of Two-Way Communication with Man,* ed. T. A. Sebeok and J. Umiker-Sebeok, 1–59. New York: Plenum Press.

Vallortigara, G.; Zanforlin, M.; and Compostella, S. 1990. "Perceptual Organization in Animal Learning: Cues or Objects?" *Ethology* 85: 89–102.

van Kampen, H.S. 1994. "Courtship Food-Calling in Burmese Red Junglefowl: I. The Causation of Female Approach." *Behaviour* 131: 261–75.

von Frisch, K. 1967. *The Dance Language and Orientation of Bees.* Trans. L. E. Chadwick. Cambridge, Mass.: Harvard University Press.

Wallace, A. R. 1870. *Contributions to the Theory of Natural Selection.* London: Macmillan.

———. 1897. *Darwinism: An Exposition of the Theory of Natural Selection with Some of its Applications.* 2d ed. London: Macmillan.

Walther, F. R. 1969. "Flight Behavior and Avoidance of Predators in Thomson's Gazelle (*Gazella thomsoni* Guenther 1884)." *Behavior* 34: 184–221.

Ward, J. 1889. *Naturalism and Agnosticism.* 2 vols. London: Adam and Charles Black.

Washburn, M. F. 1917. *The Animal Mind.* 2d ed. New York: Macmillan.

Wasserman, E. A. 1981. "Comparative Psychology Returns: A Review of Hulse, Fowler, and Honig's *Cognitive Processes in Animal Behavior.*" *Journal of the Experimental Analysis of Behavior* 35: 243–57.

Watson, J. B. 1913. "Psychology as the Behaviorist Views It." *Psychological Review* 20: 158–77.

Watson, R. A. 1966. *The Downfall of Cartesianism, 1673–1712.* The Hague: Martinus Nijhoff.

———. 1979. "Self-Consciousness and the Rights of Nonhuman Animals and Nature." *Environmental Ethics* 1: 99–128.

———. 1981. "Self-Conscious Rights." *Ethics and Animals* 2: 90–92.

Wells, H. G.; Huxley, J. S.; and Wells, G. P. 1931. *The Science of Life.* 2 vols. Garden City, N.Y.: Doubleday.

Weizenbaum, J. 1966. "ELIZA—A Computer Program for the Study of Natural Language Communication between Man and Machine." *Communications of the ACM* 9: 36–45.

———. 1976. *Computer Power and Human Reason.* San Francisco: W. H. Freeman.

Wheeler, W. M. 1939. *Essays in Philosophical Biology.* Cambridge, Mass.: Harvard University Press.

Wickler, W. 1968. *Mimicry in Plants and Animal.* Trans. R. D. Martin. New York: McGraw-Hill.

Williams, B. 1978. *Descartes: The Project of Pure Enquiry.* Atlantic Highlands, N.J.: Humanities Press.

Williams, G. C. 1966. *Adaptation and Natural Selection.* Princeton, N.J.: Princeton University Press.

Wilson, A. C. 1985. "The Molecular Basis of Evolution." *Scientific American* 253(4): 164–73.

Wilson, E. O. 1975. *Sociobiology: The New Synthesis.* Cambridge, Mass.: Harvard University Press.

Wilson, E. O.; Durlach, N. I.; and Roth, L. M. 1958. "Chemical Releasers of Necrophoric Behavior in Ants." *Psyche* 65: 108–14.

Wilson, M. D. 1978a. *Descartes*. London: Routledge & Kegan Paul.

———. 1978b. "Cartesian Dualism." In *Descartes: Critical and Interpretive Essays,* ed. M. Hooker, 197–211. Baltimore: Johns Hopkins University Press.

Wittgenstein, L. 1953. *Philosophical Investigations*. Trans. G. E. M. Anscombe. New York: Macmillan.

Wooldridge, D. E. 1963. *The Machinery of the Brain*. New York: McGraw-Hill.

Wyers, E. J., and Menzel, E. W. 1980. "Behavior and Reality." *American Psychologist* 35: 968–70.

Wyles, J. S.; Kunkel, J. G.; and Wilson, A. C. 1983. "Birds, Behavior, and Anatomical Evolution." *Proceedings of the National Academy of Sciences of the United States of America* 80: 4394–97.

Young, R. M. 1970. *Mind, Brain and Adaptation in the Nineteenth Century*. Oxford: Clarendon Press.

———. 1985. *Darwin's Metaphor*. Cambridge: Cambridge University Press.

Index